TEACHING
FAITH AND MORALS

Catechesis
for
Personal and Community
Renewal

by
Suzanne M. De Benedittis

WINSTON PRESS

Library of Congress Catalog Card Number: 81-50551
ISBN: 0-86683-621-7

Printed in the United States of America

5 4 3 2 1

Winston Press, Inc.
430 Oak Grove
Minneapolis, MN 55403

Excerpt from Margaret Wold, "Incarnation in Mission," *Changes* (Institute of Changing Ministries, University of Southern California) 1980, I (3), p. 4, used with permission.

Excerpt from Kent Hoffman, "The Dark Night Ongoing Surrender Survival Kit," *The Catholic Agitator*, September 1980, p. 6, used with permission.

To
my friend
whose love sees me through

Special thanks go to the people at Winston Press, especially to Cyril A. Reilly, my editor, to Dolores Ready, and to Dolores Curran, who have encouraged this work all along the way. To the staff of the Chancellor's office at Loyola Marymount University, a very special thank you: to Reverend Charles S. Casassa, S.J., who in an exemplary way witnesses the values of Ignatius and his commitment to catechesis, for making his personal secretary available, even after I had resigned from the University; and to Agnes Stephens, for typing and retyping the manuscript, always with a cheerful word and an encouraging prayer. To Wilkie Au, S.J., and to his students, thank you for a critical reading and helpful comments.

To Dad and Mary for their prayers, and to countless friends whose loving care and prayer have tempered how I see and what I say—a profound thank you, for the good in this work is a reflection of you.

TABLE OF CONTENTS

DIAGRAMS

CHARTS

INTRODUCTION

People today are looking for a life-style that is satisfying and makes sense. Both within the churches and among the unchurched, people are searching for a renewed morality. Many are looking for a way of life that respects the wisdom of tradition, reflects biblical roots, and projects the believer into a future filled with realistic hope in place of current despair.

The life-style of the early Christians gives us a glimpse of what people may be searching for today. Grouped in small communities, people let go prevailing fears and despair and consciously chose to live a hopeful attitude that colored their whole outlook and inspired all their words and actions. The bishop, the one selected as chief minister responsible for the community's needs, assisted by priests and deacons, preached the Word of hope and worked to see the Word take root in the community. The community's faith was made evident in its life-style. Reaching out to all, to Jews and to Gentiles, the Christians' healing touch and caring style said as loudly as their stories that they had indeed found the Way.

Thankfulness for letting go of self-centered fears and interests and for at-oneness with all was embodied in daily activity. The culmination of this living of love was the celebration of the Eucharist. The Christian community was emerging. And it was regarded by others as so different that they would marvel: "See how they love one another!" Some outsiders yearned to belong to this group whose life-style was so extraordinary. Each member, they noticed, made a significant difference. Their differences, charisms, or gifts all contributed to the quality of life of both individuals and the community. Newcomers sought initiation. They were catechized, baptized, confirmed, and admitted to living the fullness of this message within a community which extended its service to all humankind. Eventually the Way of these Christians became official in the Roman Empire, and Christianity slowly evolved to become the religion it is today.

If we look more closely at the catechetical ministry in the early Church we see not only the bishops, priests, and deacons, but the entire community of faith participating in catechesis. We see catechumens and the faithful sponsoring them; we see those who instruct by word and those who teach by action. The Church today is calling for the same involvement by all who profess that they believe in the Word.

Today the catechetical ministry has been officially extended beyond bishops, priests, and deacons to include such people as catechists, coordinators, youth ministers, diocesan directors, and many more. Other Christians are actively involved in the process even though they as yet have no official title—for example, a senior citizen who does volunteer work in the CCD office. Still others have failed to recognize their responsibility for catechesis. But whether we have titles or not, whether we recognize our responsibility or not, the very fact that we are Christians means that we are called to educate one another. As Pope John Paul II points out in *Catechesi Tradendae*, the task of catechesis concerns us all.

The purpose of this book is to show how all of us who are members of that community called the parish are already involved in one another's religious socialization—and how by becoming conscious of the influence we have on one another and by recognizing and sharing our own gifts, or charisms, we can more effectively minister as catechists, each in our own way. Although this book is written from a Roman Catholic background, it should be valuable for all Christians involved in education in faith and morals and concerned with enabling believers to connect their faith and actions in a life-style that bespeaks their harmony. The book assumes a vision of Catholic Christianity evident in recent Church documents and current theology. Making the assumptions explicit, the book suggests approaches for translating theology into sound catechetical practices. For this it relies on the findings of contemporary psychology and presents them to show how they affect education in faith and morals.

My intent is to stimulate discussion that leads to Spirit-filled action, not only among catechists but among all who are striving to live their baptismal promises. Ways will be presented for community members to explore, adapt, and experience a renewed faith in the community we commonly call our parish. The challenge for me, and if accepted, for the community of faith, is to demonstrate how renewal is at one and the same time individual and communal. For a renewed moral life to emerge, for a community that proclaims a faith embodying love in action to become evident and continuing, everyone in the parish is needed. Everyone committed to the community of faith needs to be consciously engaged in living in a style that clearly evidences a response to God's invitatory call. Hence this book is addressed not only to those directly involved in religious education but to all who are striving to respond to the covenant call to live their Baptism.

It is meant to engender dialogue with, and among, pastors, priests, religious coordinators, religious educators, parents, and all the People of God. For even as "followers" we are called to be leaders. Like leaven, we are called to enliven our communities by our commitments professed in the story of our daily lives. In discussion, action, prayer, and solitude each of us, it is hoped, will more clearly recognize our giftedness and gracefulness, even as we come to grips with our shadow, or sinfulness. Thus as gifts freely given to one another, we may come to recognize the Caller and our call to contribute our charisms from the abundance with which we have been so richly endowed. Embodying gracefulness, the community's efforts at evangelization and catechesis can move beyond verbal proclamation. And once again people will acclaim these Christians: See how they love one another!

The moral catechesis presented in this book shows how our human nature develops, and how we in the twentieth century can be true to ourselves and be like Jesus. Luke, paraphrasing Isaiah, tells us that after forty days in the wilderness culminating in the classic temptations, Jesus returned to Galilee filled with the Spirit. As was his custom on the Sabbath day, he went to the synagogue. Given the book of Isaiah the prophet, he stood up and read, "The spirit of the Lord has been given to me, for he has anointed me. He has sent me to bring the good news to the poor, to proclaim liberty to captives and to the blind new sight, to set the downtrodden free, to proclaim the Lord's year of favor." Closing the book, Jesus continued, "Today this scripture has been fulfilled in your hearing." In the remainder of Luke's chapter 4 we see that Jesus went forth doing good, bringing a healing touch and affirmation to the people he met (Luke 4:14-44; cf. Isaiah 61:1-2 and 58:6-8).

In this passage we see Jesus not only reading the words from Isaiah but *living them out* day after day. Moreover, we see the *whole* person of Jesus—head, heart, hands, and spirit—engaged in living his belief, and in a *community* context. To put it in more sophisticated contemporary terms, we see Jesus realizing the intimate connection between mythos and ethos, and acting publicly in a manner evidencing that his intellect, emotions, spirit, and senses all understood and felt the meaning of Isaiah's words.

Diagram 1
PSYCHOLOGICAL PREDISPOSITIONS
FOR HOLISTIC CATECHESIS

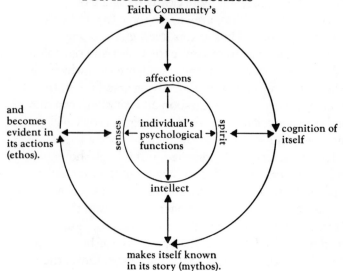

This book, then, is based on two premises derived from Jesus' own belief and practice: (1) that myth and ethic, or faith and morals, are as intrinsically one as the two sides of a coin; and (2) that for effective education in faith and morals, the whole person intellect, affections, spirit, and senses needs to be involved with the whole community (see Diagram 1).
An individual's predispositions to be primarily affectionate or intellectual or spiritual or sensual influence his or her beliefs and actions. They also influence and are influenced by the community's faith and morals—that is, the community's affections, spirit, rationality, and sensibility.

Blessed be God the Father of our Lord Jesus Christ,
who has blessed us with all the spiritual blessings
of heaven in Christ.
Before the world was made, he chose us, chose us in
Christ,
to be holy and spotless, and to live through love
in his presence,
determining that we should become his adopted sons,
through Jesus Christ
for his own kind purposes,
to make us praise the glory of his grace,
his free gift to us in the Beloved,
in whom, through his blood, we gain our freedom,
the forgiveness of our sins.
Such is the richness of the grace
which he has showered on us
in all wisdom and insight.
He has let us know the mystery of his purpose,
the hidden plan he so kindly made in Christ from
the beginning
to act upon when the times had run their course to
the end:
that he would bring everything together under Christ,
as head,
everything in the heavens and everything on earth.
And it is in him that we were claimed as God's own,
chosen from the beginning,
under the predetermined plan of the one who guides
all things
as he decides by his own will;
chosen to be,
for his greater glory,
the people who would put their hopes in Christ
before he came.

Now you too, in him,
have heard the message of the truth and the good
news of your salvation,
and have believed it;
and you too have been stamped with the seal of the
Holy Spirit of the Promise,
the pledge of our inheritance
which brings freedom for those whom God has taken
for his own,
to make his glory praised.

—Ephesians 1:3-14

1. CATECHESIS FOR PERSONAL AND COMMUNITY RENEWAL: AN OVERVIEW

This chapter defines the terms catechesis *and* holistic catechesis, *showing how the latter is but an emphatic way of referring to all the elements involved in the process of catechizing. To do that, the chapter begins with a review of the goals, source, and signs of catechesis. Then it argues that education in faith and education in morals are but two sides of the coin of catechesis. From this understanding the chapter goes on to assert that to be effective, catechesis must address the entire person—intellect, senses, affections, and intuitions—and must involve the entire community. The chapter concludes by defining the psychological functions which are the components of a holistic catechesis and then mentioning broad approaches that address each. Throughout, the chapter stresses that recent Church teaching and catechetical documents call for a holistic approach as a way of renewing Christian community and notes that what may seem contemporary and novel in the approach is actually a return to pristine forms of catechesis.*

WHAT IS CATECHESIS?

Catechesis is the "resounding" or "echoing" of the truth fully revealed in Christ. Literally, the word *catechesis* derives from the Greek *katēchein*, "to echo." Originally, the term referred to the oral repetition expected of children in school. And so we can imagine the chanting of responses as learners echo an answer over and over again, forming a chain with their singsong words.

In *Catechetics in Context*, Berard Marthaler notes that modern usage has extended the meaning of catechesis to include "the kerygma, the preparation for the sacraments as well as more advanced instructions to nourish and sustain a living faith in the community and its individual members."[1] The Higher Institute of Catechetics (of Nijmegen, Holland) describes catechesis even more broadly as "throwing light on the whole of human existence as God's salvific action by witnessing to the mystery of Christ through the word, for the purpose of awakening and fostering the faith and prompting man to live truly in accord with that faith."[2]

Marthaler distinguishes catechesis from catechetics. A more technical term, catechetics is "the systematic presentation or study of the nature, goals, means and principles of catechesis."[3] He refers to Joseph Colomb's differentiation of catechesis from religious education. Colomb identifies catechesis with the kerygma, the proclamation of good news, but regards religious education as focusing on the objective aspect of the message, teaching doctrine.

Colomb cautions catechists that without formal instruction, catechesis remains confused and incomprehensible. Pure objective instruction, however, would not be catechesis, he cautions, for it lacks force and makes no impact on the hearer.[4] John Paul II makes the same point. His *Catechesi Tradendae: The Apostolic Exhortation of Pope John Paul II on Catechetics* defines catechesis as "an education of children, young people and adults in the faith, which includes especially the teaching of Christian doctrine imparted, generally speaking, in an organic and systematic way, with a view to initiating the hearers into a fullness of Christian life."[5] The pope warns that in our catechetical renewal, routine (the one extreme) can lead to stagnation, lethargy, and paralysis and that improvisation (the other extreme) can beget confusion. He concludes that to maintain the necessary balance between formal and informal, or experiential, education "it is important for the Church to give proof today, as she has done at other periods of her history, of evangelical wisdom, courage and fidelity in seeking out and putting into operation new methods and new prospects for catechetical instruction."[6]

Echoed in each of these definitions is the theme that instruction, or the cognitive approach, is necessary but that formal religious instruction alone is not catechesis. This theme is made explicit in later chapters of this book. Catechesis, religious education, or education in faith and morals[7] as I understand it, stems from the living God calling us to faith through the resonance or echoes of one another's belief and behavior. Hence, the prime instrument for catechesis is not a textbook or a program but the Christian, living and vibrant.[8] No matter how clearly textbooks or programs may spell out the reasons for our faith, they are but tools in the hands of the catechist. Nor is the context of catechesis the classroom; it is the Church or parish community.

Given this understanding, catechesis becomes a process whose outcome is that the catechized live in tune with one another and in reverent harmony with all creation, so that in whatever they do, they work to bring a healing rhythm into the world, just as Jesus did. They work to recreate the face of the earth. In cooperation with the Holy Spirit they strive to make a symphony out of the dissonances, disasters, disease, and sin surrounding us all. The resonance of such a reverent community renders a compelling witness. In such a context, the words spoken as instruction are not only heard and regarded as ideals, but in fact are felt and understood as evidence of an empowering mystery really being lived. For faith comes through hearing and feeling the Good News made visible in action and seeing holy words actualized in graceful deeds. Effective catechesis fosters maturity of faith.

CATECHESIS AND HOLINESS. The texts of both the General and the National Catechetical Directories illustrate that an extensive catechesis is needed to foster maturity of faith—that is, to help us grow in holiness or wholeness, which is the fullness of life to which we are called. In other words, maturity of faith has to do with holiness, wholesomeness, a healed personality. It is evident in personal integrity and in recognizing our organic relationship with every element of creation. This maturity, holiness, or at-oneness with all is reflected in intimate concern for the community and in a caring interdependence with all comprising the universe. To the person of mature faith—for example, Mother Teresa of Calcutta—all creatures are godly. And each of us is called to live the vision of the universality of God's presence, although not necessarily in the same circumstances as Mother Teresa's. John Paul II, quoting from Ephesians, emphasizes this very point when he states that to catechize is to lead a person to study the mystery of Christ in all its dimensions, to help everyone see the plan, know Christ's love, and be filled with the fullness of God.[9]

To address this all-encompassing task, catechesis must employ a variety of methods which respect individual differences in learning styles and yet are comprehensive enough to recognize the source of holiness or maturity of faith and utilize all the signs that foster it. That is, to be effective, catechesis must address the whole person—the head and heart and hands and spirit of man and woman—and to do so it needs to involve the entire community of faith. *To Teach as Jesus Did* defines this traditional approach, which I term "holistic." The bishops stress the interconnection of cognitive, affective, and experiential education—essential elements in a holistic catechesis. They state that "the educational mission of the Church is an integrated ministry embracing three interlocking dimensions: the message revealed by God *(didache)* which the Church proclaims; fellowship in the life of the Holy Spirit *(koinonia)*; service to the Christian community and the entire human community *(diakonia)*."[10] Foreseeing our tendency to compartmentalize and then to dichotomize, the bishops continue with a caution.

> While these three essential elements can be separated for the sake of analysis, they are joined in the one educational ministry. Each educational program or institution under Church sponsorship is obliged to contribute in its own way to the realization of the threefold purpose within the total educational ministry. Other conceptual frameworks can also be employed to present and analyze the Church's educational mission, but this one has several advantages: it corresponds to a long tradition and also meets exceptionally well the educational needs and aspirations of men and women in our times.[11]

The catechetical dimensions of message, community, and service correspond respectively to the education of the head, heart, and hands. But to be truly holistic, a fourth dimension is called for: the education of the spirit. In the National Catechetical Directory the bishops allude to this dimension when they address worship. As I see it, worship which culminates in the eucharistic liturgy actually flows from *community* and symbolically represents the Christian *message* and social *ministry*. From this point of view meaningful worship calls for education of the spirit, which includes education of one's intuitions and imagination to enable the believer to recognize God at work in the signs and symbols surrounding us.

SOURCE AND SIGNS OF CATECHESIS. There are signs to facilitate the belief and corresponding behavior that God's word is revealed in Jesus Christ *and* is at work in our lives, a belief the Catechetical Directory designates as the source of catechesis. The signs manifesting God's self-communication in the world the Catechetical Directory lists as biblical, liturgical, ecclesial, and natural. It is interesting to note that the signs themselves can be related to the dimensions of community, spirit, doctrine, and behavior—the four elements comprising a holistic catechesis.

The Directory notes that *biblical signs* refer to the varied and wonderful ways recorded in Scripture by which God reveals himself. Biblical signs moreover are not only expressions of a past revelation; if understood with open hearts they help us recognize God working throughout history and help us feel God's presence stirring us and challenging us to respond as a Faithful People. Biblical signs help us feel God's presence in the ongoing dialogue life has with us each day.[12] *Liturgical signs* express the sanctification of human life. They mediate God's saving, loving power. In the liturgy, community members symbolize their unity with one another and with God as they participate in ritual celebration. The *ecclesial signs* of God's saving activity are classified in the Directory as both doctrinal or creedal formulations and the witness of Christian living. By pointing out that both doctrine and living witness are ecclesial signs, the Directory indicates the unity of faith (cognition) and morals (actions) in religious education.

Regarding *natural signs* of God's providence and saving power, the Directory stresses the task of examining the meaning and value of everything created, including the products of human effort. It exhorts catechists to teach adults to evaluate correctly and faithfully contemporary cultural and sociological developments, new questions of a religious or moral nature, and the interplay between temporal responsibilities and the Church's mission to the world. Catechesis "must give an intellectually satisfying demonstration of the gospel's relevance to life."[13] In doing this, "Catechesis must develop more and more a correct understanding of the faith, and thereby show that the act of faith and the truths which are to be believed are in conformity with the demands of human reason."[14]

In these four kinds of signs, but especially in our doctrines and creeds, transcendent mysteries and timeless truths are formulated in temporal terms, the bishops point out. Although doctrines and creeds suffer the limits of language, they are indispensable instruments for handing on the faith. But we must not mistake the tool for the reality it helps us grasp: "Therefore it is valid to distinguish between the truth itself and the language or words in which it is expressed. One and the same truth may be expressed in a variety of ways."[15]

Moving from a discussion of the verbal expression of our faith to the meaning behind the words, the bishops stress that the Church witnesses its faith through its way of life, its worship, and the service it renders. For example, the day-by-day experiences of forgiveness and reconciliation are ecclesial signs that the Church is a healing community not only in word, but even more so in deed. Also,

> Concern for and ministry to the poor, disadvantaged, helpless, and hopeless are signs that the Church is a servant. Uniting in love and mutual respect people from every corner of the earth, every racial and ethnic background, all socioeconomic strata, the Church is the sign of our union with God and one another effected in Jesus Christ.[16]

Although we make distinctions for analytical purposes and for formal instruction, we can see from these two examples that in actuality the Christian way of life, its worship, and service are one. Except for verbal distinctions, in real life all three aspects are so intimately connected that the bishops conclude that the Christian community characterized by its stewardship "catechizes its members by its very life and work, giving witness in a multitude of ways to God's love as revealed and communicated to us in Christ."[17]

FAITH AND MORALS AS ONE. The biblical, liturgical, ecclesial, and natural signs of catechesis indicate the integral unity of faith and morality. Hence, when the Directory stresses that the task of catechesis is to foster maturity of faith, it implies that the task also includes fostering moral maturity, since faith without good works is dead. A living faith is expressed in action;

people witness to their true faith by the behavior which characterizes their life-style. As an old saw puts it, actions speak louder than words—so loud that at times one cannot hear the words being spoken. For example, we may verbally proclaim "Our hope is in the Lord. He is our strength and our salvation." Or we may preach or teach or tell our children that faith in God means that we believe God really cares about us and will always provide for us in all that we need. But if deep inside ourselves we continually feel helpless and hopeless, and if our actions witness to the fact that we do not really believe or trust anyone, then we are giving a confused and confusing Christian witness. Or if someone comes up to you and says, "My, how good it is to see you!" but then avoids eye contact and moves on before you can acknowledge the greeting, the body language says that this person does not really feel good about seeing you.[18]

Education in faith—in which the focus is knowing intellectually—must go hand in hand with education in morals—in which the focus is enacted affections that are intelligible and infused with spirit. Otherwise, the lesson actually learned may contradict the words being taught, and an innocent youngster may become unsettled, a reflective adolescent may perceive the words as hypocritical, a mature adult may recognize their hollowness and walk away. Education in both faith and morals, the two sides of the coin called catechesis, serves to correct the imbalance that results from teaching words that do not come from or reflect one's life experiences. To ring true, education in faith and morals calls for a holistic catechesis addressing cognitions and affections, spiritual and physical realities, and embracing the whole community as catechists and catechized.

CHARACTERISTICS OF A HOLISTIC CATECHESIS

Although the label may be contemporary, the holistic approach is not new. It is a return to teaching as Jesus did. It is a return to what formerly characterized the Catholic tradition when catechesis, or religious education, was an initiation to wholeness, to a full way of life. This holistic approach involved the whole person and the whole community in the process.[19] Over time, though, by modeling itself on schools and their techniques, religious education became primarily an intellectual activity. It was assumed that if the faith were presented with intellectual clarity, a whole-hearted response would follow; the Graeco-Roman notion of knowing abstractly was confused with knowing experientially. In recent times, however, theologians, catechists, and the bishops themselves are calling us back to our original approach.[20]

AIMS OF A HOLISTIC APPROACH. The National Catechetical Directory asserts that the purpose of catechesis is to make a person's faith become living, conscious, and active, through the light of instruction. The Directory stresses that to achieve this aim, catechesis must be a lifelong process for the individual and a constant and concerted pastoral activity of the Christian community. Hence, the essential elements of the religious life, which for many centuries were the preserve of a professed few, must once again be made available so that *all* Christians can mature in holiness.[21] A holistic approach models itself on the religious life as it aims to balance physical and mental work and prayer. A holistic approach recognizes the need for guidance, leisure, and care for oneself and for others, all of which seem necessary for a mature faith—which I recognize as a simplicity and openness to life coming from the lived belief that God is at work in all. And so the believer's responses to all forms and levels of creation are but part of an ongoing dialogue with God, part of the cooperative process of renewing the face of the earth.

In more pragmatic terms the Directory reiterates the aims of a holistic approach to catechesis. It states that although "our final goal is in eternity, faith in God and union with Christ entail an obligation to seek solutions for human problems here and now."[22] Presenting Jesus Christ as the one who most fully revealed the meaning and destiny of human life, the Directory points out how Christ reveals the response we are to make to our calling to live in love. Simultaneously, he empowers us to make an affirmative response to this invitation to live love. The power is that of God's own Spirit (Love) dwelling within each of us.

The Spirit prompts people to seek what is good and helps them to advance in such virtues as charity, joy, peace, patience, kindness, forbearance, humility, fidelity, modesty, continence, and chastity. (Cf. Gal 5,22f)

Christ teaches that love of God and love of neighbor spring from the same Spirit and are inseparable. (Cf. 1 Jn 4, 12f,20f) We are to love all human beings, even enemies, as we love ourselves; even more, we are to obey Christ's new command to love all others as He has loved us. (Cf Jn 13,34;15,12f)

By this command Christ tells us something new— about God, about love and about ourselves. His command to love is "new" not simply because of the scope and unselfishness of the love involved, but because it summons human beings to love with a divine love called charity, as the Father, Son, and Spirit do. This call carries with it the inner gift of their life and the power of their love, for Christ does not command what is impossible.[23]

As I understand them, these passages present the whole aim of what I have termed the holistic approach to catechesis: to bring about a life-style that makes love *real*, that makes justice visible in action. To achieve this aim, education in faith and morals has to go beyond the classroom or schooling model. It has to engage more than the learner's reasoning ability. Christian moral education must of course develop the learner's reasoning ability, include memorization of essentials such as the Beatitudes and the Commandments, and provide for clarification of values. To be effective, however, it has to continue the process of developing the individual's full potential: the affective and behavioral as well as the intellectual and spiritual. Witness the saints and heroes of our tradition. They were not canonized because of their astuteness or knowledge but because of the evident goodness of their lives. Is this not our goal for religious education? To achieve this goal, a multi-faceted, holistic approach is called for. Such an approach issues in education in which faith and morals are intrinsically and actively related. It issues in people whose professed belief and actual behavior are consonant with each other.

SCOPE OF A HOLISTIC CATECHESIS. When we reflect on the meaning of the words the Directory uses in reference to the goal of catechesis, it seems fair to say that its scope is awesome. To live God's love in everyday life is an awesome expectation.

Although this book will describe methods of living out a mature faith, let us be aware that faith is basically a gift. It is our belief as Catholic Christians that this gift has been freely, graciously given to each of us and that it is our fundamental option to respond to, or refuse, the gift. If we refuse to live lovingly, if we choose to devise our own methods and go our own way through life without making God, who is Love, real and tangible within our world, then we are essentially choosing death.

Faith eventuates in action. The realization of God in our midst is our affirmative response to the gift of faith; and as the dictionary reminds us, *to realize is to bring into concrete existence.* Hence this realization of our faith in God is a daily requisite; day in and day out, on high days and low days, faith calls for a lifetime engagement.

It is an awesome catechesis which proposes to enable us to know, love, and serve God, neighbor, and self integrally in this world, so that our fullness of life will extend to the next. If such moral exhortations as the two Great Commandments are not parodies of vain hope tantalizing us with unachievable ideals, then the scope of catechesis is awesome, too.

It is true that the realization of these ideals is a grace. But just as Aquinas develops his moral theology on the premise that grace builds on nature, so too must education in faith and morals build on nature. That is, a holistic catechesis must be an ongoing process addressing all ages and stages of believers in modes appropriate to their full human nature as well as to their particular needs and levels of development. Hence we must keep in mind the following points in order to balance the teaching of *intellectual information* eventuating in the learning about certain things, and *affective formation*, culminating in learning to respond wholeheartedly.[24]

1. Affective education, or the education of the emotions, may at first glance seem formidable or faddish. From its definition, however, one soon realizes that it has traditionally been an essential element of catechesis; only in recent times has it become trivialized. *Human Teaching for Human Learning* defines the scope of affective education as "the identification for specific educational concern of the nonintellective side of learning: the side having to do with emotions, feelings, interests, values, and character."[25] Hence reflection upon life experiences, upon one's

feelings, moods, and attitudes falls within the scope of a holistic approach and is therapeutic. However, it can become shallow if it is devoid of doctrine, devoid of the Good News that empowers us to break out of those cycles that bind and drain and, sadly, sometimes even damn.

2. Meanings, terms, stories, fomulas, creeds, and the array of answers to life's ultimate questions form a part of catechesis. But unless there is genuine interest or felt need on the part of the catechized, no real learning occurs. Hence for catechesis to be education in faith and morals and not subtle indoctrination, the doctrine taught has to be fitted to the learner's needs and hungers, life experiences, and critical events.[26] Too much information given too soon will most likely result in aversion on the part of the learner. It is like feeding a full dinner to an infant or to someone who is ill. We nudge and coax and cajole until they swallow, only to discover later that they have spit it out. Their tolerance is limited; they could not absorb all that might be good for them. In effect, they have become sickened by the good, so that at a later time when they would have been properly disposed to savor and appreciate the message, they tend to avoid it. For catechesis to be well received, we must use affective, experiential, and conceptual approaches working in tandem and in a developmental sequence. Later chapters will both make this principle clearer and describe approaches for implementing it.

3. When affective and cognitive elements are integrated or flow together in individual and group learning, we have *confluent education.*[27] In its better moments catechesis, like education in general, has been confluent. But too often one aspect has been neglected in favor of the other. The signs of our times demand a conscious reinstatement of both. In fact, although both cognitive and affective elements are necessary, they do not address the full scope of education in faith and morals. What is needed is a more comprehensive approach, or a holistic catechesis.

HOLISTIC CATECHESIS DEFINED. A review of the findings of psychology and of education, especially as these disciplines address the spiritual and moral dimensions of the person, and an understanding of the educational outcome the Church is seeking in catechesis, are the bases for the approach I call holistic catechesis—a term used to describe the type of religious education which the Church, in all its variety of models and dimensions, calls for today. By a holistic catechesis I mean education in faith and morals which involves the whole person of the learner and the whole community of faith in a reciprocal relationship of instructor and one being instructed. A holistic approach consciously and properly addresses (1) the intellectual domain; (2) the affective domain, especially as it affects conation, which is the expression of will; (3) the spiritual domain, which includes imagination and intuition; and (4) the physical domain, the realm of the senses. Because of the organic relationship between the learner and the physical and social environment and the effects of one upon the other, a holistic catechesis provides meaningful ways to make the most of salvific or therapeutic relationships.

FUNCTIONS AND CONCOMITANT APPROACHES. A brief description of the functions of each of these domains and of concomitant approaches which together comprise a holistic approach to catechesis is in order here. A detailed explication of the what and why and how to of each is the subject of subsequent chapters.

　　1. *The intellectual domain.* Although there are 120 conceivable mental abilities,[28] for our purposes the functions of the intellectual domain include the individual's thinking ability, memory, critical reflection, and understanding. The development of the intellectual domain enables us to *understand* better what Catholic Christianity is *(kerygma)*, to *recall* our story as Christian *(anamnesis)*, and to *communicate* it with greater candor and clarity *(didache)*. Development of the intellect *(ratio, right reason)* enables the faithful to better understand the place of revelation and tradition in our lives and to make more fitting and mature moral decisions in response to life's questions. However, the subjective aspect (the developmental level of the learner) and the objective aspect (the content presented) must be consonant. The catechist needs to order the content and to present it in a balanced and systematic manner. John Paul II cautions that "the method and language used must truly be means for communicating the whole and not just a part of 'the words of eternal life' and 'ways of life.' "[29]

2. *The affective domain.* Although conceptual knowledge, that is, knowledge of the facts of our faith, is good in its own right, it does not by itself produce commitment to the faith. Evaluative knowledge, which is a knowing with the heart, is also necessary; and evaluative knowledge is an outcome of affective education. By the affective domain is meant the affections and aversions, feelings, moods, attitudes, or qualities that characterize us. The qualities which distinguish a person, such as joy or pessimism, eagerness or apathy, worry or tranquility, are the subjects of education in the affective domain. The affective domain gives us a feeling for life. It functions to make us *feel* alive, to experience our individuality as being alive. Thus even if the feelings are distorted, as in paranoia, for example, it is that very fear, that *being afraid*, that enables the paranoid individual to experience himself or herself *as being alive.* To rephrase Descartes, "I feel; therefore I am."

Education in the affective domain enables the catechized to order their passions and energies rightly so that they can appreciate or have a feel for all that they are learning. Affective education frees them to respond wholeheartedly, rather than compulsively, to the message: to the truth, goodness, and beauty of God's revelation within their neighbors and themselves. Without such appreciative knowledge it is impossible to have a community of the faithful, the *koinonia* that is essential to Christianity. Community is not a concept that, once evoked, invokes the reality. Community is *experienced.* For committed Christians, the building of community is a lifelong process calling for the engagement of all who are convinced it is right to respond to the covenant call. It calls for the purification of baser motivations to free believers to see ever more clearly God's providence and to respond to it in an ever more fitting manner.

Self-knowledge is necessary for the catechized to respond to life freely, with hearts open to be filled with love, rather than with hearts constrained by fear or pseudo self-sufficiency. In the education of the affections we come to know ourselves, our strengths and our limits, our fracturedness, and our need for healing—for being healed and extending healing to one another. Education of the emotions enables the catechized to deal effectively with libidinal energy. By means of affective education they are prepared for a transformation or conversion *(metanoia).*

If they are willing to be transformed, to have a change of heart, the catechized witness to a life-style that is a freely chosen commitment rather than an accident of birth, a habit, or a means of assuaging fear of eternal damnation which manifests itself in a compulsive religiosity.

By clarifying their values affectively (which may call for individual and/or group counseling) and by dealing with defenses that disable the self and destroy community, the catechized are empowered to make mature moral choices. Their moral style will be like Jesus', whose morality exemplifies the Beatitudes and the corporal and spiritual works of mercy. That is, their motivation will be the intent to realize the good rather than to merely avoid evil. For it is by freely choosing to do good rather than merely omitting to do evil that we actualize love. But in order to do good willingly we need to understand our motivation and intentions, our moods and attitudes, fears and hopes, joys and pains. It is in this manner that the education of the emotions not only serves a therapeutic function for the individual but serves a salvific function in freeing the community to grow toward fullness of life.[30] Approaches which address the affective domain include techniques for self-actualization and human relations, individual counseling, and group dynamics.[31]

3. *The spiritual domain.* A holistic catechesis strives to actualize persons of mature faith, who in turn give shape to a mature community of faith. Such a community is at one in a sacred work (*liturgia*). It sees itself empowered by the Holy Spirit to renew the face of the earth by the witness of its life-style. In its rituals and sacraments the community symbolically reenacts its communion with the Creator and all creation. In so doing it celebrates its basic belief that daily life is a mystery to be engaged in rather than a problem to be avoided. Bringing about reconciliation and freeing the spirit in each to experience the Spirit in all calls for intuitive knowledge, a function of the spiritual domain. In this context the spiritual domain includes the creative imagination and intuition. It is that part of our psyche which brings forth aesthetic meaning, moral insights, creative alternatives to moral dilemmas—in short, wisdom.

Whereas the function of the affective domain is to make one feel alive, the function of the spiritual domain, of intuition and imagination, is to make one feel connected with the Transcendent, with the "greater than" or "the other world." Intuition and imagination are the bases of creativity and invention. Imagination functions to evoke and create not only visual images but also auditory, tactile, and kinesthetic experiences. Imagination and intuition help us see old things in new ways. Intuitions come as gifts and enable us to transform old realities into new ones, as, for example, Jesus did at the Last Supper when he transformed Passover bread into his body. Intuition and imagination bring to us both goblins and fairy tales, demons and angels, art and music, extrasensory perceptions, such as clairvoyance, and, more commonly, foresight. Intuition and imagination are non-rational functions but are not necessarily irrational—except for those whose spiritual vision has been deadened and who therefore can make sense of reality only through logical analysis or pragmatic calculations. For example, although sociology offers pragmatic explanations for worship such as attendance at Sunday Mass, to the believer such calculations or even rational explanations make little sense. The believer is engaged on another level—that of the Spirit.

Intuition, which for our purposes means attunement to the Spirit, is cultivated through receptive prayer, or meditation. What many are seeking from Eastern philosophies, what more advanced psychologies are just beginning to discover as a powerful tool for personal transformation, and what those on the cutting edge of holistic education are striving to introduce into the public schools as ways of bringing interior calm to the individual and unity or peaceful harmony and openness in the classroom, the Church has always encouraged, especially for those serious about the spiritual life. Meditation, a supposedly esoteric discipline to bring about this state of mind, demands simplicity and the discipline of detachment. It calls for letting go of one's preconceptions, emptying the self of preoccupations so that the soul can recognize its gifts and its oneness with all. Meditation is a basic means for cultivating intuition, so necessary for the discernment of spirits.

Intuition is that psychological function by which we can see beyond the facts and so perceive intangibles in a given situation. Carl Jung, a pioneer in the study of the religious dimension of the psyche, describes this phenomenon: "My psychological experience has shown time and again that certain contents arise from a psyche that is more complete than consciousness. They often contain a super-analysis or insight or knowledge which consciousness has not been able to produce. We have a suitable word for such occurrences—intuition."[32]

Through the cultivation of intuition, one's spiritual awareness is heightened. The vast reservoir of the unconscious becomes accessible, bringing to the fore the individual's gifts and talents. He or she is enabled to live life at its heights. This state is referred to as mysticism. True mysticism does not eventuate in inaction. Rather it is the matrix of an ebb and flow, of action and contemplation. In *Charismatic Renewal and Social Action: A Dialogue*, Cardinal Suenens and Dom Helder Camara remind us that authentic Christians raise their hearts to God while extending their hands to the people. They urge the Charismatic renewal to stress both of the Great Commandments: love of God and love of neighbor. In their view, "A Christian who is not Charismtic—in the full sense of the word, that is to say, open to the Spirit and docile to his promptings—is a Christian forgetful of his baptism. On the other hand, a Christian who is not 'socially committed' is a truncated Christian who disregards the gospel's commandments."[33]

In teaching Christians to pray, to meditate and contemplate, to experience the fullness of their sacramental lives, catechesis is educating people into mysticism. Christian mysticism in turn leads to social action (*diakonia*). The life of Catherine of Siena, like that of other sainted mystics, will attest to this balance of prayer and action.

4. *The physical domain.* Intuitions go awry and symbolic or sacramental formulae become hollow if they don't somehow become tangible in the material realm of everyday reality. If our prayers do not really signify Good News—that is, if they do not bring about the good in daily life—then they are empty; they have lost their sacramental meaning. If we focus on the spiritual to the detriment of the physical, we can readily lose touch with the real world and get caught up in our own words and in gods of our own making. Dichotomizing creation into sacred and secular spheres results in violence. Whether actively engaged in or passively permitted, violence is a result of not seeing God in everyone and everything. It is ignoring the cry of the Spirit

groaning "Abba" within all of us. Busy with its own misshapen views, misguided mysticism is the refusal to hear the pleas of our brothers and sisters, of rivers and trees, of the whole ecology. It is expecting the *deus ex machina* to come forth and save the day if we but pray.

By contrast, a holistic catechesis respects the mystery that we are both body and spirit; hence it enables us to develop a meaningful spiritual life grounded in a sound sensuality, in an engagement with all that is good. A spirituality that comes from a holistic education in true Christian faith and morality results in compassion, concern, and care for the physical domain, the realm of the senses. By the physical domain is meant everything that has to do with our bodiliness. It extends to all that is a part of our physical composition: the earth, water, air, and energy. The material domain includes all that we sense—that is, what we see, smell, taste, hear, touch, or feel. Its function is to assure survival. Education of the physical, of the domain of the senses, is essential to promote reverence for life. Basically, it is education for both individual and universal survival. But it begins with the individual. For only as we learn to care for ourselves can we care for another; we cannot give what we do not have. Hence we cannot love our neighbor as ourselves if we do not love ourselves.

A holistic catechesis makes provisions for the Christian to look at himself or herself and to affirm all that is good. In recognizing the worth or loveliness of all one's powers, including one's bodiliness or sensuality, the Christian realizes that the glory of God is indeed man and woman fully alive. Those so catechized admit in what they say and do that Jesus has come to bring us fullness of life, and that we are ever so gifted—if only we will open our eyes to our gracefulness, our goodness, our power to make a difference with our lives here and now in this world.

Enjoying and employing all of one's charisms, the self lives fully. Seeing every other as another self and ministering accordingly, the catechized comes to be at one with all; and so one becomes universal and loves universally. Experiential religious education, or education for justice, enfleshes our faith and our moral language. Actual involvement with the poor, the handicapped, the scorned, and those deprived of civil or human rights—in a spirit of compassion, as opposed to compulsion—

makes all the difference in the world. By this means, all involved—teachers, learners, givers, and receivers—are evangelized. All are thereby existentially instructed in the Way, a life-style characteristic of the early Church. In this Way the catechized learn to live like Jesus.

The introduction noted how Jesus spent forty days in the wilderness in prayer. Renewed in spirit, he returns home, proclaims and fulfills the word of the Lord God. Ministering to the blind, the poor, the oppressed, Jesus extends himself to all. So too the goal of a holistic catechesis is the development of reasoning Christians who know and joyfully actualize the ideals of Jesus by doing justice out of reverent respect for the God-given dignity of all people and all creation. Such a catechesis calls for the development and integration of the thinking, feeling, intuiting, and sensing functions of the individual. According to Carl Jung, this is the epitome of personal development, and the means for accomplishing it have all been part of our Catholic tradition. We have traditionally recognized the fullness of personal development as holiness. Using different words to describe it, theology and psychology have both demonstrated how this fullness of life is possible. Both disciplines have shown how Jesus exemplifies the fully functioning person.[34] Since the focal point of all catechesis is Christocentric, can we do less?

NOTES

1.   Berard L. Marthaler, O.F.M. Conv., *Catechetics in Context: Notes and Commentary on the General Catechetical Directory* (Huntington, IN: Our Sunday Visitor, Inc., 1973), p. 35.

2.   *Fundamentals and Programs of a New Catechesis* (Pittsburgh: Duquesne University Press, 1966), p. 88.

3.   Marthaler, *Catechetics*, p. 35.

4.   Joseph Colomb, *Al servizio della fede* (Torino-Leumann: Elle Di Ci, 1969), I, pp. 7-8, as cited in Marthaler, *Catechetics*, pp. 35, 37.

5.   John Paul II, *Catechesi Tradendae: Apostolic Exhortation on Catechetics* in *Origins* (Washington, D.C.: National Catholic News Service, 1979), p. 334 (#18).

6. Ibid., p. 334 (#17).

7. Some authors call catechesis a pastoral activity but claim that religious education is primarily an academic enterprise. However, since few scholars can agree on the specific differences between these terms, *catechesis* and *religious education* are used synonymously in this book. See Marthaler, *Catechetics*, p. 35.

8. National Conference of Catholic Bishops, *Sharing the Light of Faith: National Catechetical Directory for Catholics of the United States* (Washington, D.C.: United States Catholic Conference, 1979), pp. 126-129 (#205-213) and p. 154 (#249).

9. John Paul II, *Catechesi*, p. 331 (#5). The reference is to Ephesians 3:9, 18-19.

10. National Conference of Catholic Bishops, *To Teach as Jesus Did: A Pastoral Message on Catholic Education* (Washington, D.C.: United States Catholic Conference Publications Office, 1973), p. 4 (#14).

11. Ibid., pp. 4-5 (#14).

12. *National Catechetical Directory*, pp. 22-23 (#43).

13. *National Catechetical Directory*, p. 24 (#46).

14. Sacred Congregation for the Clergy, *General Catechetical Directory* (Washington, D.C.: United States Catholic Conference, 1971), #97.

15. *National Catechetical Directory*, p. 24 (#45).

16. Ibid.

17. Ibid.

18. See Julian Fast, *Body Language* (New York: Evans, 1970).

19. See The Murphy Center for Liturgical Research, *Made Not Born: New Perspectives on Christian Initiation and the Catechumenate* (Notre Dame: University of Notre Dame Press, 1976).

20. *Becoming a Catholic Christian: A Symposium on Christian Initiation* (New York: Sadlier, 1979).

21. An underlying argument here is that the process of living an individual-communal spirituality, which until recently was considered the preserve of the professed religious or of mystics and considered supererogatory for the common Christian, needs to be adapted and become common fare for all

who intend to profess Christianity in word and in deed. In this sense catechesis is not a duty to be performed for some few. It is a lifelong process involving all who have made a commitment to live as Christians.

22. National Catechetical Directory, p. 49 (#86).

23. National Catechetical Directory, p. 51 (#91).

24. John Paul II, Catechesi, p. 335 (#20-22) on "Specific Aims of Catechesis," "Need for Systematic Catechesis," and "Catechesis and Life Experience."

25. Stuart Miller, as cited in George I. Brown, Human Teaching for Human Learning (New York: The Viking Press, 1971), p. xvi.

26. National Catechetical Directory, p. 101 (#176).

27. Brown, Human Teaching, p. 3.

28. J. P. Guilford, "The Structure of Intellect," Psychological Bulletin 53(1956):267-293, describes the content, operations, and products of the intellect in greater detail. Benjamin S. Bloom et al., Taxonomy of Educational Objectives, Handbooks I and II (New York: Longmans, Green, 1956), provides an extended classification of educational goals for the cognitive and affective domains. What Bloom calls cognitive, I see as intellectual, for cognition also includes a knowing with one's heart, spirit, or body.

29. John Paul II, Catechesi, p. 337 (#31).

30. Cf. The Personality and Human Relations (PRH) Institutes, which deal with the affective life and seeking God. They originated in France in the 1960s under Andre Rochais. They are being conducted by religious and are becoming popular among Catholics on the West Coast. For more information on this catechetical approach write to the PRH Office, W. 4000 Randolph Road, Spokane, WA 99204; or call (509) 328-2976.

31. See Bruce Joyce and Marsha Weil, Models of Teaching (Englewood Cliffs, NJ: Prentice-Hall, 1972), part II, "The Personal Sources."

32. C. G. Jung, Collected Works (London: Routledge & Kegan Paul, 1960), as cited in Thomas A. Kane, The Healing Touch of Affirmation (Whitinsville, MA: Affirmation Books, 1976), p. 68.

33. Cardinal Leon-Joseph Suenens and Dom Helder Camara, Charismatic Renewal and Social Action: A Dialogue (Ann Arbor, MI: Servant Publications, 1979), pp. 2-3.

34. See John A. Sanford, The Kingdom Within: A Study of the Inner Meaning of Jesus' Sayings (Philadelphia: J. B. Lippincott, 1970).

2. ON THE DEVELOPMENT OF FAITH: CATECHESIS FOR UNDERSTANDING THE MESSAGE

This chapter examines the way the message of faith is received at the various stages in one's life. First the chapter summarizes the work of Piaget, Goldman, and Allport in this regard. Then it presents Allport's characteristics of mature belief. Following that is Fowler's description of how one matures in faith. The second part of the chapter offers some catechetical approaches that are respectful of the needs and limits of the learner at the different developmental stages. Although it focuses on the intellectual cognition of faith, the chapter begins to substantiate the two premises on which this book is based: (1) It alludes to the intimate connection between faith and morals both within a community (mythos ↔ ethos) and within the individual (belief ↔ action); (2) The catechetical approaches begin to show that for an understanding of faith to be effective in transforming the lives of the catechized, the message has to be proclaimed holistically—that is, intellectually, affectively, spiritually, and sensually.

The substance of the chapter is consonant with Paul's exhortation to the Corinthians: "When I was a child, I used to talk like a child, and think like a child, and argue like a child, but now I am a man all childish ways are put behind me."[1] Its content is summarized in a statement from the National Catechetical Directory:

Because the life of faith is related to human development, it passes through stages or levels; furthermore, different people possess aspects of faith in different degrees. This is true, for example, of the comprehensiveness and intensity with which they accept God's word, of their ability to explain it, and of their ability to apply it to life. Catechesis is meant to help at each stage of human development and lead ultimately to full identification with Jesus.[2]

Psychologists researching the development of faith spell out in detail the phenomenon of human development alluded to by

Paul and by the National Catechetical Directory. Before
reviewing the research let us put the theories into a catechetical
context by briefly noting pertinent Church teaching. According
to Vatican II's *Christus Dominus*, the purpose of catechesis is to
make a person's faith become "living, conscious, and active,
through the light of instruction."[3] But since catechesis aims to
enrich the faith life of individuals, it presupposes evangelization,
which is a closely related form of ministry. The purpose of
evangelization is to arouse the *beginnings* of faith, to bring the
Good News into all strata of humanity in order ultimately to
renew humanity by transforming it from within. Like catechesis,
evangelization aims at interior change, at the development or
conversion of "the personal and collective conscience of people,
the activities in which they engage, and the lives and concrete
milieux which are theirs."[4] Hence the National Catechetical
Directory states that neither evangelization nor catechesis is
complete if it does not take into account the constant interplay
between Gospel teaching and human experience. It emphasizes
that social change and renewal are goals of catechesis as much as
they are of evangelization. The bishops state that "to consider
evangelization only as a verbal proclamation of the Gospel robs
it of much of its richness; just as it does not do justice to
catechesis to think of it as instruction alone."[5]

   Moving from evangelization and catechesis as processes of
faith development to their expression, we find that faith is
expressed in *words and deeds,* according to the Directory. Believers
grow in insight through study and contemplation of tradition
and Scripture, which are the deposit of the word of God
committed to the Church. The community of believers expresses
its faith by means of words, such as creeds and dogmas, moral
principles, and teachings. The words come alive in the deeds of
the Church community. These deeds include both worship
(especially the celebration of the Eucharist) and actions
performed to build up Christ's body through service to all. The
Directory makes clear the intimate connection between the
words of faith and moral action: "While it is true that our
actions establish the sincerity of our words, it is equally true that
our words must be able to explain our actions."[6] Thus faith
involves intellectual acceptance and active response. Through
faith we have a new vision of God, of the world, and of

ourselves. In faith we not only accept the Christian message; *we act on it,* "witnessing as individuals and a community to all that Jesus said and did. Catechesis thus 'gives clarity and vigor to faith, nourishes a life lived according to the spirit of Christ, leads to a knowing and active participation in the liturgical mystery, and inspires apostolic action.' "[7]

CONTRIBUTIONS OF PIAGET AND GOLDMAN

Reviewing the work of Ronald Goldman will help us understand how the richness of the deposit of faith is assimilated by the variety of believers who form the Church. Goldman's research on the development of religious thinking from childhood through adolescence is consistent with that of Gordon Allport and James Fowler in that each notes how the individual can grow from a childish faith to maturity of belief—that is, from an egocentric understanding of religion as something extrinsic and even magical to a greater interiority and at-oneness with all. Goldman, like Fowler (and Kohlberg, who will be treated in the next chapter), explores the individual's development from the standpoint of a structuralist theory of knowledge, which is Jean Piaget's contribution to how we structure knowledge—that it, how we know what we know. To understand the theories of the development of religious thinking, faith, and moral reasoning let us look at what structures of knowledge presuppose.

PIAGET'S STRUCTURALIST THEORY OF KNOWING. Structuralism assumes that we receive and respond to the world (information, data, or what we think about) in a variety of ways, patterns, or structures. Structuralism proposes that the mind organizes all its input by employing these patterns or structures to construct the ideas, concepts, and beliefs that give form to (constitute) the substance of thinking and valuing.[8] From this structuralist standpoint Piaget argues that differences in mental abilities are not the result solely of biological maturation or of the unfolding of innate talents. Nor, he maintains, is mental development solely a function of the environment's influence on a passive or neutral individual, as if the mind were a blank slate or a computer being programmed. Piaget regards learning as the interplay between an active, structuring self and an equally dynamic environment. Mental development is a function of combining nature and nurture, native capacity and interaction with the social environment in a way that leads to transcending one's original perspective. As the individual interacts, over periods of time, with significant others and events that are at the same time accepted and questioned, human thinking develops. Hence the thinking of children systematically differs in significant ways from that of adults.

Thinking develops according to certain uniform patterns (structural stages) which, according to Piaget, are universal; they are found in all cultures and human groupings. These structures are invariant in the sequence of development; that is, each step or stage builds on the preceding one, so the developing individual cannot skip over one step to get to the next higher one. Each more advanced stage of cognitive development transforms and incorporates the best features of the earlier stages. Chart 1 summarizes the stages (structures or patterns) of intellectual development.[9]

Chart 1
PIAGET'S STAGES OF INTELLECTUAL DEVELOPMENT

Stage	Approximate Age Range	Major Achievements Affecting Religious Thinking	Major Intellectual Limitations Affecting Faith
Sensori-motor	Birth—two	Recognition of patterns, that objects have permanency	Egocentrisim: cannot differentiate between self and external world
Preoperational, or Prelogical thinking	Two—six	Functioning with symbols (such as language, role-playing, and imitation)	Cannot differentiate between symbols and objects they represent
Concrete operational thinking	Six—twelve	Thinking independently of the experience	Cannot differentiate between thoughts about reality and actual experiences of reality
Formal operational thinking	Twelve on	Abstract thinking (hypothetical, counterfactual, and propositional)	Scope of one's imaginery audience and personal fable is limited

GOLDMAN'S STAGES OF RELIGIOUS THINKING. To understand the development of religious thinking, Goldman applied the criteria for stages of intellectual development established by Piaget to the responses of children and adolescents to questions about the Bible, the Church, prayer, God's nature and activity in the world, divine providence, and the punishment of evil. His research revealed a high correlation between the ages of the respondents and the types of answers they gave. Like Piaget, Goldman found major stages in the development of religious thinking, with transitional stages connecting them. Goldman's major stages are those of pre-religious thinking, sub-religious thinking, and personal religious thinking.

Pre-religious thinking is characteristic of young children, five to nine years old. It is similar to Piaget's prelogical thinking. At this stage the individual is unable to go beyond literal meanings. Since the child has neither life experience nor the mental capacity to check out conclusions in light of evidence, pre-religious understandings are often illogical and inconsistent. A child will assert that "God can be unfair if he wants, 'cause he can do anything" while at the same time affirming that God loves everyone.[10] Concerned with God's vengeance, the child believes that naughty people are not only unloved but vehemently punished; God divides people into good and bad, loved and unloved, favored and nonfavored, worth saving and not worth saving.

The Bible is considered a book of magical and holy veneration written by God himself and therefore entirely and literally true. As one child explained, the Bible was "dictated by God, and Jesus took it down on his typewriter."[11] Jesus is viewed as an angelic boy and perfect man (because all grown-ups are perfect). He is frequently confused with God, who is conceived in anthropomorphic terms as living in heaven, a place situated in the sky, and making occasional visits in person to the earth, although not as often as in olden times because now people are naughtier.

Even when the child at this stage prays for others, his or her prayers are largely egocentric and materialistic. Thus in praying for friends, the child prays that God will make them be good friends. "The child feels his prayers come true for magical reasons, or they don't come true because he has been naughty or impolite. He enjoys church to a limited degree, especially the singing, but experiences some fears about it, as well as physical fatigue."[12] God and Santa Claus are equal in stature at this stage. Because the pre-religious child is not yet logical, many religious ideas are drastically misunderstood.

Sub-religious thinking occurs roughly from ages nine to thirteen; the child is in a stage between fantasy and adult logic as he or she is developing what Piaget terms concrete operational thought. Although the pre-adolescent can reason, it is only about concrete, specific things. And so at this stage the learner has a propensity for accumulating facts and dealing with concrete information rather than engaging in logical discussions about the faith, since he or she is not yet capable of reflective reasoning.

Cruder, anthropomorphic ideas of God are receding, and a dualistic way of making sense of God's activity in the natural world is developing at this time. In becoming aware of scientific matters while still holding infantile ideas of God's arbitrary intervention in the world, the individual begins to dichotomize the theological and the scientific. Understanding the Bible literally, the child reveres it as an authority, even though recognizing its multiple authorship and minor mistakes. Jesus is regarded as a normal, serious-minded boy whose significance stems from his miracles. The devil is seen as more menacing than in the previous stage, being regarded as the evil spirit or mastermind behind all evil actions, as though the child has become more aware of the fact of evil. At the threshold of thinking that love and justic may be compatible, the child is still unable to overcome the problem of evil people and regards God as occasionally unfair. True altruism and prayers of self-examination begin to occur at this period; the individual expresses the desire to be better morally and is most open to learning formal prayer.[13] The church at this stage is a place of worship where adults go to learn about God and Jesus and where the child is helped to be a better person.

Personal religious thinking is the watershed in religious conceptual development and occurs about the age of thirteen. As learners begin to break out of concrete modes of reasoning, they start to think abstractly and in terms of hypotheses or propositions. They are now able to conceive of God in a symbolic and abstract manner. It is only by analogy that physical terms are used to describe God, who is regarded as essentially unseen and unseeable, unimpeded by physical limitations, omnipresent to all. With less capable adolescents, however, there are still traces of anthropomorphism. Because the natural and supernatural worlds are still separate in the early adolescent's thinking, conflict about miracles is evident. The Bible is now seen in a truer light, although some still cling to it as infallible in all matters, while others tend to reject it because of the earlier uncorrected misconceptions of authoritarian literalism. Punishment is now related to degrees of guilt, and God is regarded as just. No longer are entire groups readily condemned as evil. Goldman says, "A realistic Christology is also evident, where a normal boyhood of Jesus is recognized with normal childhood imperfections as necessary if Jesus was to have been truly man. Jesus is now identified with his mission and the Jesus of history is seen as the incarnation of the Christ."[14]

During adolescence prayers become more altruistic. Prayers of confession, seeking forgiveness, and asking help with school work sharply increase. It is believed that prayers which are contrary to God's will go unanswered. God is felt to be present in prayer and in a sense of peace, calm, or joy. Church is now understood as a fellowship of believers, and churchgoing is seen as a natural expression of belief and a means of making one a better person. Goldman notes a curious occurrence, however. At a time when real religious insights are now possible, there is a strong tendency for negative attitudes to occur, particularly in less capable learners. He concludes that the intellectual difficulties posed by the need to move from a childish to an adult framework may lead many to negating religion as seemingly easier than wrestling with its problems. Thus some tend to give up religious belief and retreat into indifference or hostility.[15]

ALLPORT'S CONTRIBUTIONS TO UNDERSTANDING MATURE FAITH

Like Goldman, Gordon Allport in *The Individual and His Religion*, a classic study of the development of mature religious belief, describes an egocentric, magical, wishful period of *raw credulity*, most clearly seen in the individual who believes indiscriminately in the evidence of his or her senses or imagination. For the credulous believer, whether child or adult, words are as good as facts. If faith development remains arrested at this stage, the believer's primitive credulity lasts throughout life and is characterized by an unquestioning, childish, authoritarian, and irrational religious sentiment.

The doubts and questions of adolescence normally disrupt childish credulity. In seeking to make sense of conflicts, Allport tells us, critical thinking develops. This in turn leads to agnosticism, to a faith seeking understanding. Through critical questioning the individual begins to move from extrinsic to intrinsic reasons for belief as he or she accepts some things and rejects others as unreasonable or unworthy of belief. Rather than extrinsically assenting to articles of faith (which is paying lip service without making a belief evident in one's life-style), the individual who is internalizing the faith begins to act on what he or she assents to, and in a committed way. Hence, as Erik Erikson (to whom we shall refer in the chapter on the development of virtues) states, fidelity (faithfulness) is the product of the successful resolution of the conflicts and doubts characteristic of adolescence.

Religious awakening in the adolescent may be traumatic, semi-traumatic, or gradual, Allport points out. Thus one may move from childish credulity to a somewhat more mature belief as a result of a crisis, or conversion experience, or from an emotionally stimulating event. But for the majority, mature religious belief awakens gradually out of the process of synthesizing doubts and affirmations characteristic of productive thinking.[16]

Adult faith, in Allport's terms, is characterized by a *mature religious sentiment*. This sentiment is a "disposition built up through experience, to respond favorably and in certain habitual ways to conceptual objects and principles that the individual regards as of ultimate importance in his own life, and as having to do with what he regards as permanent or central in the nature of things."[17] Paraphrasing Allport in an essay entitled "From Magic to Faith," Henri Nouwen describes mature faith as a perspective which does not create new things but adds a new dimension to the basic realities of life: "It brings our fragmented personality into a meaningful whole, unifies our divided self. It is the source of inspiration for a searching mind, the basis for a creative community and a constant incentive for an ongoing renewal of life."[18]

Allport states that the development of faith is a lifetime process. It develops as a unique combination of the individual's (1) bodily needs, (2) spiritual values, (3) temperament, (4) hunger for meaning, and (5) response to the surrounding culture.

1. *Bodily needs* include food, water, shelter, health, safety, and companionship, which, Allport points out, serve as a stimulus and way of approaching God, especially at times when these needs are critical.

2. *Spiritual values*, which Allport calls psychogenic interests, are the desires for goodness, beauty, truth, and holiness; these too lead us toward God as we experience them, say, in a sunset, or experience their lack and so pray for justice, harmony, or unity.

3. Allport's listing of the five bases on which personal faith develops affirms the premise undergirding a holistic catechesis; especially so is his notation about how our *temperament* strongly affects our religious sentiment. An individual's religious expression is a reflection of his or her orientation toward introversion or extraversion, toward thinking or feeling, intuiting or sensing. Thus what one recognizes as valid or meaningful is often a function of his or her psychological orientation, just as what the individual tends to discount may be the very thing that personality needs for balance or wholeness.[19] Diagram 2 exemplifies these orientations.

According to psychologist Carl Jung, each individual

Diagram 2
PSYCHOLOGICAL FUNCTIONS

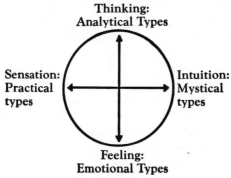

Thinking:
Analytical Types

Sensation:
Practical
types

Intuition:
Mystical
types

Feeling:
Emotional Types

unconsciously tends to organize reality primarily by means of one of these four modes or psychological functions: thinking, feeling, sensing, intuiting. The mode that predominates in an individual takes psychic energy away from its polar opposite. Thus one's very strength is also one's weakness, since too much energy spent in one direction makes for an unbalanced life and a distorted view of reality. For example, when mystical types are told to "come down from the clouds," what is meant is their need to be more practical. They need to "get their feet on the ground" and be in touch with sensible reality. If they do not, they are dismissed as impractical, unbalanced, or "out of it." So too the pragmatic are chided for not being able "to see the forest for the trees" when they tend to become overly concerned with detail and lose the greater vision of life.

Hence while thinking or analytical types may prefer an ordered or logical approach to religion, the feelingful or affective tend to favor the effervescence and charisma arising from communal prayer. The sensate or physically inclined may seek "hands on" experiences and engagement in social action, while the intuitive or spiritual types may find mystical moments of contemplative prayer to be their most meaningful religious expressions. Each individual has a preferred mode of approach to God. Allport concludes that individuals' theological and ritualistic preferences tend to differ "according to their emotional thresholds, according to the quality of their prevailing mood, and according to their tendency to express or inhibit feeling. Moreover, they are likely to be sharply biased in favor of these preferences, and correspondingly critical of others who find a different sort of religion better adapted to their needs."[20]

4. One's *hunger for meaning* further nuances religious expression. The way each individual responds to ultimate questions about the meaning of life, death, sickness, and evil differs and stems from one's developing religious sentiment. Just as the capacity for comprehension differs, so does the ability and inclination to make use of empirical, scientific explanations or of religious symbolism and metaphors to answer life's questions. Thus, just as no two people have identical intellectual difficulties or powers, so no two reach identical solutions or identical religious understanding and expression.

5. In a similar manner, the believer's *response to the surrounding culture*, in combination with the hunger for meaning,

temperament, spiritual values, and bodily needs, strongly influences that individual's religious development and makes for a unique personal faith and morality. The same culture that presents opportunities for one, presents obstacles to another. All these factors lead Allport to conclude that "there are as many varieties of religious experience as there are religiously inclined mortals upon the earth."[21]

THE MATURE RELIGIOUS SENTIMENT. For Allport, personal faith is a function of the individual's unique response to the givens of physical and spiritual desires, temperament, search for meaning, and influence of culture, and although these givens are influential in our becoming, they do not determine outcomes. Each unique person, or self, shapes what that individual becomes; hence despite the existential givens there is freedom of choice or free will in our reponses to life. Totally different responses to the same situation may be seen as one individual's faith deepens in surviving a catastrophe, while another's is shattered by the same event. The difference may be the function of intrinsic as opposed to extrinsic faith.

   Extrinsic religion, Allport says, is a matter of conforming to Church tenets and rules that are not integrated into one's life and so do not facilitate the development of wholeness. Spiritual fragmentation is documented in studies which reveal that those with an extrinsic religious commitment evidence prejudiced, conforming, and authoritarian behavior.[22] *Intrinsic belief*, however, is reflected in a mature religious sentiment. This sentiment or personal faith is the ultimate attempt individuals make to enlarge and complete their own personality by finding the supreme context in which they rightly belong.[23] Since individuals are continually in process of becoming all they can be, their religious sentiment, or expression of faith, even when mature, is still becoming even more so and hence will not be absolutely consistent. Nonetheless there are attributes that mark it off from an immature faith. According to Allport the mature religious sentiment is: "(1) well differentiated; (2) dynamic in character in spite of its derivative nature; (3) productive of a consistent morality; (4) comprehensive; (5) integral; and (6) fundamentally heuristic."[24] Although he distinguishes each quality from the others, in reality they overlap, as can be seen in the following explication of the characteristics of mature faith.

1. *Well-differentiated.* A well-differentiated faith is the outgrowth of critical reflection leading to successive reorganization of one's beliefs. The individual who is maturing questions the oversimplified products of earlier, egocentric thinking and blind conformity to institutional or parental views. He or she is no longer comfortable with literal beliefs and second-hand faith. The need is felt to make religion one's own. In order to appropriate the faith, the individual will discard the beliefs of the child and put on those of an adult. To arrive at a more personal understanding and an intrinsic faith commitment, the believer moves from a roseate, naive view of the Church and comes to see it in all its glory and its weakness, its strength and its sickness. Mature faith enables one to see how the Church has acted as both the faithful and the unfaithful bride of Christ, and still the believer remains steadfast. The mature believer recognizes that we are the ones responsible for both the good and evil outcomes, and so, with eyes wide open to the demands of faith, as opposed to raw credulity, the mature believer intentionally chooses to cooperate with the Holy Spirit to renew the face of the earth.

A well-differentiated faith is balanced, encompassing all dimensions of the person: the rational, emotional, mystical, and conative. A mature believer understands and has a proper attitude toward doctrinal and moral matters, knowing where he or she stands, and acting accordingly. An immature or undifferentiated faith lacks balance and confuses accidentals and essentials. For example, a study of attitudes among Catholics conducted a number of years ago showed that "many were more concerned about the laws of fast and abstinence than they were about the commandment to love all, even enemies."[25]

2. *Dynamic.* Although the religious sentiment is prompted by organic cravings and desires, mature faith develops its own dynamism. Whether in an adult or in a child, immature religion is mainly concerned with self-justification and comfort, indicating that the drives and desires of the body still sustain it. In contrast, mature religion is less a servant and more a master of its drives and desires, as it is no longer goaded and steered exclusively by impulse, fear, or wish. Instead, it tends to control and to direct these motives toward a goal that is no longer determined by mere self-interest.[26] The dynamic nature of mature faith is

neither fanatical nor compulsive. Fanaticism is fed by immature agencies. Allport says of the fanatic sentiment that "Rather than admit criticism that would require the arduous process of differentiation, such a sentiment stiffens and fights intolerantly all attempts to broaden it. In compulsive religion there is a defensive ruling-out of disturbing evidence."[27] On the other hand, mature faith is ardent without being unduly zealous; it maintains an enthusiastic espousal of its objectives and an insatiable thirst for God.

3. and 4. *Consistent and comprehensive.* Mature belief transforms one's character by directing action. It produces a consistent morality, aligning what one does with what one believes. The mature religious sentiment provides the ideals which motivate the maintenance of ethical standards, so that thought, feelings, and action are integrated in the same direction. Comprehensive in character, mature faith manifests a unifying philosophy of life that takes all elements into account and gives meaning to all one's beliefs and behaviors. In Tillich's terms, it serves to integrate for the individual those dimensions of depth or height or ultimacy which inform the very heart of culture. It is the ultimate concern which qualifies all other concerns as preliminary and which itself contains the answer to the question of the meaning of our life.[28] But mature faith is more than a philosophy of life.

5. *Integral.* Although those mature in faith have a seriousness of purpose, they also display a sense of humor, which is a sign of wisdom, since they are able to forgive themselves and all others. Mature faith integrates one's bright side and one's shadow and all areas of life and human knowledge into a harmonious belief system, enabling the individual to face the problems of evil and of limited freedom. Mature faith is evidenced in humility and tolerant behavior. A mature religious sentiment reflects a forgiving graciousness, which is wisdom since it has grown beyond the intolerance or prejudice that comes from blindness to one's own weaknesses and sins and from their projection onto others.[29] An example of such projection and prejudice is found in the biblical account of the men eager to stone the adulteress to death. When Jesus told them that the one without sin could cast the first stone, they all went away; Christ had forced them to look inward. Immature faith looks outward

and is quick to put blame on others. Mature faith recognizes human limitations. Hence the Christian who is developing a mature religious sentiment devotes his or her energies to *correcting conditions instead of condemning people caught in them.* The life of Jesus, like the lives of those canonized as saintly, witnesses to the fact that faith integrates all aspects of life, transforming evil into good.

6. *Heuristic.* The last characteristic of mature faith, Allport tells us, is that it is not set in its ways. Instead, mature faith is heuristic. Like a guiding light, it is a belief one holds and works from until it has confirmed a truth or helps the believer unveil a more valid or more comprehensive belief. Ore who believes heuristically is conscious that our beliefs limit or expand our growth toward wholeness, that our beliefs profoundly affect our physical, mental, emotional, and spiritual health. And so the individual with heuristic beliefs reflects the wisdom Paul shared with the Corinthians by discarding childish beliefs for more fulfilling ones. The mature in faith are wise enough to know that it is better to put new wine into new wineskins than into old ones. Letting go old ways of being and putting on the new is what a dynamic faith—a heuristic belief system—is about.

In letting go the old, mature faith exposes us to risks we must take if we are to become all that we are called to be. The history of our salvation illustrates the risks that faith calls for, as we can see from the example of those who let go their old way of being by risking to follow Moses through the Sea of Reeds into a new life. An example of belief that is not heuristic is evident in the behavior of the rich young man who was dissatisfied with his comfortable way of life and yet was afraid to take the leap of faith; he feared to risk a new way of being that would come about in response to Christ's invitation, "Come, follow me." Mature faith calls for wholehearted response to life's demands even without absolute certainty. Allport sums it up by saying that mature faith is compatible with "an heuristic commitment that has the power to turn desperation into active purpose."[30] Fashioned in the crucible of doubt during the dark night of the soul, a mature religious sentiment is well acquainted with all the grounds for skepticism yet enables the individual to live serenely in faith. From successive acts of commitment with their beneficent consequences, the individual's faith strengthens, and moments of doubt gradually lose their potency for keeping the believer impotent.

VALIDATION OF FAITH. Allport points to ways in which one can assess the validity of faith and notes what mature faith asks the believer to risk. Faith can be confirmed in various ways, according to Allport, depending on the individual's psychological propensity. Fittingly, holistic catechesis appeals to all propensities, or modes of belief. For the thinking type, *rational arguments*, such as Aquinas's or Aristotle's proofs for the existence of God, serve to validate faith. These may leave others cold, especially those who prefer *reasons of the heart*. For such people, validation lies in the very fact that they continually hunger for what no earthly experience can satisfy, and this indicates to them that we are made for more than this world.[31] The unshakeable certainty that the mystics have from their *intuitions* confirms for them the existence of God. Such a validation of faith is not completely understood by others whose religious sentiment is confirmed primarily in a *pragmatic manner*. For them the will to believe, as described by William James, validates faith as it generates higher values, provides strength, meaning, and purpose in living. "Good, believed in, finds itself embodied simply because faith changes aspiration into realization, transforms the possible into the actual."[32] In other words, for the pragmatic to truly believe in the Beatitudes and in Jesus as our model, one's life has to *embody* these ideals; they become actualities. However, if one pays lip-service to Christlike caring for all humanity but regards it as too idealistic for this world, then one does not *really* have faith (although there may be intellectual assent); for if our lives remain untransformed, the Gospel goes unrealized.

Whether one is primarily intellectual, affective, spiritual, or practical, in all mature faith is an *intention*, that is, a mental act expressed in one's life-style. It is a stretching forth of our entire being, aiming at the future, striving to bring into reality a goal that is more or less clearly envisaged. It is not indifferent to the means employed. For the mature believer, to desire an end is to desire the appropriate means to achieve that end. Jesus put it quite simply: "It is not those who say to me, 'Lord, Lord,' who will enter the kingdom of heaven but the person who does the will of my Father in heaven."[33]

FOWLER'S CONTRIBUTIONS TO UNDERSTANDING FAITH DEVELOPMENT

Whereas Goldman's research focused on religious thinking in children and adolescents, and Allport contributed to our understanding of mature faith, James Fowler presents a theory that encompasses faith development from womb to tomb. Working from the Piagetian point of view that cognition develops in stages, Fowler describes six steps, or stages, in the process of faith development. Each stage describes a more mature relationship or response to the surrounding environment and to significant others. Yet "Each stage may be *the* most appropriate stage for a particular person or group. Each stage describes a pattern of valuing, thinking, feeling and committing which is potentially worthy, serene and 'graceful'."[34] In the words of the National Catechetical Directory, the developmental character of faith is like a relationship or friendship between persons. "As the quality of a friendship between human beings is affected by such things as their maturity and freedom, their knowledge of each other, and the manner and frequency of their communication, so the quality of a friendship with God is affected by the characteristics of the human party."[35]

In *Life Maps*, Fowler portrays faith as "a person's or community's way-of-being-in-relation to an ultimate environment."[36] He explains that the character of the ultimate environment as apprehended in faith (which for us is God as revealed in Christ) informs and permeates our way of being in relation to other persons and groups, and to values, causes, and institutions that give meaning, form, and pattern to life. Elsewhere Fowler states that faith is a knowing, a construing, or an interpreting which fixes on our relatedness to those sources of power and values which impinge on life in a manner not subject to personal control. Faith is the knowing or mental construction of reality by which we understand ourselves as related to God.

When one understands faith in an active sense, that is, as a "verb," faith is distinguished not only as a relationship but also as a knowing which fuses reason and passion, intellection and affection. In faith we have a disposition toward God or the transcendent. As Fowler puts it, "One may trust, give loyalty, have love or admiration for the transcendent; or one may fear, resent, distrust, or revolt against it. Thus, faith qualifies and gives tone to one's entire way of understanding, reacting to, and taking initiatives in the world."[37] Hence faith-knowing involves *valuing*. "It involves resting one's heart upon something, trusting someone, committing oneself to someone or something."[38] Fowler's theory affirms the contention that mythos and ethos influence each other, as each stage represents a kind of consciousness or knowing reflected in action that is working toward a relationship of being at one with the cosmos, of recognizing one's self in all and all in one's self. Lastly, Fowler cautions against misuse of the theory when he refers to the stages as filters or lenses which can assist us to look at an individual's faith; while they focus and clarify some areas, they blur or obscure others. Hence the stages can be regarded as a heuristic device to help illustrate the journey to mature faith; they are not a value scale to determine relative worth of individuals or groups.

STAGES IN THE DEVELOPMENT OF FAITH. The six stages or ways of structuring faith are developmental movements from more simple and undifferentiated to more complex patterns. As an individual moves through the stages his or her faith manifests a growing self-awareness. Chart 2 is Fowler's summary of a structural approach to understanding the development of faith.[39] What follows is my understanding of how religious education is taking place at each stage—assuming, of course, that there is some validity to Fowler's theory.

Stage 1: Religion as mood. Fowler states that intuitive-projective faith is typical of children ranging from four to eight years of age. At this stage the child's faith-knowing is filled with fantasy and magical notions. Highly impressionable and imitative at this time, the child can be powerfully and permanently influenced by the words, examples, moods, and gestures of significant adults, especially parents and relatives. The forms of faith observed provide channels for the child's own projections of numinous intuitions and fantasies with which he or she tries to come to terms with a world perceived as unlawful, magical, and unpredictable. For example, in a home where fear predominates, the child may project an image of God as an old man in the sky who will strike us if we are bad. Where hope predominates, the child may project an image of God as a Santa Claus who sends us gifts if we are good.[40] At this stage religion is caught much more than it can be formally taught. The moods and attitudes

Chart 2
FOWLER'S STRUCTURAL-DEVELOPMENTAL APPROACH TO FAITH

STAGES	A. FORM OF LOGIC (MODIFIED PIAGET)	B. FORM OF WORLD COHERENCE	C. ROLE-TAKING (MODIFIED SELMAN)
1. Intuitive-Projective	Preoperational	Episodic	Rudimentary empathy
2. Mythic-Literal	Concrete operational	Narrative-dramatic	Simple perspective-taking
3. Synthetic-Conventional	Early formal operations	Tacit system, symbolic mediation	Mutual role-taking (interpersonal), "third person" perspective
4. Individuative-Reflexive	Formal operations (Dichotomizing)	Explicit system, conceptual mediation	Mutual, with self-selected group or class
5. Paradoxical-Consolidative	Formal operations (Dialectical)	Multisystemic, symbolic *and* conceptual mediation	Mutual, with groups, classes, and traditions other than one's own
6. Universalizing	Formal operations (Synthetic)	Unitive actuality, "One beyond the many"	Mutual, with the commonwealth of Being

D. LOCUS OF AUTHORITY	E. BOUNDS OF SOCIAL AWARENESS	F. FORM OF MORAL JUDGMENT (MODIFIED KOHLBERG)	G. ROLE OF SYMBOLS
Located in and derivative of child's attachment/ dependent relationships to parents or parent-like adults. Criteria of size, power, and visible signs of authority	Family, primal others	Punishment-reward	Magical-Numinous
Located in incumbents of authority roles and made (more or less) salient by personal proximity and trust-inspiring qualities	"Those like us" (in familial, ethnic, racial, class and religious terms)	Instrumental hedonism	One-dimensional, literal
Located in traditional or consensual perspective of valued group and in persons authorized or recognized as personally worthy representatives	Conformity to class norms and interests	Interpersonal concord; law and order	Multidimensional, conventional
Located in personally appropriated pragmatic or ideologically established perspectives and in spokespersons or group procedures or outlooks consistent with such perspectives	Self-aware adherence to chosen class norms and interests	Reflective relativism or class-biased universalism	Critical translation into ideas
Located in the dialectic between critically self-chosen beliefs, norms, and values and those maintained in the reflective claims of other persons and groups and in various expressions of cumulative human wisdom	Critical awareness of and transcendence of class norms and interests	Principled higher law (universal-critical)	Postcritical rejoining of symbolic nuance and ideational content
Building on all that went before, authority now located in the judgment purified of egoistic striving and attentive to the requirements of Being	Trans-class awareness and identification	Loyalty to Being	Transparency of symbols

and life-style of the adults who comprise the child's
world envelop his or her consciousness, informing the youngster
about what faith in God is. Without intending to be so, the
child is empathic. Like an empty vessel, he or she is readily
infused with whatever mood persistently prevails. In this
feelingful manner the child comes to regard God either as one to
be relied on and turned to, or as one to be feared and appeased.

Stage 2: Religion as story. Children between the ages of six
and twelve typically display mythical-literal patterns of belief. But
instances of adolescents and adults who are at this stage
demonstrate that stage level is not automatically a function of
chronological age or biological maturity. The individual at this
stage of development begins to separate the real from the unreal
on the basis of practical evidence. Concrete thinking is
beginning, and a more orderly empirical world is emerging.
"However, there is usually a very private world of speculative
fantasy and wonder. This is a world of hope and terror; of
reassuring images and myths in daydreams; of undermining fears
in nightmares and waking consciousness."[41]

With concrete thinking in operation, the believer's
understanding is literal. Tied to the world of sensory experience,
the individual is limited in the use of abstract concepts. Hence
symbols are referred to specifics and are understood by literal
correspondence with elements of concrete experience. Whereas
God was formerly perceived as more numinous, now the most
favored images or symbols of God are anthropomorphic. This
tendency to use concrete analogies helps explain why dramatic
narrative and myth, which capture and order the child's
imagination, are the favored modes for constructing and
communicating a sense of transcendent meaning at this stage of
development. More adequate empathy is developing as the skill
of projecting oneself imaginatively into the position or situation
of another is beginning. The individual, however, still looks up to
and models on trusted adults for validation of conclusions and
for an understanding of social boundaries, or the limits of one's
group—of how far one is to be empathic.

The circle of trusted adults begins to extend beyond the
family. It includes teachers and other school authorities, friends
and their families, church leaders or members, and personages
from the vicarious world of television, movies, sports, and
reading. From this broadened social environment, characteristics

such as the family's ethnic or racial heritage, religious affiliation, and social class standing become important aspects of the child's self-image. Identifications with the in-group, "those like us," are strong, while images of "those who are different" can be harsh stereotypes. A very negative image of oneself and one's group can develop if the child comes to regard the characteristics of his or her own family or group as inferior. In this case the stereotyped image of "those different from us" is given an excessive positive evaluation and one's own group identity is unduly negativized.

Stage 3: Religion as authority. The earliest transition to a state of synthetic-conventional faith is at age eleven; the earliest transition from it is at seventeen. For many Stage Three comes later and lasts longer. A significant number of adults display this type of faith through middle age and into older adulthood. Essential to this stage is the structuring of the world and the ultimate environment in interpersonal terms undergirded by a faith in others that is surrounded by ambiguities of "mystery" which stem from real contradictions. Nonetheless there is a coherent and meaningful synthesis of a now more complex world within the believer.

Becoming sensitive to how they are regarded by "significant others," individuals at Stage Three become dependent on these people as authority figures for "their sense of identity, and for sanctioning the beliefs, values, and action guidelines by which they shape a way of moving into and taking hold of life."[42] Conformity to these external authorities is not an easy matter, whether the believer is an adolescent or an adult. The arena of action and relationships is now larger and extends to include family or other intimate groups, such as a religious community. It is also enlarged by attachments arising from work or school, politics, peers, leisure activities, or public life. From these arenas, as also from one's fantasy and the media, there emerge both individual and collective authority figures on whose expectations, evaluations, and judgments the person relies. The problem is that these "authorities" do not always agree.

To overcome the contradictions among authorities and to have a coherent faith and identity, the individual synthesizes the values and judgments of various others by either compartmentalizing or by creating a hierarchy of values. The person who compartmentalizes acts one way with one group and another way with an authority figure or group whose values are different. Thus we can see individuals who act one way at home and another way when in public. For instance, someone in the business world, where the expected norm is to acquire as much capital gain as possible by whatever means available, will work for this end and at the same time when in church may make generous donations because this is the expectation emanating from the pastor, preacher, or whoever is respected as the authority. Consideration of means and ends and consistency of behavior from one arena to another do not enter the picture or pattern of faith at this state, since the believer is not yet critically self-aware. Besides compartmentalizing beliefs, another way of resolving disparities is to create a *hierarchy of authorities.* By regarding peers and their values—for instance, those in the business world—as of primary importance, and by subordinating other authority figures to them, the individual gives coherence to his or her world.

The believer's picking and choosing among authorities is dominated more by feelings toward them than by conceptual reasoning. There is heavy reliance upon interpersonal virtues, such as sincerity and loyalty, to judge the truth or value of perspectives that potential authorities represent. The individual tends to accept the values of those authority figures whose positions *feel* right. Trust-evoking qualities and the appropriate physical appearance of potential leaders or representatives of ideas or movements tend to invest them with authority. Just as a deep concern at this stage is "What will *they* think of me?" so "To be credible, a spokesperson must usually 'look the part,' possess a conventionally expected style and mannerisms [whether it be leftist or rightist, counterculture or traditional], have the approval of some personally valued institution or institution-like group, and come across as sincere, genuine, and truthful."[43] In sum, appropriate dress and physical appearance is authoritative at Stage Three.

Stage 4: Religion as ideological certainty. Individuating-reflective faith is not evident before age seventeen at the earliest. Fowler has also found that for some the transition to this stage does not occur until their thirties or forties, and that there are adults of all ages who have been in a Stage Three-Four transitional state for years because they are dissatisfied with former conventionalities but are without materials or models to develop more mature faith patterns.

At Stage Three believers derive identity from prominent persons, from the adoption of the faith of their fathers. Their beliefs are more a function of ascription, of conforming to the expectations of significant others. At Stage Four believers are aware of their identity as part of a group, but now faith is personalized (individuated or internalized) by *reflection*. Faith is now determined by the individual's own outlook or sense of self.

As the individual takes responsibility for his or her own commitments, life-style, beliefs, and attitudes, he or she moves beyond the previous encircling dependence upon significant others for the construction and maintenance of an identity and faith. Stage Four, however, does often develop under the tutelage of powerful ideologies, religions, or charismatic leaders. It develops in the effort to find or create "identifications and affiliations with ideologically defined groups whose outlook is expressive of the self one is becoming and has become, and of the truth or truths which have come to provide one's fundamental orientation."[44]

With the development of critical reflection, the individual who earlier synthesized belief in a conventional manner now faces universal polar tensions, such as relative vs. absolute values, subjectivity vs. objectivity, individuality vs. belonging to community, and self-fulfillment vs. service to others. The polarities are usually resolved by collapsing the tensions in one direction or the other and by dichotomizing reality into either/or categories.

Accountability for authenticity, congruence, and consistency in the relation between one's self and one's outlook becomes important. Group boundaries and knowing whom to include and whom to exclude are also important, since the continued existence and integrity of one's own group is a matter of concern. In justifying one's own truth in the face of competing perspectives, persons at this stage "typically distort their construction of others' perspectives in unconscious ways, [so that they tend to] honor *caricatures* of the perspectives of other groups, not recognizing that they are caricatures."[45] The acceptance or rejection of a potential authority figure or ideological or religious perspective is based on how well the claims fit with the truth, or "reality," as the individual perceives it. The individual now regards symbols, myths, and rituals as meaningful only if their message can be translated into usable concepts. In so doing, the believer loses a richness of meaning that lies beyond words. Rather than allowing the myth or symbol to transform the believer's understanding, at this stage the individual will accept only what can be translated into an explicit idea or proposition; the concern is for explicit meaning and internal consistency and for protecting the boundaries of self and outlook.

Stage 5: Religion as the way of the cross. Fowler asserts that paradoxical-consolidative faith is relatively rare. Transition to it is uncommon before age thirty. It is often a mid-life development, if it comes at all. For this stage of faith to develop, one must have experienced suffering and loss, responsibility and failure, and the grief that comes with making irrevocable commitments of life and energy. There is evidence that the modern-day *anawim*, that is, the disadvantaged and those who suffer class, racial, sexual, or ethnic discrimination and oppression, and who have made the difficult transition from Stage Three to Four, frequently confront Stage Five issues and develop that perspective earlier than the more advantaged. "This is not surprising, since survival and coping, for such persons, depend upon being able to take the perspective of the dominant and advantaged groups and their representatives."[46] The person at Stage Five has the ability truly "to walk a mile in another's moccasins." He or she can take on the role of another individual or group, putting on their world view in all its complexity.

Although the limits and distortions of Stage Four's ideological and communal identifications become evident to the individual at Stage Five, one does not become a relativist who asserts that one person's faith is as good as another's. Instead, the believer holds his or her vision with a provisional ultimacy. Conscious of its inadequacy and open to new truth (which is the heuristic dimension of a mature religious sentiment), the individual is committed to the absoluteness of the truth which is recognized as inadequately comprehended and expressed. The tensions that were collapsed at Stage Four by favoring one aspect of truth and ignoring other aspects are now embraced. When necessary, paradox is accepted as an essential characteristic of truth.

The person at Stage Five lives in tension between the claims of egocentric or group-centered loyalties and loyalty to the all-encompassing community of humankind. The believer's complex or more mature world-view is not reducible to any one of the many communities or points of view which contributed to its formulation. "While the normativity of tradition, scriptures, customs, ideologies and the like is taken seriously, these no longer are solely determinative for the person. Personal methods and discipline have developed for maintaining a living relationship with, participation in, or deference to the transcendent or the ultimate conditions of life."[47]

Moving from an exterior or ideological motivation, the believer is now developing a more interior sense—in Allport's terms, a mature religious sentiment. Stage Four's faith offered solutions to the pull between seeking self-fulfillment and commitment to the welfare of others by downplaying one or the other. At Stage Five faith comes to grips with the tensions of being ethically responsible but finite. In this pull or tension is the way of the cross for the believer. The individual is now burdened with the awareness of the degree to which free will or choice is always limited in fateful ways by a person's or group's history or situation.

"In the understanding and pursuit of justice at Stage Five, the indicative (seeing what justice requires) and the imperative (doing what justice requires) are inseparable."[48] Believers now act on the imperatives of love and justice extended to *all* persons and groups and are inevitably anguished at the limits of their own group or church. At Stage Five the faithful maintain a commitment to "the worth of ethical action and its costliness even while accepting the realities of intractable ignorance, egocentricity, and limited abilities and interests—in oneself and in human beings generally."[49]

The structure of faith, though more complex than at previous stages, carries forward their capacities. Thought and feeling, reason and passion, cognition and commitment are blended. Working through the polarities of Stage Four, the believer now enjoys a "second naivete." Having faced the questions and problems which were incomprehensible in the earliest stages, the individual is now prepared to live with ambiguity, mystery, wonder, and apparent irrationalities. The faithful no longer need to force meanings and value judgments onto reality, interpreting things in a reductionistic manner—as, for example, assuming that our cause is just and that God is on our side, blessing us, when we win a war.

Symbols, myths, and rituals now regain effective aesthetic importance (as opposed to being regarded rationally). They are allowed to make an impact on their own terms. This postcritical seeing through symbols affords one the opportunity to grasp life and reality in fresh depth and with enlarged possibilities. It allows for renewal, for a *metanoia* or change of mind, that brings a new way of being from a new way of seeing.

Stage 6: Religion as the fullness of simplicity. Few advance to Stage Five, and even fewer to Stage Six, universalizing faith. For those who advance to Stage Six, defensiveness and egocentrism are gone. Affirmation of others no longer means a denial of oneself. Distorting loyalties and biases toward one's own interests and investments in clan, class, region, religion, or nation no longer prevail. Participation in the Ultimate is direct and immediate. The Kingdom of God is a live, felt reality. With a sense of self as at one with God and all of creation, the believer's community is now universal. The unity of all creation is no longer a glib verbalism or mere ideological belief. It is felt and sensed as real and permeates all the believer's decisions and actions. The individual at this stage lives in the world as a transforming presence but is not of the world, since he or she sees more than the here and now. "Such persons are ready for fellowship with persons at any of the other stages, and from any other faith tradition. They seem instinctively to know how to relate to us affirmingly, never condescendingly, yet with pricks to our pretense and with genuine bread of life."[50] Disclosing the narrowness of our views simply by the grandeur of their visions of universal community, they in effect threaten our limited, pragmatic sense of justice. "In penetrating through the usual human obsession with survival, security, and significance, they threaten measured standards of righteousness, goodness, and prudence."[51] By relating to us concretely, they also evoke our potential to grow.

Persons at Stage Six frequently suffer at the hand of the less developed. Some are scoffed at and ignored for the seeming foolishness of their simplicity. Others become martyrs to the visions they incarnate. Witness the life of Jesus. More contemporary exemplars include Martin Luther King, Jr., Mahatma Gandhi, Mother Teresa of Calcutta, and Dag Hammarskjöld, to name but a few now acclaimed saints and heroes. Their leadership initiatives often involve nonviolence, reverence and respect for life which, without intending to do so, constitute affronts to our less-simple pragmatism, realism, and conventional notions of relevance. Their faith endures the misunderstandings, slander, and violence of those who cannot comprehend the simplicity of the Kingdom of God, and of those who do and are thereby threatened to the core. Fowler suggests that if the faithful at Stage Six can overcome the danger of ethical and political paralysis and the despair which may come from seeing just causes subverted by less universal interests, and if they do not become too mystically merged in the Eternal Now, they can offer "solutional approaches which introduce genuine novelty and transcendent possibilities into situations of conflict and bitterness and deeply contested interests."[52] Their faith is a model to us, inspiring, renewing, and sustaining a vision of cosmic meaning. In Kazantzakis's terms they are "Saviors of God" in a world that too often loses sight of God.

CATECHETICAL IMPLICATIONS AND APPROACHES

This review of the contributions of Goldman, Allport, and Fowler helps us understand how the message of faith comes across to individuals at different stages in their life journey. From Goldman's research we learn to respect the developmental limits that surround an intellectual approach to imparting the message. From Fowler and Allport we gain psychological verification of the need for lifelong religious education—a theme stressed by both Pope John Paul II and the Catechetical Directories. Allport's work also brings to our attention the need for adult religious education to assist the faithful to articulate a mature religious sentiment, one that is flexible and open to Truth and to the Spirit wherever the Spirit may be.

To extrapolate catechetical methods from Allport's allusions to personal styles of belief, we see that to respect the variety of believers who form the Church, catechesis cannot be primarily

religious instruction, primarily an appeal to the intellect.
Catechesis must give equal attention to the head and the heart,
the spirit and the senses of the believer. By addressing each
psychic function of the individual, a holistic catechesis (1) will
attract *all* types of believers—thinking types and the feelingful,
mystics and the pragmatic—and speak to their needs; (2) will
begin with the believer's psychological preference and will work
to bring balance or fullness of life experience to the believer by
encouraging, for example, the opening of the heart to feel
compassion, or the deepening of one's spirit in prayer, or
whatever function may be underdeveloped because the
predominating one unwittingly takes up most of the believer's life
energy and time (see Diagram 3 on page 58).

FAITH AS A DEVELOPMENTAL JOURNEY. The following
exercise serves to make the theories presented in this chapter
take on personal meaning where applicable. It can also be used
to introduce the topic of faith development in the religious
education of adults.

In a relaxed position, allow cares and concerns to float
away. Gently become aware of your breathing. With all senses
attuned (sight, smell, taste, touch, hearing), become aware of the
presence of God in your life here and now. Receive whatever
image, sensory impression, or feeling comes to you.
Listen. . . . Now travel in time and memory to an earlier
impression of God. Engage it with all your senses (as appropriate)
and with your feelings. Be aware of the events surrounding this
image, of the beliefs that supported it. Travel once more in
memory to an even earlier prevailing image of God. Continue
this process until you have reexperienced the variety of
predominant images of God, religious sentiments, or beliefs, you
have had from earliest childhood to the present.

Upon completion of this journey you may wish to jot down
or sketch your prevailing images of God. Note how each
reflected your faith at the time. Reflect on what each has to tell
you about God's working in you and about the people and
events that have assisted in your faith development. If you
engage in this exercise in a group, be aware of what you have
learned about yourself and share what your faith journey has to
teach you about methods and approaches to catechesis.

EARLY CHILDHOOD FAITH EDUCATION. In doing this reflective activity with various groups of adults, I found that the early childhood experiences they reported tend to confirm Fowler's findings that religion is "caught" rather than taught at this stage. A striking example comes from a Jewish-Catholic Women's Dialogue in which one participant stated that she drew a blank regarding early childhood. All that came forth was a feeling of emptiness. In describing her background the woman reported that both her parents lost their faith when they barely escaped the Holocaust. She was brought up in a home devoid of any religious ritual, with no mention ever made of God. It is telling that her memory and feelings are of emptiness. In the same group a Mexican-American nun spoke of her earliest memories in glowing terms. She told of being cradled in her grandmother's arms as the older woman prayed the rosary aloud. She even recalled the statue on the dresser and reported feeling good, reexperiencing the warmth and security that came with this fond remembrance.

The major implication for early childhood education in faith and morals seems to be that the medium is the message. The religious behavior and overall life-style witnessed daily is the "doctrine" being learned and stored in the child's consciousness. It is these prevailing moods or attitudes, feelings or affects, that penetrate our spirits even deeper than words can. Embedded in our consciousness, they are summoned throughout later life. Hence we teach reverence for life by revering the child. We teach awe and love by being awe-filled and loving. We teach respect for just authority by respecting authority. Sadly, we also teach fear, moral cowardice, thoughtlessness, and the like by our life-styles. Whatever we are living becomes the context or social environment that is being absorbed preverbally and transformed into the filter or lens through which the believer, even in later life, sees and responds to faith messages. Hence Montessori-like experiences involving "hands on" activities in an environment evidencing goodness, love, joy, and security seem essential for effective early childhood religious education.

ELEMENTARY FAITH EDUCATION. Words put a label on experiences and provide an intellectual handle for us to better grasp those experiences. By means of stories and prayer formulas effectively transmitted, the catechist, parent, teacher, or community not only maintains an atmosphere which tells of God as caring and taking delight in creation, but also introduces the learners to living doctrine. Given that six-to-twelve-year-olds are most receptive to stories and observances symbolizing our beliefs, we can capture and inspire their imagination by recapturing the art of storytelling. By means of narrative dramatization, or story-telling, the catechist can engage their hearts and minds and spirits and leave them longing for more.[53] To illustrate this method let us imagine Native Americans (or even the early Israelites) sitting under the hush of a starry sky, around a crackling fire, and in its light and warmth recounting the beneficence and grandeur of the Great One. If we can enter the mood created by the environment, we can begin to appreciate the impact of words spoken in appropriate settings. Multi-modal—that is, rational and affective and sensory— impressions can be made on the learners through the restoration of this art form that has been for the most part abandoned in our academic approach to religious education.

By reviving this oral tradition the trusted adult, as storyteller, would be able to reconnect self and learners with the Infinite. In this manner, instead of being presented abstractly, God comes to be understood experientially as we recount God's working in our everyday lives. As the listeners tell their stories too, it becomes evident how the story of salvation is continuing in our lives even to this day. The learners' faith consciousness is thereby heightened to infinite horizons and deepened to focus on social reality and the everyday world. In Fowler's words, by providing vehicles of identification and affiliation, religious stories, myths, rituals, music, symbols, and heroic figures "become means of evoking and expressing the child's or person's faith in a transmundane order of meaning, as well as being guarantors of present and future promise."[54]

The art of storytelling respects the findings of Goldman's research, as the child is not being inundated with concepts beyond his or her level of cognition. Instead, the learner is being initiated thematically into the great mysteries of our faith by means of stories retold and relived. From the experiences recounted, the themes essential to an understanding of our faith will emerge. Creation, reconciliation, thanksgiving, sacrifice, and other themes that help us understand God's working in our lives can, in turn, be developed experientially by means of activities, such as planting a garden, or by mimes, dances, or plays which the children produce and perform for others.

In moving from the traditional classroom to this more varied, although still systematic approach, it will take much longer to teach Catholic doctrine. What is learned, however, is learned by heart and mind and body, not just by the intellect. The following example serves to illustrate this point and, it is hoped, will stimulate your own creativity.[55]

LEARNING FROM EXPERIENCE. In preparing children for the Eucharist we can engage them in a series of experiences culminating in the baking and the breaking of bread. Inviting older learners to serve as assistants, we can work with the little ones, over the course of a year or so, to plant grain, raise sprouts and perhaps even some wheat, grind grain to make flour, and use it (together with store-bought flour) to bake bread—enough to enjoy hot from the oven and for each to bring some home to share. In each session (which would be monthly or bimonthly and would take longer than an hour) the learners would actually have their hands on and would be attending to that reality whose spiritual significance is also being explained.

By means of this kinesthetic approach to learning, the doctrine taught is more apt to be heard and understood. Each experience serves as the grounding to make relevant the teaching about a Creator who cares and looks forward to our growth, or about a Savior who gives of himself for our nurture and salvation as the grains did to become bread. In this manner the catechized can understand how the Holy Spirit, like leaven, is at work transforming us, giving us new life if we are open to be changed from lumps of dough into delicious bread. And they learn that we who call ourselves Christians are, like Jesus the Bread of Life, called to feed the hungry by sharing our gifts. In short, the practice of the presence of God, the ability to recognize God working in ordinary reality, is being cultivated in a manner which turns abstract talk of God being everywhere into a truth felt and lived.

LEARNING FROM TEXTBOOKS. There is a place for the printed word, too. Textbooks, as the National Catechetical

Directory make clear, "are guides for learning, summary statements of course content, and ready instruments of review."[56] As tools for catechesis, textbooks enable those young in the faith to recall and recount what they have learned. Textbooks, however, are not the starting point, nor the end point, of catechesis. Their function is to crystalize the message by providing a conceptual summary of the doctrine the learners are experiencing. Those who believe that experiences to engender learning can be bypassed to save time and that the printed word in the text is sufficient must ask themselves what is the purpose of religious education. Is it intended to teach formulas and words about eternal life? Or is it meant to engage the whole person in a journey of faith enabling the believer to encounter the Word?

LEARNING FROM OTHERS. Fowler's research indicates that it is not the printed word, but the narrative or story, that gives coherence to experience and orders the child's imagination. However, as the believer matures in faith, he or she moves from reliance on the story to reliance on the authority figure who is its spokesperson. A classic example of this is the conviction with which learners exclaim, "But teacher said...." Given that a significant number of believers of all ages are at this stage of faith development, it is not surprising that the National Catechetical Directory stresses that the success of catechesis depends on the "human and Christian qualities of catechists, more than their methods or tools."[57] In recognizing that it is the person more than the printed word, and personal qualities more than methods, which are the bases of effective catechesis, the Church urges the spiritual formation of catechists. We are reminded that as witnesses to the Gospel, catechists "must be fully committed to Jesus Christ. Faith must be shared with conviction, joy, love, enthusiasm and hope."[58] Is this the present state of the art in parishes and schools? Are those teaching religion doing so because they are prevailed upon? or because they are *prepared and enthusiastic?* Since the mediators are the message at this stage, are they filled with spirit and knowledge of both doctrine and methods, and do they have the aptitude and ability to communicate the Gospel message?

Given that the personal qualities of the catechist are essential for effective catechesis, more basic questions must be asked of those of us in positions of responsibility. First, how seriously do we pray for and avidly seek out those with the charism or talents to relate to youth? to youngsters? to adults? Secondly, how much are we willing to invest in their religious education so that they can more aptly serve us in their respective ministries of adult religious education, youth ministry, elementary religious education, and the like? Lastly, how much are we, as schools or parishes, willing to pay to attract *and maintain* dedicated professional catechists in these ministerial careers? Pastors or parish councils who believe that professional catechists should volunteer services or be satisfied with subsistence-level stipends are not only urged to reflect on the lack of justice in their assumption. They are urged to pay heed to the *Apostolic Exhortation on Catechetics,* in which the pope tells us it is not a pragmatic matter of human calculation, but an attitude of faith to "offer catechesis [our] best resources in people and energy, without sparing effort, toil or material means, in order to organize it better and to train qualified personnel."[59] Hence the truth of our desire to renew our parish or school is evident in the bottom line of our budgets. The money allocated to catechesis indicates our priorities.

FOSTERING MATURITY OF FAITH. Psychologists of personal development are finding that throughout our lives we develop, stabilize, and then terminate a series of age-linked life structures. Life structure is the term used by Daniel Levinson to describe the pattern or design of an individual's life at a given time. As one life structure becomes inadequate we go through a transition period which serves to terminate the former and initiate a new one. Among Levinson's conclusions is that we use only parts of ourselves in creating a new life structure. Hence important parts are not integrated into it. However, as we restructure our lives we have the opportunity to create a more comprehensive fit between our daily life and our interior selves, particularly those aspects left out of previous life structures.[60]

Levinson's findings in this regard relate well to Fowler's and are pregnant with possibilities for youth ministry and adult religious education. If the person at Fowler's Stage Four is seeking ideological certainty *and* an expression of his or her own individuality, it behooves us to pay heed to Allport's recommendation that we provide for a variety of religious experiences and to Goldman's recommendations that adolescence is the time to begin a critical-reflective study of the faith. In this manner the faithful will achieve ideological certainty. However, if this intellectual approach is our sole focus, believers may well shift into a cult or sect later as they make transitions in life structures. Perhaps the movement among our youth away from the faith of their fathers and mothers and into contrary life-styles (often rigidly embraced) is a function of this phenomenon. These youthful believers may well be seeking to compensate for what has been left out of their faith education, so that the polar opposite of what has been inculcated and now seems shopworn may tend to feel truer, fresher, or more fitting to their life experience—and so they embrace it as *their* faith. To prevent this we need to provide for the various dimensions of the believers' needs and interests.

To assist the individual to make a self-chosen, rather than a reactionary or other-imposed, act of faith, catechesis has to be holistic; it has to provide for the variety of life experiences, needs, and interests of each of us and to create opportunities for us to integrate each so that wholeness, or holiness, eventuates. Thus for thinking types it is appropriate to begin with the message (*didache*). It can be conveyed in home groupings, lectures, or classes in Scripture, Christology, Church history, sacraments, or the moral life. From there it needs to be combined with community building, service to *anawim*, and liturgical prayer if our words are intended to authenticate the Word. For the message taught is not a mere repetition of ancient doctrine presented for intellectual stimulation; the verbal teaching of doctrine is necessary but by itself insufficient to affect the process of professing the truth in love.[61]

Whereas an intellectual approach may be the original beckoning point for some, conviviality may well be the catechetical port of entry for the more feelingful. Fellowship, or the building of heartfelt community (*koinonia*), is "at the heart of Christian education not simply as a concept to be taught but as a reality to be lived."[62] Our bishops tell us that "Christian fellowship grows in personal relationships of friendship, trust and love."[63] Hence socials, retreats, parish productions or school plays, baby-sitting services, parish co-ops, suppers, sharing groups, and the like can serve as catechetical processes if they provide opportunities for intentional religious socialization[64]— that is, if these engagements model the Christian life and serve as opportunities to invite believers to come hear the Word in order to better articulate their faith, to engage in communal prayer, especially the Eucharist, and to engage in serving those in need.

For those more interiorly inclined, liturgical participation (liturgia), the culmination of community in Christ Jesus, may be the commencement of their catechesis. If effectively celebrated, the liturgy elevates us beyond ordinary time, a phenomenon that appeals to the mystical types. Liturgy also ritualistically represents who we are, whose we are, and for whom we are intended. By concluding with a blessing and an exhortation to go forth to love and serve the Lord, the liturgy grounds us again, energizing us to minister to one another. Service (diakonia) is thus sanctified by the recognition that the liturgy and other catechetical instruction give a way which is integral to living fully. It is through practical service that religion begins to make sense to pragmatic types. Practical service to the present-day anawim in turn gradually moves believers from an egocentric and limited self-concept, through the way of the cross, eventually into an understanding of the self as universal, at one with all—a belief requiring full maturity of faith.

Diagram 3 graphically summarizes this holistic approach to catechesis. Note the integral interrelation of all components so that any aspect can be the starting point, depending on how well it fits the condition of the learner. If any component is neglected, wholeness is lacking, and catechesis is fragmented. A holistic catechesis appeals to all types of believers, develops all the psychological functions, and fulfills the Church's expectations of education in faith and morals.

ADULT FAITH DEVELOPMENT: AN APPROACH. The following is a method for beginning adult faith education. (Later chapters conclude with more detailed approaches for a holistic catechesis.) An example of a starting point to help adults let go the beliefs of childhood and become consciously aware of those of an adult would be a retreat or ongoing study group whose structure would contain the following elements: (1) A concise and clear theological exposition, such as key ideas from Rahner's

Diagram 3
HOLISTIC CATECHESIS

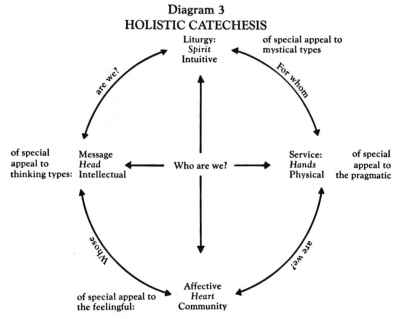

The Shape of the Church to Come. (2) A description of the development of faith structures to enable participants to recognize and better understand their own developmental process. To personalize the presentation, lead the participants through the exercise on "faith as a developmental journey" presented earlier in this chapter. (3) A presentation elucidating the characteristics of mature faith, or the mature religious sentiment. (4) Time and solitude for each adult to write out his or her philosophy or beliefs about life in order to become more affective and spiritual. Each can symbolically represent the philosophy or belief about life that he or she holds or aspires to by drawing a spiritual coat-of-arms or shield using colors, and inscribing the word or name the believer wishes to give to his or her life. In small groups have participants share their drawings. (5) A closing liturgy, at which these personalized ideals (charters and shields) can serve as gifts for each to place on the altar for blessings as they strive to "live by the truth and in love [and] grow in all ways into Christ, who is the head" (Ephesians 4:15). (6) A special time at the end of the liturgy for the celebrants to return these gifts by calling each person by name and anointing each one's forehead or hands with some blessed oil as a sensate symbol of empowerment to live the faith being professed. (7) Encouraging the faithful to keep these "sacramentals" as reminders, or evocative images, of the ideals to which they are committing themselves and striving consciously to realize in cooperation with the Holy Spirit. A year later they can bring these symbols to the next such retreat, mission, or parish renewal study group to once again review and renew their vision.

NOTES

1. 1 Corinthians 13:11.

2. National Conference of Catholic Bishops, *Sharing the Light of Faith: National Catechetical Directory for Catholics of the United States* (Washington, D.C.: United States Catholic Conference, 1979), p. 100 (#174).

3. *Decree on the Bishops' Pastoral Office in the Church (Christus Dominus, #14)*, as quoted in *National Catechetical Directory*, p. 18 (#32).

4. *On Evangelization* (Paul VI, 1975, #18), as quoted in *National Catechetical Directory*, p. 19 (#35). See also Romans 12:2.

5. *National Catechetical Directory*, p. 19 (#35).

6. Ibid., p. 31 (#59).

7. National Conference of Catholic Bishops. *To Teach as Jesus Did: A Pastoral Message on Catholic Education* (Washington, D.C.: United States Catholic Conference, 1973), p. 6 (#19), with a reference to the Vatican II document on *Christian Education*, #4.

8. Jean Piaget, *Structuralism* (New York: Basic Books, 1970). See also Jean Piaget, *The Language and Thought of the Child* (New York: Harcourt and Brace, 1926); *Judgment and Reasoning in the Child* (New York: Harcourt and Brace, 1928); and *The Child's Conception of the World* (New York: Harcourt and Brace, 1929).

9. See Richard M. Lerner, *Concepts and Theories of Human Development* (Reading, MA: Addison-Wesley, 1976), pp. 158-175, for a fuller explanation.

10. Ronald Goldman, *Readiness for Religion* (New York: Seabury Press, 1965), p. 14.

11. Goldman, *Readiness for Religion*, pp. 14-15.

12. Ronald Goldman, *Religious Thinking from Childhood to Adolescence* (New York: Seabury Press, 1964), p. 231. See also Gordon Allport, *The Individual and His Religion* (New York: Macmillan, 1950), pp. 31-36.

13. Goldman, *Religious Thinking*, p. 236.

14. Ibid., p. 240.

15. Ibid., p. 241.

16. Allport, *Individual and Religion*, p. 38.

17. Ibid., p. 64.

18. Henri J.M. Nouwen, *Intimacy: Pastoral Psychological Essays* (Notre Dame: Fides/Claretian, 1969), p. 19.

19. See Ira Progoff, *Jung's Psychology and Its Social Meaning* (New York: Anchor Press/Doubleday, 1973).

20. Allport, *Individual and Religion*, p. 13. He notes that Roman Catholicism and Hinduism are quasi-ecumenical in providing a place within the fold for a great variety of temperaments. Organized religions which cannot find a place for the different types of religious expression must provide for greater variety or else resign themselves to their limitations both in ecumenism and in attracting believers.

21. Allport, *Individual and Religion*, p. 30.

22. See Gordon Allport, *The Nature of Prejudice* (Reading, MA: Addison-Wesley, 1954).

23. Allport, *Individual and Religion*, p. 161.

24. Ibid., pp. 64-65.

25. John Elias, *Psychology and Religious Education* (Bethlehem, PA: Catechetical Communications, 1975), p. 112.

26. Allport, *Individual and Religion*, p. 72.

27. Ibid., p. 73

28. See Paul Tillich, *Dynamics of Faith* (New York: Harper and Row, 1957).

29. Progoff, *Jung's Psychology*, p. 75.

30. Allport, *Individual and Religion*, p. 83.

31. Ibid., pp. 154-155. Allport affirms his position by quoting from C. S. Lewis and a Muslim legend in this regard. He concludes poetically, "In that thou seekest thou hast the treasure found. Close with thy question is the answer bound."

32. Ibid., pp. 159-160. Allport here distills William James, *The Will to Believe and Other Essays* (New York: Longmans Green, 1897).

33. Matthew 7:21.

34. James W. Fowler, "Stages in Faith: The Structural-Developmental Approach," in *Values and Moral Development*, edited by Thomas C. Hennessy, S. J. (New York: Paulist Press, 1976), p. 191. At the end of this article both Alfred McBride, O. Praem., and James E. Hennessy, S.J., react. Both state their appreciation for what Fowler proposes but caution that the theory has a long way to go to demonstrate objective verification of what is proposed.

35. *National Catechetical Directory*, p. 100 (#173).

36. Jim Fowler and Sam Keen, *Life Maps: Conversations on the Journey of Faith* (Waco, TX: Word Books, 1978), p. 24.

37. Fowler, "Stages in Faith," p. 174.

38. Fowler, *Life Maps*, p. 24.

39. Ibid., pp. 96-99.

40. Fowler, "Stages in Faith," p. 192.

41. Fowler, *Life Maps*, p. 49.

42. Ibid., p. 61.

43. Ibid., p. 63.

44. Fowler, "Stages in Faith," p. 199.

45. Fowler, *Life Maps*, pp. 71-73.

46. Ibid., p. 80.

47. Fowler, "Stages in Faith," p. 199.

48. Fowler, *Life Maps*, p. 82.

49. Fowler, "Stages in Faith," p. 201.

50. Ibid., p. 185.

51. Fowler, *Life Maps*, p. 88.

52. Fowler, "Stages in Faith," p. 203.

53. Bishop Fulton J. Sheen exemplified the art of storytelling, enabling the narrative to become dramatically alive to the listeners. Our Nigerian students recount that storytelling and the presentation of parables and paradoxes are the common methods of moral teaching among their people.

54. Fowler, *Life Maps*, p. 195.

55. See Goldman, *Readiness for Religion*, for many more examples of life themes as approaches to religious education.

56. *National Catechetical Directory*, p. 158 (#264). See also p. 154 (#249).

57. Ibid., p. 126 (#205).

58. Ibid., p. 126 (#207).

59. John Paul II, *Catechesi Tradendae: Apostolic Exhortation on Catechetics* in *Origins* (Washington, D.C.: National Catholic News Service, 1979), p. 333 (#15).

60. Daniel J. Levinson, *The Seasons of a Man's Life* (New York: Random House, 1978), pp. 40-63.

61. *To Teach as Jesus Did*, p. 6 (#20 and Ephesians 4:15).

62. Ibid., p. 7 (#23).

63. Ibid., p. 7 (#24).

64. See John H. Westerhoff III and Gwen Kennedy Neville, *Generation to Generation* (Philadelphia: United Church Press, 1974), especially chapter 2.

3. ON THE DEVELOPMENT OF MORALS: CATECHESIS FOR MATURE CHRISTIAN RESPONSE

A holistic catechesis calls for informing and developing reflective reasoning and critical thinking in respect to both faith and morality. This chapter on the development of mature moral judgment presents predominant ways of understanding Christian morality, then details the Church's teaching on conscience and the moral life. Next it describes how the Christian can make mature moral decisions that are true to oneself and to the Church's teachings. After a review of the psychology of moral development the chapter concludes by presenting implications and approaches for a moral catechesis.

The following quotation from the National Catechetical Directory provides the context for this chapter:

Catechesis in morality is an essential element of catechetical ministry.

The Gospels contain Jesus' moral teaching as transmitted by the apostolic Church. The epistles, especially those of St. Paul, denounce conduct unbecoming to Christians and specify the behavior expected of those who have been baptized into Christ. (Cf., e.g., Eph 4, 17-32; Col 3, 5-11).

Through the ages moral teaching has been an integral part of the Catholic message, and an upright life has been a hallmark of a mature Christian. Catechisms have traditionally emphasized a code of Christian conduct, sometimes summarized under three headings: a sense of personal integrity; social justice and love of neighbor; and accountability to God as a loving Father who is also Lord of all.

Catechesis therefore includes the Church's moral teaching, showing clearly its relevance to both individual ethics and current public issues. It takes into account the stages through which individuals and communities pass as they grow in ability to make moral judgments and to act in a responsible, Christian manner. *Catechesis expresses the Church's moral teaching clearly and emphasizes the faithful acceptance of this teaching—an acceptance which carries a twofold responsibility on the part of individuals and the community: to strive for perfection and give witness to Christian beliefs and values and to seek to correct conditions in society and the Church which hinder authentic human development and the flourishing of Christian values.*[1]

In order to discuss with clarity the development of moral reasoning and the formation of conscience it is necessary to define the nature of ethics, morality, and conscience. Although the terms ethics and morality will be used interchangeably in this book, properly speaking ethics is moral philosophy—that is, an *individual's* philosophical thinking about moral questions, problems, and judgments. Daniel Maguire, in *The Moral Choice*, defines ethics as the "art-science which seeks to bring sensitivity and method to the discernment of moral values."[2]

But morality, as described by William Frankena, is an *institution*, just as language, state, and church are institutions. It is a social enterprise, not just an individual's discovery or invention for self-guidance. Morality exists before us. We are born into it, become its participants or live in reaction to it; and even after we die, morality continues. Social in its origins, sanctions, and functions, morality is "an instrument of society as a whole for the guidance of individuals and smaller groups."[3]

Although morality has elements in common with both law and etiquette or custom, it is distinct from both. Morality calls for the use of reason and of prudence, yet it is more than these. "Morality starts as a set of culturally defined goals and of rules governing achievement of the goals, which are more or less external to the individual and imposed on him or inculcated as habits."[4] The individual's conscience (superego) is formed by internalizing these goals and rules. As reasons are given with the moral instruction, the individual's conscience develops, moving from an "irrational kind of inner direction to a more rational one in which we achieve an examined life and a kind of autonomy, become moral agents on our own, and may even reach a point when we can criticize the rules and values of our society,"[5] as did Socrates, to the ultimate advantage of all.

Morality, as a social institution, can promote rational self-guidance or self-determination, as it concerns itself with what befits or does not befit persons as persons. Morality is concerned with life-style. Its foundation is "the experience of the sacredness and valuableness of persons and their environment."[6] It is not only concerned with principles of right and wrong, good and bad, duty and obligation, but more so for Christians, with understanding these in light of virtue and sin, redemption and reconciliation as we seek to fulfill our vocation to live as Christians.

Conscience, in the words of Vatican II's "Pastoral Constitution on the Chruch in the Modern World" (*Gaudium et Spes*), is what accords us our human dignity. It is the most secret core and sanctuary of a man or woman, wherein we are alone with God, whose voice echoes in our depths. "In a wonderful manner conscience reveals that law which is fulfilled by love of God and neighbor. In fidelity to conscience, Christians are joined with the rest of men in the search for truth, and for the genuine solution to the numerous problems which arise in the life of individuals and from social relationships."[7]

In a broad sense conscience is self-consciousness. It is a function of our existence as reflective and self-critical social beings always aware of the approval and disapproval of our actions by other men and women. It is that power or faculty which reveals to each of us who we are and who we must be as human beings called to respond to God's love.

STYLES OF MORAL CONSCIOUSNESS

In *The Responsible Self*, H. Richard Niebuhr presents three major ways of understanding Christian morality. Throughout the history of human beings' quest for self-understanding as moral agents, as individuals in charge or their own conduct, the most common style of moral consciousness has been to understand the person as a fashioner: creative, artistic, goal-achieving. Another major style has been that of regarding the person as a law-abider, a citizen, or an obedient servant. In place of these Niebuhr proposes a more comprehensive metaphor or image for understanding ourselves: that of the moral agent as a responder, one living in a dialogue, in relationship to others.

TELEOLOGICAL ETHICS: FOCUS ON ENDS. By portraying the person as a fashioner, Niebuhr describes the teleological approach to ethics, an approach which focuses on the end (telos), the good sought after. In this style of moral consciousness, all human action is goal-directed. It is done for a purpose, and as such is directed to a future good. This image of the person as a maker, technician, goal-seeker, or shaper of life has been refined and criticized in its use by idealists and utilitarians, hedonists and self-realizationists, among others. It has a wide range of applicability in life, since being human and having a purpose go well together. Even the determinist or behavioral specialist has a goal in sight in setting forth a step-by-step program of behavior modification; so too does the seeker of the Beatific Vision. This is the style of moral consciousness proposed by Aristotle, who began his Ethics: "Every art and every inquiry, and similarly every action and pursuit, is thought to aim at some good."[8] It is the style espoused by his Christian disciple Aquinas, who in syllogistic fashion concludes: "Therefore all human actions must be for an end."[9] And Aquinas argues that our end is to see God face to face.

In this view of the moral life, Christ came to show us the way home, to enable us to find our way back to the Father, for sin had blinded us. Sin, as understood by the teleologist, is "missing the mark" (hamartia). It is losing sight of our ultimate goal, the Beatific Vision, as we stray, beguiled by lesser goals or goods. Salvation comes with the restoration to us of the vision of God. "Salvation is the restoration of the goal that had been lost and so also the healing of the diseased powers."[10]

DEONTOLOGICAL ETHICS: FOCUS ON RULES. Whereas teleological ethics portrays Jesus as Herald, pointing the way to the Father, deontological ethics presents another major metaphor for understanding Christian morality. Viewing Jesus as the obedient servant (deontos), it portrays the moral life as one of obedience to God's laws; hence the focus on rules. This great symbol of the person as serving the law, as law-abider or citizen, prevails with those who do not view life as techné, as a skill or craft, nor living as an art. They argue that in crafting something both the end and the means are relatively under our control; hence an artisan can reject unsuitable material. But, they say, we cannot reject our bodies, sensations, impulses. They have been given to us; it is not under our control whether to have them or not. All we can realistically do is to regulate, rule, or control them. Thus, they conclude, our moral life is more like politics than it is like art, as we come to self-awareness in the midst of dos and don'ts, directions and permissions, commands and prohibitions, approvals and sanctions.

Deeming politics the art of the possible, a deontological moral consciousness raises the question: "What is possible to us in the situation in which we find ourselves? That we should rule ourselves as being ruled, and not much more."[11] For although we can and do rebel against some rules and regulations, it is morally necessary to consent to some laws and to give ourselves rules, or to administer our lives in accordance with some discipline, to bring about unity of the self and community within society.

In this style of moral consciousness, right life is obedient life. Obedience to commandments is necessary for justification; transgression of these commands or rules is sin and calls for repentance. "Salvation is the *justification* of the transgressor, his *acquittal* before the universal court despite his guilt."[12] It calls for restitution such as the substitutionary punishment incurred by Christ to pay the price to redeem, or buy back from sinful bondage, those willing to live under a new or higher law.

RESPONSIBLE ETHICS: FOCUS ON DIALOGUE. Although some use the language of justification, acquittal, and other legal imagery, Niebuhr believes that it is neither this way nor by means of ultimate goals, such as the Beatific Vision, that we understand our moral lives. Arguing that it is in dialogue and interaction that we become ourselves, Niebuhr presents another image for understanding Christian morality. He presents the idea of responsibility, that is, of the person-as-answerer, engaged in dialogue, acting in response to action upon him or her. He notes that it is common experience to be interacting, to answer questions addressed to us, to defend ourselves against attack, reply to injunctions, and meet challenges. All our actions can be understood as responses, answers, to actions upon us. Just as biology, sociology, and psychology have taught us to regard ourselves as being in the midst of a field of natural and social forces, acted upon and reacting, attracted and repelling, so too, Niebuhr argues, we must regard our personal and social histories.[13]

CRITIQUE OF MORAL STYLES AND ANALYSIS OF RESPONSIBILITY

The legal imagery found in our theology, such as justification by faith, substitutionary atonement, the righteousness of God, and the like, reflects the deontological style of moral consciousness. It subordinates the good to what is right, or legally ordained. However, for the teleologist, who views living morally as a skill or an art, law is subordinated to setting one's sights on the good, on what is worth working toward. For the teleologist, ". . . the right is to be defined by reference to the good; rules are utilitarian in character; they are means to ends. All laws must justify themselves by the contribution they make to the attainment of a desired or desirable end."[14] For the deontologist "Only right life is good and right life is no future ideal but always a present demand."[15]

Although both approaches have merit, they remain essentially unharmonized, especially in light of practical questions about individual or social responsibility. For example, what are parents to do in respect to their teenager's unwanted pregnancy? As Catholic Christians shall they condone? disown? forgive? This moral dilemma, like so many encountered in daily life, has no evident rules or goals to enable its solution. Yet it calls for the assumption of responsibility on the part of all involved to do what is fitting before God and humans, to do what is befitting the Christian, who, like Jesus, is committed to living love. Such a response calls for more than a preconceived notion of what is good or right. On the social level, too, the traditional approaches to morality break down. In a moral issue of universal magnitude, such as world hunger, what is good or right to do? Teleologically, as Christians are we really working toward the goal of eliminating this problem? Are we contributing resources and personal efforts to achieve this good? Is this our focus or aim? If our response is no, then we are confronted with the question of how we can call ourselves Christians in light of the ideals proposed from the Sermon on the Mount down through the Church's social teachings. If we are deontologists, the questions remain: Do we have any meaningful rules in light of this present demand? What are Christians commanded to do in respect to world hunger? Is it sinful not to feed the hungry? These and other examples of both individual and social moral issues illustrate the inadequacy of the traditional metaphors for understanding the moral life.

In their stead Niebuhr proposes a phenomenological approach to bring home the reality of Christian morality. Reflecting on the phenomena of social emergencies and individual suffering, he notes that although ideals, hopes, drives, and laws play a part, the actual decisions made—decisions on which the future depends and from which new laws or rules issue—are made in response to action upon us, the society or the individual. Our action is guided by interpreting what is going on. Active, practical self-definition arises from response to challenge rather than from the pursuit of an ideal or from adherence to some ultimate laws. We define ourselves by doing what we regard as fitting a situation. Opportunity on the one hand, and limiting events on the other, form the matrix in which we define ourselves by the nature of our responses.

ELEMENTS OF RESPONSIBLE MORAL ACTION. Niebuhr says that to be human is to interact. To be moral (or responsible), one's action must be in response to interpreted action upon oneself. Responsible action seeks to answer the question: "What shall I do?" by addressing a prior question: "What is going on?" or "What is being done to me?" rather than "What is my end?" or "What is my ultimate law?"[16] As we answer the question about what is going on or being done, accountability becomes evident as the responsible self looks both backward to what has gone on and forward, anticipating answers to his or her answers. Hence all action becomes interaction, becomes part of a total conversation. Like a word spoken in a sentence, no action is isolated. We are all part of a community of agents, formed by a continuing society and continuing its formation by our discourse or interaction. Responsibility lies in the individual who stays with his or her action, accepting the consequences in the form of reactions, and looking forward in a present deed to the continued interaction.

In sum, responsible moral action includes the four elements of response, interpretation, accountability, and social solidarity, according to Niebuhr. It is action in response to action upon us. It is not a reflex or mere reaction, but an interpretation of the action upon us by which we hold ourselves accountable—that is, expecting answers to our answers or actions. In doing so we are recognizing a continuing community (social solidarity) in which we are acting.

From this understanding of morality as the ability to respond, Niebuhr notes affinities not only with much modern thinking but with the biblical ethos which represents the historic norm of the Christian life. He believes that instead of examining deontological oughts and teleological ideals, we can better understand our Covenant call and respond more fittingly if we keep before us the question: "To whom and for what am I responsible and in what community of interaction am I myself?"

RESPONSIBILITY AND INTEGRITY OF LIFE. After he gives a phenomenological exposition of responsibility in society, in time and history, and in absolute dependence on the Transcendent, or God, Niebuhr's conclusion, restated in terms of Christian spirituality, is that the practice of the presence of God is essential for Christian responsibility, for integrity of life. "When I respond to the One creative power, I place my companions, human and subhuman and superhuman, in the one universal society which has its center neither in me nor in any finite cause but in the Transcendent One."[17]

This integrity of life or moral unity, traditionally referred to as sanctity, calls for awareness of the needs, strengths, and limitations of both the individual and the whole human race and all creation. It calls for a recognition of God as present within each one and yet beyond all. Integrity is present when we are aware of whose we are, when duplicity among roles and expectations is no longer acceptable to us. Moving beyond playing contradictory roles or trying to please significant others at all costs, the responsible self is consistent and true to Self, for in all his or her responses the self is responding to God who is Love. Operating from this center of awareness of the presence of God within oneself, the individual is thereby able to discern in all objects, events, or situations "one action, one intention, one final context of all the actions upon me, whether these issue from natural powers or from men, from Its or Thous. The self which is one in itself responds to all actions upon it as expression of One intention or One context."[18]

RESPONSIBILITY, SIN, AND SALVATION. In the responsible style of moral consciousness, sin means living in such a way that God is unknown as God, unknown as good, unrecognized as loveworthy and loving. It is moral myopia, living out the myth of death, as opposed to that of life. It is bringing in a closed, a damning future as opposed to transforming the past to make ready the Way of the Lord. Sin is the refusal to respond to Love. It is the refusal to be held accountable in assisting to bring in the Kingdom. It is the refusal to see life in a new way, refusal to be willing to receive it as gift graciously given.

The bishops' pastoral on the moral life describes sin as Niebuhr does. *To Live in Christ Jesus* defines sin as "a spirit of selfishness rooted in our hearts and wills which wages war against God's plan for our fulfillment. It is the rejection, either partial or total, of one's role as a child of God and a member of His people, a rejection of the spirit of sonship, love and life."[19]

In the state of sin our vision tends to become limited and fixed. Losing sight of the whole, we lose our integrity. As beings of many interests (individual, social, familial, political, economic, aesthetic, and the like) we become torn within by demands from without. Finding ourselves in conflict, we tend to seek easy solutions which make for uneasy truces within ourselves and with others. Focusing on the limited picture, whether it be Communism, Catholicism, Nationalism, Capitalism, or any other ism, we lose sight of the whole. Resolving divisions by being responsive to limited circles and closed societies, we perpetuate sin as we fear the stranger, ignore the alien, and shut ourselves off from the outsider, thereby refusing to respond to the universal community, to the larger world which includes us all.

A state of fracturedness, restlessness, and neurosis prevails and haunts us as we hunger for unity in Love. As Augustine poignantly prayed, "Our hearts are restless until they rest in You." He also pointed out that to live fully we simply need to love God—and then we can do as we will. For in loving, in responding to God who is Love, there can be no sin. Yet, in the words of our bishops, we find ourselves in a sad condition of sin:

Everywhere we encounter the suffering and destruction wrought by egoism and lack of community, by oppression of the weak and manipulation of the vulnerable; we experience explosive tensions among nations, ideological, racial, and religious groups, and social classes; we witness the scandalous gulf between those who waste goods and resources and those who live and die amid deprivation and underdevelopment—and all this in an atmosphere of wars and ceaseless preparations for war.[20]

This present condition describes what Niebuhr refers to as the ethics of death, or survival ethics. It represents the myth that death is the end of life, that there is no Other on whom we can rely. In this dog-eat-dog, competitive rat-race of daily life, we believe we must fend for ourselves individually and protect our limited selves and societies from the seemingly imminent and inevitable. And, in spite of our fears, an ever-so-quiet voice within groans, crying out in the wilderness of our souls, "Make ready. The way is at hand." However, with an overdeveloped rationality, we too often turn from these intimations, intuitions from the Spirit, and dim our consciousness with drinking or drugs, aphrodisiacs or overwork.

And yet salvation is at hand. "Through Jesus Christ, through His life, death, resurrection, and reign in power, we have been led and are being led to *metanoia*, to the reinterpretation of all our interpretations of life and death."[21] Through the response of this man who, sent into life, enlivened death by rising again, we are given the option of choosing life or choosing death as our style of moral consciousness. Instead of fearing the other as the ultimate death-dealer, through Christ we are reconciled to God. For Niebuhr, "Salvation now appears. . .as deliverance from that deep distrust of the One in all the many [whom we encounter] . . .Redemption appears as the liberty to interpret in trust all that happens as contained within an intention and a total activity that includes death within the domain of life, that destroys only to re-establish and renew."[22]

He concludes that responsible moral action is obedient to law but goes beyond all laws. It is form-giving but, even more so, form-receiving, for it is fitting action informed by Love. "It is action which is fitted into the context of universal, eternal, life-giving action by the One. It is infinitely responsible in an infinite universe to the hidden yet manifest principle of its being and its salvation."[23] Stated simply, responsibility affirms: "God is acting in all actions upon you. So respond to all actions upon you so as to respond to his action."[24]

CONSCIENCE AND SIN

The understanding of conscience as the consciousness of who we are called to be as responsible selves fits the long history of our Christian tradition. And it elucidates recent Church teachings as found in the documents of Vatican II and the social encyclicals. Living in accord with conscience, or "having a good conscience," requires more than mere obedience to imposed laws or obligations. Research in moral development is implicitly validating the Church's teaching that being true to one's conscience (to the voice of God within us) at times necessitates going beyond the norms of societal or Church expectations.[25]

The inviolability of our conscience as transcending norms or rules is attested to by Vatican II's "Declaration on Religious Freedom" (Dignitatis Humanae). It asserts that in all our activity we are bound to follow our conscience faithfully, in order that we may come to know God, for whom we are created. We must not be forced to act contrary to conscience, nor must we be prevented from acting in accordance with our conscience, especially in religious matters.[26] This same respect for the inviolability of conscience is found in Aquinas's Summa. To do otherwise, to go against one's conscience, is to sin.[27]

In Has Sin Changed? Sean Fagan tersely states that conscience involves two basic elements: (1) knowledge of right and wrong, and (2) the obligation to act in accordance with this knowledge. Experientially, conscience is felt as a judgment in a concrete situation. When we ignore or refuse to do what we know we should, there is tension because we lose our basic self-unity—the unity between belief and action. "We are torn within ourselves, we experience alienation and guilt. This is sin. It is a basic inconsistency between our knowing and our doing, and so we become divided within."[28] In line with Niebuhr, the social encyclicals, and the Gospel, Fagan continues that since we are not self-sufficient atoms, but beings in relationship with one another, the sin and lack of unity within ourselves spills outward. Hence all sin is social. "Whatever the occasion or the area of our sin, it cannot be confined or contained. Not only are we not at peace within ourselves, but on a deep level we become alienated from our fellowmen and from God. Even the material world that God meant to be our home and garden becomes a hostile environment to aggravate our inner lack of unity."[29] In the words of the bishops' pastoral on the moral life, "We sin first in our hearts, although often our sins are expressed in outward acts and their consequences."[30]

FUNDAMENTAL OPTION. In the Gospel of Luke (6:43-45), Jesus tells us that a sound tree does not produce rotten fruit, nor a rotten tree good fruit. Just as a tree can be told by its fruit, so too can every man and woman, for from the abundance of our hearts (from our fundamental option) all our actions flow. Our fundamental option is our basic or root choice with respect to the totality of our existence, its meaning and direction. Although our everyday choices and actions arise from many events in our lives and offer the opportunity for an infinite number of possible responses, at heart (at their core) our responses all point to a basic orientation, a basic affirmation or denial of the good, of Life, of God.

In *Sin, Liberty and Law*, Louis Monden states that the fundamental option is made between a yes and a no in which a person as a spirit unconditionally commits or refuses himself or herself. That option always amounts to letting oneself go: either yielding to a "becoming," to a growing toward a more complete self-realization, or falling back on an already-acquired self-possession, rejecting the new risks and the advance in self-realization. In order to realize itself, this basic option must enter into a dialogue with a complete psycho-physical situation and development, assume all acquired determinisms within its free directedness and thus bestow on them, out of that freedom, a new shape for the future.[31]

The fundamental option is the name given to the exercise of basic, or transcendental, freedom—that is, freedom which opens up life, which liberates the individual to become more fully realized. In *Principles for a Catholic Morality*, Timothy O'Connell notes that our fundamental option (as the deeper meaning and significance underlying important decisions) reflects our fundamental stance in life. That fundamental stance, which in some ways can be compared to Allport's mature religious sentiment, gives our lives direction, significance, and definition. "It is, in a very real sense, that fundamental stance which makes [our] lives human. For it affirms and expresses, as it also creates and effects, the person that [we] have chosen to be."[32] From a moral point of view the fundamental stance is, according to O'Connell, nothing other than the state of virtue or of sin, or of friendship with or alienation from God.

MORTAL AND VENIAL SIN. The refusal to risk becoming who we are called to be, which is the refusal to respond to God's invitatory love, is sin. Sin is the denial of our nature as human becoming loving. When this refusal to love perdures, sin becomes a state of being. It is a state of alleged independence from God and man and woman, an illusory self-sufficiency abrogating the responsibility implicit in acknowledging our interdependence upon one another and ultimate dependence upon God.[33] In scriptural terms, sin is hardness of heart. It is a refusal to repent, a stubbornness that will not allow for *metanoia*, for a change of heart or mind. In the words of Isaiah (6:10), reiterated in Matthew (13:13-15), and sadly so often in our own lives, sin is the heart that has grown coarse, ears that are dull, and eyes shut to love's appeal, for fear of understanding the need to turn our lives around, to be converted, to be made whole.

The National Catechetical Directory teaches that we can turn aside or away from hearing and doing God's will in both active and passive ways, by "sins of commission or sins of omission—i.e., not doing what one is morally obliged to do in a particular circumstance. (Classic illustrations are found in the story of the good Samaritan: cf. Lk 10, 25-37 and Mt 25, 41-46.)"[34] The Directory distinguishes mortal sin from venial sin thus:

> Personal sin resides essentially in interior rejection of God's commands of love, but this rejection is commonly expressed in exterior acts contrary to God's law. A grave offense (mortal sin) radically disrupts the sinner's relationship with the Father and places him or her in

danger of everlasting loss. Even lesser offenses (venial sins) impair this relationship and can pave the way for the commission of grave sins.[35]

CONSCIENCE AND MORAL DECISIONS

Given these considerations, how are we to form or, more properly, to educate consciences so that the catechized are assisted to choose life with its attendant risks, and to avoid personal sin in which death inheres? Specifically, how are we to make moral decisions that are true to ourselves, our neighbor, the Church, and the One God? A clearer understanding of conscience is necessary to address these questions which are essential for a moral catechesis.

O'Connell sets forth the three different meanings traditional moral theology has ascribed to the term conscience: (1) *synderesis*, which is the basic sense of responsibility that characterizes the human person; (2) *moral science*, or knowing the particular good to be done or evil to be avoided; (3) *syneidesis*, the act of conscience, the judgment by which we evaluate a particular action. For simplicity's sake, O'Connell refers to these as conscience/1, conscience/2, and conscience/3 respectively. Whereas conscience/1 and 3 are infallible (as will be explained), conscience/2 is fallible, and hence is the proper domain of moral education.

Conscience/1 refers to a general sense of value, an awareness of personal responsibility. Utterly characteristic of personhood is the felt sense that to be human is to be accountable. "It is to be a being in charge of one's life. This human capacity for *self-*direction equally implies a human responsibility for *good* direction. Indeed, so much is this true that we question the 'humanity' of anyone who lacks an awareness of value."[36] Apart from the bizarre aberrations of sociopaths or psychopaths (sick people devoid of any sense of right and wrong), all human beings share a sense of the goodness and badness of their deeds. This is conscience/1. The very existence of varying opinions and moral argument as to what is right or wrong points to the primordial realization that it makes a difference whether a thing is right or wrong. This realization is conscience/1. In *The Moral Choice*, Daniel Maguire describes this phenomenon as the foundational moral experience. It is "the experience of the value of persons and their environment.... It is this experience that sets us apart from beast and barbarian. It is...the badge of distinctively human consciousness."[37]

The force of conscience/1 obliges individuals to search out the objective moral value of their situation, to analyze their behavior and their world, to seek to distinguish the really good from what is not. This search, which is the exercise of moral reasoning, can be termed conscience/2. O'Connell says, "Conscience/2 deals with the specific perception of values, concrete individual values. And it emerges in the ongoing process of reflection, discussion, and analysis in which human beings have always engaged."[38] At the level of conscience/2, differences, disagreements, and errors can occur. "We seek to find and understand the concrete moral values of our situation, but we may fail. We are capable of blindness as well as insight, of distraction as well as attention, of misunderstanding as well as understanding."[39]

FORMATION OF CONSCIENCE. Conscience/2 is a fragile reality in need of education. Sincere persons who have accepted the fundamental responsibility implied by conscience/1 will seek the assistance and insights of friends, colleagues, peers, the larger culture, the wisdom of previous generations, and voices from other situations, in order to more objectively interpret their own situation.

> In a word, the sincere person will engage in the process know as "formation of conscience." For that, indeed, is a characteristic of conscience/2: it needs to be formed. It needs to be guided, directed, and illuminated. It needs to be assisted in a multitude of ways. Conscience/2, then, is quite different from conscience/1. It is not universal, at least in its conclusions and judgments. And it most certainly is not infallible. Quite the contrary, conscience/2 possesses a sort of humility, an emptiness that needs to be filled by the facts.[40]

O'Connell continues to describe conscience/2, not as arrogant or proud, but as kneeling before the truth which is the object it seeks. Here is where the Church, as teacher of moral values, has its greatest role. Both as a human institution with a long history and as an institution which the Holy Spirit guides and illumines, the Church has much to offer the prudent person willing to listen to its declarations. "But note that conscience/2 is not directly accountable to the Church. No, it is accountable to the truth and nothing else. In its search for truth, conscience/2 makes *use* of sources of wisdom wherever they may be found. And major among those sources is the Church, the religious community."[41]

Conscience/3 moves the person from searching out the truth, from thinking and analyzing facts, to intelligent action. Conscience/3 is the final declaration or judgment by which one makes a decision to do or to avoid a deed. It is the point at which the individual recognizes that there is a theoretical possibility of being wrong, but from the evidence of conscience/2 he or she is obliged to take a particular course of action as most fitting or responsible. "Conscience/3 is consummately concrete, for it is the concrete judgment of specific persons pertaining to their own immediate action. But for all that concreteness, the judgment of conscience/3 remains infallible. That is to say, it constitutes the final norm by which a person's actions must be guided."[42]

Through such action our fundamental stance is expressed and realized. If we have done all we possibly could do to inform ourselves on how to make the most fitting or most responsible moral decision we are conscious of, our actions will never be sinful, although we may later discover that objectively a certain action was wrong.[43]

MAKING MORAL DECISIONS. If we are not to obey blindly, but to intelligently weigh all factors and consequences, can we who call ourselves Christians distinguish our moral decision-making process from that of an intelligent non-believer? Yes. Respecting both the Church's wisdom and the inviolability of the individual's conscience, the National Conference of Catholic Bishops states that "we must *make decisions of conscience based upon prayer, study, consultation and an understanding of the teachings of the Church.*[44] The bishops continue with a reminder that our judgments are indeed human and can be mistaken, blinded by the power of sin or by the strength of our desires. Referring to Scripture, they advise that we not trust every spirit, but put spirits to a test to see if they belong to God. As followers of Jesus we are to have a realistic approach to conscience, accepting what Jesus taught and judging as Jesus does. Our bishops instruct us that we must do everything in our power to make informed moral judgments that respect the moral order. "Common sense requires that conscientious people be open and humble, ready to learn from the experience and insight of others, willing to acknowledge prejudice and even change their judgments in light of better instruction."[45]

Diagram 4 schematically summarizes the bishops' statement regarding the making of moral decisions by Catholic Christians.[46] In a fundamental stance of prayerful openness to truth, due attention is given to Scripture, tradition, group and individual experience. Knowledge is derived from each by employing all one's personal epistemic functions. That is, by means of intuition, reasoning, sense experience, and feelings, the individual will arrive at a balanced and fitting response, a life-serving answer to the moral question, so that in all action the conscious believer is indeed responding to God. As Maguire reminds us in speaking of "Love's Strategy," humility or modesty is especially important in ethical decision-making. Because ethics does not enjoy the simplicity of a precise science, ethical schemas, such as this diagram, can guide us but do not always totally dispel the dark. "This is disconcerting to those who look to ethics for a neat code of dos and don'ts. . . . It is [an understandable] desire to escape from the disturbing responsibility of having to decide when wracked by unbanishable doubt. This, however, is part of the burden and challenge of being both free and finite."[47]

Reference to each aspect is necessary for conscientiously informed moral decisions, whereas reliance on any one aspect alone may well prove insufficient for the conscientious resolution of a moral dilemma. If one attends to only the upper quadrants, ideals are magnified and reality is distorted. If only the bottom two quadrants are taken into account, potentially liberating ideals are disregarded. In the event that an individual truly understands Gospel values, there can be no moral dilemma about *what* to do. The sole question is *whether* or not the individual will do the truth in love. So too, if the facts and findings of the sciences are explicit and clearly understood, the only question remaining is one of volition or willingness; that is, will the person respond in conformity to the truth, or will he or she violate reason? For example, if one knows the probable effects of speeding on a curving, wet highway, will that individual conform to reason, or violate it?

Although the Gospels present human values very simply, the paradox is that most of us do not clearly understand those values. Also, since many of the findings of the sciences are not definitive in their moral implications, ambiguity sets in. To

Diagram 4
SCHEMA FOR CATHOLIC-CHRISTIAN
MORAL DECISION-MAKING

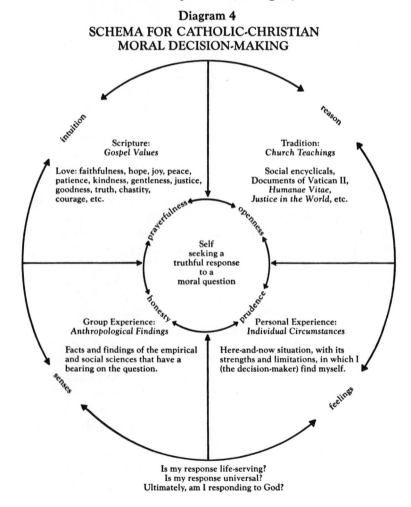

intuition · reason

Scripture:
Gospel Values

Love: faithfulness, hope, joy, peace, patience, kindness, gentleness, justice, goodness, truth, chastity, courage, etc.

Tradition:
Church Teachings

Social encyclicals, Documents of Vatican II, *Humanae Vitae, Justice in the World,* etc.

prayerfulness · openness

Self
seeking a
truthful response
to a
moral question

honesty · prudence

Group Experience:
Anthropological Findings

Facts and findings of the empirical and social sciences that have a bearing on the question.

Personal Experience:
Individual Circumstances

Here-and-now situation, with its strengths and limitations, in which I (the decision-maker) find myself.

senses · feelings

Is my response life-serving?
Is my response universal?
Ultimately, am I responding to God?

resolve the ambiguity by mere conformity to Church teachings may seem tidy but is actually irresponsible, a denial of our distinguishing characteristic as human beings: responsible freedom. With the exception of the mentally deficient, we are all graced with intellect, the faculty for critically reflective reasoning. To deny this God-given gift is seeking to evade our responsibility to mature as Christians. It is a pretense that we are not enlightened, have no knowlege of life nor of our own personal circumstances. At best, it is a pretense that we are still unthinking children. At worst, such behavior is indicative of a split personality—able and mature in daily affairs but impaired and incapable in moral matters.

INFALLIBILITY AND AUTHORITY. Unquestioning obedience is not what the Church is calling for. Such a stance puts an undue burden on our priests. It turns them into pretenders instead of ministers when they are put in the role of pretending that all moral matters have clear-cut answers that they are privy to. Vatican II's "Pastoral Constitution on the Church in the Modern World" (Gaudium et Spes) explicitly states that we may look for spiritual light and nourishment from our priests but that we should not imagine that our "pastors are always such experts, that to every moral problem which arises, however complicated, they can readily give a concrete solution, *or even that such is their mission.*"[48] And yet, "The authoritative moral teachings of the Church enlighten personal conscience and are to be regarded as certain and binding norms of morality."[49] There is no contradiction between these two Church statements if one recognizes and respects the differences between what is authoritative and what is authoritarian. *Moral teaching is not infallible.* The moral teachings of the Church have all come from the "ordinary magisterium." Although assisted by the Spirit, just as an open, honest, prayerful person would be, the Church's ordinary teachings are susceptible to error and therefore fallible. Hence the Church has never spoken infallibly in moral questions.[50] Most of the Church's teachings, however, are authoritative and for that reason call for obedience.

Authority can be exercised from either an authoritative or an authoritarian stance. All the difference in the world emerges from how one understands and exercises authority. Both terms derive from the Latin *auctor*, meaning "originator, author, augmentor, one who gives an increase." An increase of power is implied. Whereas the *authoritative* person empowers the other through service on behalf of or for that other, the *authoritarian* person empowers himself of herself at the cost of the other, who is made to serve the one in power. The two are distinguishable. Authoritative authorities are chosen by charism or election. Life-serving, assisting, ministering unto others, the authoritative are called upon to share their talents. They do not force themselves upon us but rather gain our trust, as does, for example, a hair-dresser, dentist, or auto mechanic sought for his or her expertise.

Authoritarians are the opposite, draining energy and laying burdens on those whom they purportedly serve. Supposedly enabling, they are in actuality debilitating because they deny others their capabilities. Authoritarians are self-serving. Coerced and constrained themselves, they usurp the human need for reliance and guidance insofar as they impose their wills on subordinates, exacting obedience by means of constraints and fear. Self-appointed, imposed from above, or chosen by others than those over whom they exercise authority, the authoritarian is recognized as one who *does not invite, but instead commands.*[51]

To invite is to recognize the sacredness of the other and at times even to suffer, out of respect for the inviolability of the other's conscience. Jesus' encounter with the rich man exemplifies a positive, or authoritative, exercise of power. Although Jesus as the Son of God is infallible, he did not coerce or constrain the man. He invited: "Come, follow me" (Luke 18:18-23). Although he was saddened, Jesus did not threaten the man for choosing to go away. In like manner, our bishops begin their pastoral on the moral life with an invitation and respect for our equality by addressing us as brothers and sisters in Christ. "We wish to share our faith with you. . . ." So too we as catechists, as a magisterial or teaching Church, need to keep before ourselves in thought and in our daily actions that education in faith and morals is a calling forth of the Spirit and a recognition and celebration of charisms. It is not an imposition of dictums.

OBEDIENCE TO CHURCH AUTHORITY. Moral teaching, to be authoritative, must reflect a humble exercise of guidance, always in dialogue, open to correction, sensitizing itself to the

circumstances of those it serves. Authoritative moral teaching is
not arrogant or oppressive, for it is always conscious that it is in
service to life, to truth, to showing the way to love. And so it
always stands humbly before God and the faithful. It does not
abuse authority like a tyrannical parent who may be sincere but
blind in the exercise of pseudo-apodictic power. Rather it is a
magister, sancta mater ecclesia, a teacher and mother, serving her
children, a people who by election have a teacher and a holy
mother appreciating, exhorting, encouraging them,
authoritatively leading them by actually doing and by
exemplifying the way. Authoritative moral teachings command
our respect and are thereby certain and binding. They do not
contradict the evidence of the senses, our personal circumstances,
or the Gospels. Rather they challenge us to a wholehearted
response.

Just as an individual obeys a doctor, respecting his or her
competence, we too obey the Church's authority. But just as a
doctor may sincerely and responsibly prescribe a certain
medication, unaware of its destructive side effects, so can the
Church. The individual has the responsibility to dialogue with
the authority, to find together a course that is life-serving. To do
so is to use that common sense which is traditionally termed the
virtue of prudence. On the other hand, the individual can
blindly obey, ignoring the effects such obedience has on his or
her person, ignoring the evidence of the senses and reason, and
suffer the consequences. Or, in a reactionary manner, the
individual can berate those in authority and leave the Church,
as some have done. Assuming good will and humble openness
on the part of our pastors, it is silly and unfair to berate them for
being fallible human beings. So too it is imprudent and unfair to
ourselves to ignore common sense and perpetrate immorality by
pretending a certain teaching is life-serving when in fact it is not
evoking a fullness of life but is yoking and choking the Spirit of
God whose temples we are. To discern the spirit or intent of the
law calls for moral maturity.

The Church itself, in current official statements such as the
documents of Vatican II and the social encyclicals, is calling for a
mature faith and a mature moral response. Yet at times our Holy
Mother, like our own mothers, means well but seemingly forgets
and speaks to us as if we were little children. In developmental

terms to be explained in the next section, the Church is exhorting us to respond to the Two Great Commandments in a postconventional manner, even though at times those in positions of authority expect nothing but a conventional moral response. And some few Church leaders may even be at a preconventional level themselves and so seek obedient submission by means of reprisals or promise of rewards. A study of the development of moral reasoning discloses where and how these expectations work and why and when they will break down. It also attests to the place and importance of law, rules, and commands in the development of moral maturity.

CATECHETICAL IMPLICATIONS AND APPROACHES FROM KOHLBERG'S CONTRIBUTIONS

According to Lawrence Kohlberg's research, there is evidence for a cross-cultural or, as he claims, universal pattern in the development of moral judgment. The pattern consists of three leaps in consciousness, which he terms levels. Within each level there are two steps or stages. Each successive stage follows the previous one in an invariant, or unalterable, sequence. Each step has a different quality. Each constitutes a structural whole, a complete pattern reflecting an underlying characteristic of thought organization. The patterns or stages form a hierarchical sequence, with each succeeding one reflecting higher cognitive integration and more complex differentiation of moral concepts.[54] Chart 3 summarizes Kohlberg's stages and levels of moral maturity.[55]

FROM HETERONOMY TO AUTONOMY. Both Kohlberg and Piaget (on whom Kohlberg relied) describe how the individual moves from a very physical, concrete understanding of justice undergirded by fear through a series of stages, which for those reaching full moral maturity culminates in an ideal or abstract understanding of justice, of the principles of right and wrong based on fairness and respect for the dignity of each individual person. In Piaget's terms, through a series of social interactions the child's moral understanding moves from heteronomy to autonomy. Through the cognitive dissonance

Chart 3

KOHLBERG'S LEVELS AND STAGES OF MORAL REASONING

I.   Preconventional Level: Egocentric self =center of moral views. Good and bad, right and wrong are understood in terms of the physical or hedonistic consequences of action (punishment, reward, exchange of favors) or in terms enunciated by those in authority, that is, those who have power over the individual. The level is divided into the following two stages:

Stage 1:   *Avoidance of punishment* or the avoidance of negative physical consequences of an action determines goodness at this stage. Evil is anything that hurts the Stage One individual.

Stage 2:   *Physical, pragmatic pay-off* or rewards determine what is right at this stage. It is wrong not to return a favor, for good is done with the expectation that it will be rewarded.

II.   Conventional Level: Social expectations = center of moral views. Morality is understood as blind obedience, support, and justification of the expectations, norms, and rules of the individual's family, group, or nation. At this level are the following two stages:

Stage 3:   *Approved good behavior* and conformity to stereotypical images of what is "natural" or right determine goodness at this stage. It is bad not to conform to the expectations of significant others.

Stage 4:   *"Law-and order,"* fixed rules, and social customs determine goodness at this stage. It is bad to neglect one's duties, show disrespect for authority, or do anything that questions or threatens the established social order.

III.   Postconventional Level: Principles of justice = center of moral views. Human values and principles of justice as fairness to all determine what is good at this stage. It is bad not to respect and follow the truth of one's conscience.

Stage 5:   *Legal viewpoints* that have been critically examined and accepted by all who will be affected by them determine the good. It is wrong not to respect the social contract one agrees to.

Stage 6:   *Consciousness of justice,* of the reciprocity and equality of human rights, and of respect for the dignity of human beings as unique individuals determines the good. It is wrong to go against one's conscience if it is in accord with ethical principles that are logically comprehensive, universal, and consistent.

(disequilibrium, or creative tension) produced by interacting with those at successively higher stages of moral development, the child moves from regarding moral rules or the law as imposed from above to seeing it as that which we administer to one another. Hence with appropriate methods individuals can develop from an egocentric moral realism to a democratic reflective idealism, from regarding the law or morality as coercive and unilateral to understanding it as a cooperative endeavor calling for mutual respect.

The movement from an egocentric sense of self, through seeing the self as social, to an eventual understanding of oneself in universal communion with all creation is a function of both cognitive development and cognitive dissonance. It is a function of both intelligence and tension or creative confusion which comes from interacting with those a little more morally mature. If the discrepancy in stages of moral development is too great there is no disequilibrium since the more developed is simply dismissed as odd or different, or not even noticed. However, when those around one are slightly more mature, the individual, in seeking to make sense of his or her peers, takes on their behavior and accommodates his or her own to the more mature models. It is from this repeated imitation that the novel or more comprehensive moral structure develops.[56] Thus tension in regard to moral questions can lead to greater moral maturity. If an environment is sterile, if there are no challenges to authority because everyone believes in the same manner, then there can be no moral development. There is simple conformity to norms.

If the major points of Kohlberg's theory of the development of moral reasoning are accepted, then important implications for a moral catechesis follow. After making clear these implications I will suggest and describe catechetical approaches that are consistent with Kohlberg's theory and respectful of Church teaching about conscience and moral decision-making.

PRECONVENTIONAL MORALITY: SURVIVAL OF SELF AS CENTRAL. At the preconventional level the individual's consciousness does not extend beyond his or her egocentric self. Physical survival is all important. There is no understanding of law and order; self-preservation is the motivator of all one's actions. Justice is understood as doing whatever one needs to do in order to survive. Good is equated with power; to cross the will of those in power is bad because it will incur punishment.

This first stage of moral reasoning characterizes not only little children but any individual motivated solely by fear of punishment. It is evident in persons attending Sunday Mass and obeying the commandments out of fear that they will die and go to hell if they disobey God (who is all-powerful). This mentality is also evident in the might which gangs display and the fear-filled allegiance they claim. The ghetto youngster or adolescent is protected and empowered by aligning his or her will with that of the all-powerful leader with no questions asked, since that very gesture would threaten the one in command. In this power-play it is deemed right and just to victimize the poor and the helpless, for they are regarded as deserving this treatment for being so weak.

This primitive mentality can also be seen on a social scale and among intellectually developed, but morally retarded, adults. It is reflected in those who reason that the United States of America is Number One only if we have more missiles and other weapons. The underlying reasoning in this primitive morality is that might makes right.

At this stage, displays of power, threats, reprisals, physical deprivation, and other forms of corporal punishment elicit obedience. But educationally they will contain the learner and block development, for they are not eliciting dissonance but merely reinforcing conformity to a norm of physical survival. Obviously there is no place for this type of negative discipline in catechesis.

On the other hand, behavior modification is most fitting for those at this earliest stage of moral development. By being offered rewards, the learner at Stage One is challenged to replace fear with positive gain, which is a whole new way of making sense out of survival. In the receiving of tangible rewards, those at Stage Two are reinforced in their behavior. Again, it is not only little children who exemplify this mentality. The apostles James and John may well have been at Stage Two if the following were characteristic comments and not just chance occurrence. "Master,...we want you to do us a favor....Allow us to sit one

at your right hand and the other at your left in your glory"
(Mark 10:35-37).

   If the promise of a crown of glory and of eternal rewards
has little appeal, it may indicate that the catechized is beyond
that stage of moral reasoning. Kohlberg states that the individual
ignores or scoffs at appeals made below his or her level, spurning
what is outgrown.

CONVENTIONAL MORALITY: SURVIVAL OF SOCIETY
AS CENTRAL. The popular labeling of people as saintly or
sinful, as "trouble-makers" or "good folk," often reflects a
conventional understanding of morality. With a major shift from
self-preservation to consciousness of the other as significant, the
individual moves from preconventional regard of right and
wrong as that which affects oneself to an understanding of justice
as that which conforms to one's group, church, or society's
expectations. The good is what pleases individual significant
others at Stage Three and pleases the Generalized Other, which
is the melding of many voices of society, at Stage Four.

SUPEREGO AND CONSCIENCE. The stages at this level
coincide with the child's development of a social perspective, that
is, the ability to take the role of the other. The individual is
beginning to see things from another's point of view.[57] At Stage
Three we find little children dressing up as mom, dad, priest,
sister, big brother, or another who is significant in their lives. We
can hear the children internalizing their parents' norms, donning
the dos and don'ts of their elders just as they did their apparel,
dinning their moral expectations into their own souls, and
investing themselves in these oughts, shoulds, and have-tos.[58]
The morally maturing individual synthesizes all the prohibitions
and commands ("A man is not supposed to cry," "Nice girls don't
do things like that," "A good boy always. . .," and on and on)
into a generalized voice which he or she then regards as the law,
or as God's will, or as the voice of conscience. What in fact has
been formed is the superego. And if there is no challenge to this
primitive form of conscience, mature Christian responsibility will
not develop. For what has happened is that conscience/2 has
now been informed, programmed, or indoctrinated, socialized
into a certain way of acting. If we indoctrinate or form

consciences, as opposed to educating them, the catechized may in effect be blinded to genuine human values, since their critical reasoning becomes blocked for fear of disobedience and the concomitant loss of love from the significant others.

As catechists we have a delicate task. Just as it is our responsibility to have our children internalize, love, and respect the law as life-serving, so too is it our responsibility to see that both we and they (when they have developed reflective reasoning) learn to lovingly question the law and those who serve us as authorities, whether secular or religious, to prudently prune away the wooden and to preserve and uphold whatever has justice, and not merely antiquity, as its roots.

A mature conscience is capable of this challenging task, essential for growth in love, whereas a superego serving as conscience is crippled at the very outset. John W. Glaser in "Conscience and Superego: A Key Distinction" contrasts the differences between the two. He defines *moral conscience* as the recognition of an absolute call to love and thereby to co-create a genuine future. Conscience is the insight into a radical invitation to love God in loving one's neighbor and thereby become abiding love. The *superego* is just the opposite of this conscious love going outward. "The dynamic of the superego springs from a frantic compulsion to experience oneself as lovable, not from the call to commit oneself in abiding love."[59] He contrasts the characteristics of superego with genuine conscience as follows:[60]

SUPEREGO	CONSCIENCE
commands that an act be performed for approval, in order to make oneself lovable, accepted; fear of love-withdrawal is the basis	invites to action, to love, and in this very act of other-directed commitment to co-create self-value
introverted: the thematic center is a sense of one's own value	extroverted: the thematic center is the value which invites; self-value is concomitant and secondary to this

static: does not grow, does not learn; cannot function creatively in a new situation; merely repeats a basic command

dynamic: an awareness and sensitivity to value which develops and grows; a mind-set which can precisely function in a new situation

authority-figure-oriented: not a question of perceiving and responding to a value but of "obeying" authority's command "blindly"

value-oriented: the value or disvalue is perceived and responded to, regardless of whether authority has commanded or not

"atomized" units of activity are its object

individual acts are seen in their importance as a part of a larger process or pattern

past-oriented: primarily concerned with cleaning up the record with regard to past acts

future-oriented: creative; sees the past as having a future and helping to structure this future as a better future

urge to be punished and thereby earn reconciliation

sees the need to repair by structuring the future orientation toward the value in question (which includes making good past harms)

rapid transition from severe isolation, guilt feelings, etc., to a sense of self-value accomplished by confessing to an authority figure

a sense of the gradual process of growth which characterizes all dimensions of genuine personal development

possible great disproportion between guilt experienced and the value in question; extent of guilt depends more on weight of authority figure and "volume" with which he speaks rather than density of the value in question

experience of guilt proportionate to the importance of the value in question, even though authority may never have addressed this specific value

Glaser notes that both a genuine moral world and a world of pseudo-morality and religiosity (the superego) exist in the normal person. All too often in the life of an average adult the existence and guilt-invoking influence of the world of childish morality is overlooked. In a tone similar to that of John Paul II's call for lifelong catechesis, Glaser attests to the need for adult moral education. "The maturing of one's conscience is a task that takes a lifetime; it is with us far beyond the end of adolescence. For one who has been the object more of conscience training than conscience education, this task of arriving at mature conscience will be particularly difficult, if not impossible."[61]

ADOLESCENT MORAL DEVELOPMENT. Although Stages Five and Six are more philosophical propositions than psychological patterns of development,[62] their thrust is consonant with Catholic moral teaching on human rights and issues of social justice.[63] Like the other stages and theories presented, they are put forth as models for reflection and discussion as to how we can foster maturity of faith, to grow to fullness as the People of God.

Essential for the development of mature moral reasoning is a cognitively stimulating environment, rich in opportunities to take the role of others.[64] Kohlberg states that a great deal of experience in personal decision-making is not necessary until the individual reaches the threshold of principled thinking—that is, postconventional morality. In "The Adolescent as a Philosopher," Kohlberg and Gilligan note that although all children display some clear capacity for concrete thinking, not all adolescents go beyond that level to formal, logical reasoning. In fact, for many people the development of reflective, critical thinking never occurs at all. Since the ability to think abstractly is necessary in order to make formal moral judgments, this may account for the scarcity of mature moral reasoning.[65]

Because many have not developed the ability to raise questions, they tend to conform unwittingly to whatever may be the norm, religious or social, as the tragic incident of the mass suicides at the religious community in Jonestown in 1979 sadly illustrates. Postconventional moral development presupposes internalization of the law and commandments, Beatitudes and

Gospel, and more. However, in order to grow beyond the tyranny of the superego, to live a faith that does justice out of love and compassion (as opposed to guilt and compulsion), the faithful need not only to *know* the law, which is Stage Four, conventional morality, but, more so, to *understand* it. And this comes through questioning.

Just as it is wearisome for parents to have a four-year-old continually ask, "Why? Why? Why?", so it is irksome to have adolescents continually challenge authority. Yet probing questions are proportionate to intelligence: the more inquisitive tend to be the brighter. Just as raising questions is a sign of intelligence, and therefore a right befitting the child's dignity as an intelligent human being, so too is it for the adolescent. Having recently reached the age of abstract reason, that is, having achieved the ability to think ideally, to think about ideas and ideals and not just about concrete facts, the adolescent is merely testing this God-given ability, striving to make sense of the world, the Church, and all of society's expectations by relentlessly posing the question "Why?" For adults who are insecure, or who have not developed their own critical faculty, the challenges come as a threat to their authority. And in the power-play, the adolescent may condescend by pretending to submit to the authority. Or he or she may leave the Church or family, finding them unbearably unreasonable. Or, saddest of all, the searing vision of youth may be squelched. Yet it is in the crucible of their questions that all of us can be purged of the dross which keeps us from responding wholeheartedly to the Lord who is Life.

MORAL DISCUSSIONS: AN APPROACH. Are parents, catechists, or youth ministers simply to tolerate anything and everything that is said and done? Emphatically no! Such seeming liberality is actually illiberal. It is just as oppressive as tolerating no difference of outlook. A method consonant with Kohlberg's approach and befitting those striving to strengthen a community of faith is the formation of discussion groups.

Robert Leslie's *Sharing Groups in the Church: An Invitation to Involvement* demonstrates how the drama of Christian salvation (call, conviction, grace, crucifixion, and resurrection) can be experienced within the group process.[66] His method

Chart 4
GROOME'S CHRISTIAN EDUCATION BY SHARED PRAXIS

	Purpose	*Procedure*
Step One *Present Action*	To bring to group awareness the partici-pants' present action in regard to a particular focus of their Christian faith-life.	The participants articulate their present action in response to the initial focusing question.
Step Two *Individual Story and Vision*	To return to the bio-graphical and social genesis of the partici-pants' present action, and to become aware of the future conse-quences of that action.	The participants critically remember and retell the stories, both personal and social, that explain their present action, and attempt to articulate what they envision as the consequence of that action.
Step Three *Christian Community Story and Vision*	To make present the Christian community Story in regard to the topic to which the group is attending. To imagine the Vision of God's Kingdom as it relates to the topic in hand.	The facilitator or a resource person retells the Christian community Story in regard to the focus of the group, giving a historical overview, the official teaching of the Church, and the present state of the question among the theologians. He/she adds an envisionment of the meaning of this action in the light of the Kingdom of God.
Step Four *Dialectic between the Com-munity and Indi-vidual Stories*	To critique the individ-ual stories with the community Story and to critique the com-munity Story with the individual stories.	The participants attempt to answer the question, "What does the community Story say to my (our) story, and what does my (our) story say to and ask of the community Story?"
Step Five *A Decision for Future Action*	To critique the vision embodied in present action in the light of the Vision of God's Kingdom, and to decide on a future action that will be creative of that Vision.	The participants, looking at the focus of dialogue, attempt to answer the questions, "How is my present action creative or non-creative of the Vision, and how will I act in the future?"

experientially elicits the effect and importance of the Scriptures in our lives today as participants come to convincing self-realizations from sharing their faith and doubts, hope and questions, in an accepting group.

Briefly, Leslie's method consists of these steps: (1) There is a reading or narration of a scriptural incident. (2) The group shares associations stirred up by the reading. (3) The group probes into the timeless, interpersonal depth of the story. (4) Understanding salvation history as ongoing process, the participants personalize Scripture by relating similar experiences from their own lives. For example, after discussing associations and probing the timeless, interpersonal depth of the story of Zacchaeus, the members tell of times when each felt cut off or "up a tree" like Zacchaeus. (5) The group leader then asks what helped when each felt cut off. (6) In conclusion, the sharing group discusses the meaning of a pivotal line from the story, such as Luke 19:9; "And Jesus said to him, 'Today salvation has come to this house, because this man too is a son of Abraham.' "

A somewhat more sophisticated process for small-group dialogues on matters of faith and morals is found in Thomas Groome's "The Crossroads: A Story of Christian Education by Shared Praxis." Chart 4 presents Groome's outline of the process.[67] Groome stresses that the function of the group is dialogue, not discussion. That is, the participants are to enable one another to hear the depths of their own souls and to disclose them, not to criticize, contradict, or challenge what each other is saying.[68]

Whereas Leslie's approach is affective, Groome's is a combination of feeling and of thinking. In contrast to these two methods for the development of moral judgment, to advance through Kohlberg's stages there is an approach termed the discussion of moral dilemmas or, more simply, moral discussion. An example of how this method can be used follows.

ADULT MORAL DEVELOPMENT: AN APPROACH.
Although adults and adolescents can have joint moral discussions, it seems better to begin with separate groups. When both age groups have overcome inhibitions about expressing what they really feel and believe, and when both have learned

how to dialogue, to listen with respect to both the younger and the older, then a conjoint second series can be made available.

To begin the process of adult moral education on a parish level, all can be invited by means of announcements in the parish bulletin and from the pulpit. A sample announcement and outline of an approach for adult moral development follows.

PROGRAM FOR FOSTERING MATURE CHRISTIAN MORALITY
Sample Announcement

Dear Parishioner,

You and any other adult members of your family or friends are invited to attend a series of four sessions, each two hours in length, on Mature Christian Morality, during the month of

_____.

The series will provide you with:
- an overview of the Church's moral teachings;
- a process for making responsible moral decisions that are respectful of self and true to our Catholic tradition;
- an understanding of how conscience is formed; and
- active involvement in the discussion of pertinent moral questions.

To aid in accommodating your needs, please tear off the attached and leave it in the designated box at the back of the church.

- -

Please check preferences:
I prefer sessions from

_____9:30 A.M. to 11:30 A.M.   _____Tuesdays

_____7:30 P.M. to 9:30 P.M.   _____Wednesdays

                 _____Thursdays

Moral issues I would like to have addressed include the following:

- -

Outline of Program

Session I

Objectives:

To enable participants to articulate that

- Moral judgment develops in stages over time
- Honest discussion of disturbing questions leads to creative tension which in turn can lead to moral maturation
- Understanding reasons is essential for developing a responsible Christian conscience

Procedure:
- Introduction and overview of series
- Presentation of a moral dilemma
    1. explanation of the process of moral discussion
    2. small-group discussions and probe for reasons followed by large-group summary of reasons
- Presentation of Kohlberg's stages of moral development by means of filmstrip, slide show, and/or lecture
- Questions-answers and evaluations of the session (to maintain interest, acknowledge all questions or issues raised but state that some will be dealt with in later, more appropriate, sessions)
- Suggested readings: *Moral Development: A Guide to Piaget and Kohlberg* by Gerald Duska and Mariellen Whelan (New York: Paulist Press, 1975); *Erica's School on the Hill: A Child's Journey in Moral Growth* by Patricia Burgess (Minneapolis: Winston Press, 1969)

Suggested Dilemma: What Price Truth?

All her adult life Michaela Smith has worked as a chemist at a pharmaceutical corporation. In two weeks she will receive a substantial pension and retire to a small island in a faraway country.

Cross-checking a report on a popular drug her company does not wish to remove from the market, she discovers that someone has falsified this final report which needs her signature and is due at the FDA in five days. In going through the files she finds that all the incriminating evidence has been removed. She no longer has her own records since she had destroyed them all in packing to move. There is no one else who would have the information to prove that this drug has an unusually high proportion of very damaging side effects, the most obvious being the high incidence of paralysis among long-term users.

Michaela's husband, a lawyer, advises her not to worry about it, since there is nothing she can legally do with all the evidence gone. In a few weeks they can take off for the place of their dreams if she acts as if nothing is remiss and signs the report. If she does not, she will become embroiled in a legal battle with the corporation in a case that may take years to resolve.

Discussion Questions:
- What is the moral dilemma?
- What pressures does Michaela feel?
- What should Michaela do? Why?
- Do you think Michaela has acted responsibly thus far? Why? Why not?
- What does being responsible mean?
- Is Michaela's husband acting responsibly? Why? Why not?
- What do you think is the most fitting solution? Why?

Session II

Objectives:

To enable participants to
- Learn and practice effective listening skills in a moral discussion
- Distinguish between a healthy and a neurotic (superego) conscience

Procedure:
- Brief review of last week's presentation of the stages of moral development, perhaps by means of a handout and a call for questions
- Presentation of a moral dilemma
    1. review of dynamics of the discussion process
    2. small-group discussions and probe for reasons, followed by large-group summary
- Lecture on the differences between superego and conscience and on conditions necessary for the formation of a mature Christian conscience
- Questions-answers and evaluation of session
- Suggested readings: *Has Sin Changed?* by Sean Fagan, S.M. (Wilmington, DE: Glazier, 1977); *Moral Development, Sin and Reconciliation for Parents and Children* by Mary Perkins Ryan and David P. O'Neill (West Mystic, CT: Twenty-third Publications, 1977)

Suggested Dilemma: Will God Forgive Me?

Coming from a very strict Catholic family of which she is proud, Rita is about to graduate from a Catholic university and hopes to follow in her father's footsteps in the family business.

Since high school days she has dated Rick. After the spring formal he informed her that he could wait no longer, that it would take at least two more years before he could even think about marriage, and that unless she made love with him he would find another friend. In a moment of passion she consented (unprepared and somewhat naive, since the subject of artificial birth control was never discussed in her family nor taught at school).

She has just learned that she is two months pregnant. Disgusted with herself and with him, Rita had already broken up with Rick a few days after their affair. She told him that she hated him for leading her on and that she never wanted to see him again. Angry at herself for being so stupid, she doesn't know if she can forgive herself. She feels angry at God too, because she has prayed and prayed asking his forgiveness for that stupid sin she committed with Rick—and he has made her pay for that one stupid mistake.

Seeking out abortion information, she begins to feel overwhelming guilt and a sense of despair. She is now in the university chaplain's office, distraught as he counsels her to trust her family and to have the baby and then give it up for adoption. She responds, "I can't. I just can't. You don't know my family. They'll literally disown me. I know that for a fact. And I couldn't just carry the baby and then give it away. I want to raise my child. Father, do you know if there's a family I can live with for the first few years, until I finish school and get settled in a job? I can't go it alone. And I can't turn to my family. Who can I turn to for two or three years of help? Where will I go? What am I to do? I don't see any way out. I feel like killing myself. Maybe I should just go drown myself. That'll solve the problem. Or will God forgive me if I have an abortion?"

Discussion Questions:
- What is the moral dilemma?
- What pressures is Rita feeling?
- What should Rita do? Why?
- Do you think Rita has acted responsibly thus far?

Why? Why not?
- What does being responsible mean in this situation?
- Does the Christian community have a responsibility toward Rita and the unborn child? If yes, what is it?
- Is the chaplain counseling responsibly? Why? Why not?

Session III

Objectives:
- To encourage the faithful to accept their responsibility to mature morally
- To provide them with a process for making mature moral decisions that are true to oneself and respectful of Church teaching

Procedure:
- Brief review of previous sessions
- Presentation of a moral dilemma
    1. quick review of the moral discussion process
    2. small-group discussions and probe for reasons followed by large-group summary of reasons
- Lecture on Catholic Christian moral teachings; expose participants to:
    - the bishops' pastoral, *To Live in Christ Jesus*
    - stages of moral development reflected in this document
    - a process for making mature moral decisions as a Catholic Christian, as evident in the document (see Diagram 4 in this chapter)
- Questions-answers and evaluations of the session
- Suggested readings: *To Live in Christ Jesus* by the National Conference of Catholic Bishops (Washington, D.C.: USCC, 1976); *Principles for a Catholic Morality* by Timothy E. O'Connell (New York: Seabury, 1978)

Suggested Dilemma: What Is God's Will?

Rosemary Peters is twenty-seven, married six years, has two toddlers, and is pregnant with a third. Her husband, suffering severe emotional problems, often beats her and the little ones. Daily Mass and Communion have sustained Mary throughout the years.

She is presently separated and, after much prayer, is filing

for divorce. Whenever she suggested they see the parish priest or
go for marriage counseling, her husband became abusive to the
point where she almost miscarried.

Her employer Frank, whom she has known since childhood
days and always liked, was widowed a year ago. After Rosemary
separated, Frank proposed marriage to her. She realizes that she
is falling in love with this compassionate Christian gentleman.

Rosemary discusses this with a priest in confession. He
informs her that the original marriage is considered valid, that
therefore a remarriage could not be blessed by the Church and
she would thereby remove herself from the sacraments.
Rosemary is upset, since she desires to remain an active,
practicing Catholic and enjoy a happy marriage. In becoming
aware of how much she loves Frank, Rosemary is torn as she
realizes it is just as unthinkable to give up the sacraments as it
would be to give up Frank's love and married companionship.

Discussion Questions:
- What is the moral dilemma?
- What are some of the issues involved?
- What should Rosemary do? Why?
- Has Rosemary acted responsibly thus far? Why? Why not?
- Has the priest acted responsibly thus far? Why? Why not?
- What is the Church teaching about divorce? about
  reception of the Eucharist? On what principles is it
  based? Is it reasonable? Does it foster maturity of faith?
  Why? Why not?
- What do you think is the most fitting thing for
  Rosemary to do?

Session IV

Objectives:
  To enable participants to
- Conduct their own moral discussion
- Recognize that reason is necessary but insufficient to live
  faithfully as a Catholic Christian
- Come forth with their own response about whether or
  not they wish to
  1. continue with moral discussion groups
  2. engage in a faith that does justice

Procedure:
- Brief review of previous sessions
- Presentation of a moral dilemma
  1. have small groups engage in the moral discussion
  2. observe groups, monitoring to be sure that all know how to conduct moral discussions
- Summary and evaluation of series
  1. in small groups have participants discuss the following: Do we wish to continue moral discussions in neighborhood groups in individuals' homes? Moving from discussion to Christian moral action, are there areas of concern that cry out for justice? How can we as a parish group of caring Christians begin to respond?
  2. Large-group summary: Regroup those with similar desires, e.g., to continue moral discussions, or to work together on a project of social concern. (More specifics for organizing action groups will be given in a later chapter.) Allow for introductions and exchange of names, addresses, phone numbers among the regrouped. Have each group set up a mutually convenient time and place to continue in their development of a mature Christian morality.
  3. Provide an agape or some fitting prayer of thanksgiving for successful conclusion of all that is beginning.
- Suggested readings: *This Is Progress*, a creative translation of Pope Paul VI's encyclical (Chicago: Claretian Publications, 1968); *Charismatic Renewal and Social Action* by Cardinal Leon-Joseph Suenens and Dom Helder Camara (Ann Arbor, MI: Servant Books 1979)

Suggested Dilemma: What Does It Mean to Be Catholic?

Your teenage son, who is a very sensitive youth, has just come home from school and starts telling you, "Today in our political science class we tabulated the results of our survey and interviews. Did you know that the highest incidence of racism falls right within our parish boundaries? Did you know that we found substantial evidence that our parish council president controlled the realty board and saw to it that no blacks could buy into this area? And you know what else? That minority family at the 7:00 A.M. Mass every Sunday are called the Vasquezes....I spoke to both Mr. and Mrs., and they said they'd be honored to have Mr. Vasquez lector at that Mass on Sundays. But would you believe it! Mr. Parish Council reported at the last meeting that he had personally asked all likely candidates and could find none—so there would be no lector at the 7:00 A.M. Mass on Sundays. What is that guy doing? Does he know what it means to be Catholic?"

And before you can respond, he continues, very deeply upset, "I just don't understand. What does it mean to be a faithful Catholic? Did you read in the paper about that wealthy parish that refused to help the poor? It said that something about its principles kept it from diverting funds to the poor. Parishioners interviewed explained that the poor had welfare, so they already had their money. Instead of helping build a shelter for the homeless poor, these people used $400,000 to redecorate their church. In the new stone front they had carved, 'To the honor and glory of God.' Yet in the bitterest part of winter they wouldn't allow the poor to sleep in the church basement; it might smell up the place. And six old men, five women, and a couple of children froze to death. What does it mean to be Catholic? Why don't people seem to care? Doesn't the Gospel have anything to do with our religion? Or are Catholics hypocrites?"

Discussion Questions:
- What is the moral dilemma?
- What is the young man feeling?
- Do you consider him ornery for raising these questions? Why? Why not?
- What do you tell him? Why?
- What does being a responsible Catholic Christian mean?
- What are some real social-moral issues affecting your parish?
- What do you think are some fitting solutions to these moral questions? Why?

MECHANICS FOR CONDUCTING MORAL DISCUSSIONS: The moral dilemmas suggested for each session are intended to stimulate cognitive dissonance and to provide a context for the specific session's lecture. The content for each lecture can be taken from this chapter and from the suggested readings. Having those readings and other related books for sale at each session has encouraged more intellectually oriented participants to embark on moral and spiritual reading.

Chart 5 is reproduced from Barry K. Beyer's "Conducting Moral Discussions in the Classroom"; it outlines a process for conducting moral discussions.[70] It can be adapted to any group.

Chart 5
BEYER'S STRATEGY FOR GUIDING MORAL DISCUSSIONS

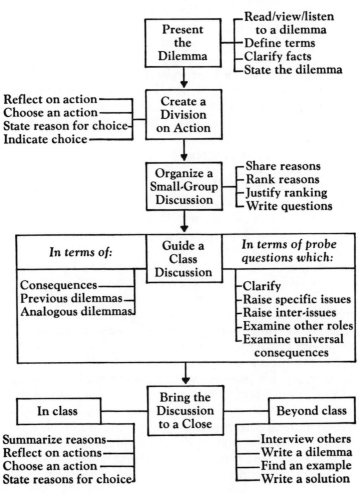

After the facilitator orally presents or distributes copies of the dilemma for each to read, for the sake of clarity someone in the audience is asked to state exactly what the moral dilemma is in that story. All should know that a moral dilemma is the conflict arising between two or more competing values. Once the entire group is clear as to what constitutes the dilemma (e.g., Michaela is torn between signing the report so that she can enjoy her retirement with her husband, and becoming embroiled in a battle to tell the truth about a dangerous drug), then each individual is to decide what action is to be taken and *why*.

By taking a show of hands regarding the action mentioned at the end of Chart 5 (e.g., how many think Michaela should sign the report? How many think she should not?), a division is created in the audience. The facilitator has two options: to form small groups of like-minded responders (e.g., all those who think Michaela should not sign the report, keep your hands raised and join in groups of five or six each) or to form mixed groups (e.g., all those who think Michaela should not sign the report, keep your hands raised and everyone reassemble so that each group has three "yeses" and three "noes").

In the small groups, the participants are to select a facilitator and a reporter. The facilitator's function is to see that all the questions are answered, that no one or two monopolize but that everyone gets an opportunity to respond, and that for the action chosen each participant gives his or her reasons why. Tolerance of differences of opinion both in choice of action and in reasons given for choices is essential. If the prime facilitator or anyone in the group imposes "the right answer" the process is defeated. It is in hearing others' reasoning that our own becomes disturbed, awakened from its own structures. Over time, after enough disconcerting reasons are taken in, the individual's thinking expands to the next higher stage.

Note that it is reasons, not excuses, explanations, or rationalizations that provoke interest by disturbing our thinking and forcing us to reflect more deeply. A reason is something that is logically consistent, something that any thinking human being would do in the specific circumstances. For example, when a child asks, "Why must I do the dishes?" it is reasonable to reply that "each one takes a turn in our family and now it is your turn, since the dishes need to be done as part of necessary sanitation." But to say, "Because I told you to do them!" is unreasonable. By being forced to accommodate the point of view of the other in order to achieve equilibrium or peace of mind, our moral thinking process becomes more and more expansive and comprehensive, as our mind probes ever more deeply into an understanding of what it means to be just, to be fair, to be human. Interestingly, these are the very characteristics that are essential for maturity of faith as described in the previous chapter.

After twenty-five to thirty minutes of small-group discussion, reassemble all into a large group. With the help of a timer, have each group's reporter give a two-minute summary of the group's discussion, being sure to list the reasons given. These could be written on newsprint during the small-group discussions and posted now, or they can be put on a chalkboard. To close the moral discussion, the participants can rank for themselves which reasons they consider most cogent and which least convincing, and note why.

It is necessary to make clear to all that we refrain from pontificating, deriding, or shaming. To say to someone, "How can you give that reason!" or "Don't you know better?" or "How can you call yourself a Catholic?" can kill the opportunity for that person to grow through that stage and at a pace consonant with God's grace working within him or her. As we all know, being put down by another or being told we are wrong does not change us. It only puts us on the defensive and causes polarization. Trying to get the group to find the one right answer or the best reason is counterproductive. Imposing norms for internalization from without violates the very process of stimulating the inborn hunger for understanding justice from *within* the learner. As stated earlier, inculcation of norms, which is indoctrination, issues in moral retardation, the development of superego instead of mature conscience. As the fallen-away or unchurched attest, it leads to the rejection of faith as too rigid or unjust.[71]

By trusting the Spirit at work within each, by tolerating the variety of stages one another are maturing through, and by entreating one another with heartfelt respect and provocative, open discussions, we are making ready the way of the Lord, enabling all to mature to their fullness as the People of God. It is only by conscious recognition of why we do what we do that we can grow beyond formalities and conventions and commit ourselves freely to do the truth in love. And it is only when our actions are no longer coercive obligations, but freely expressed, heartfelt responses to the Spirit that we have grown to the fullness of Christian moral maturity.

NOTES

1. National Conference of Catholic Bishops, *Sharing the Light of Faith: National Catechetical Directory for Catholics of the United States* (Washington, D.C.: United States Catholic Conference, 1979), p. 21 (#38). Italics added.

2. Daniel Maguire, *The Moral Choice* (New York: Doubleday & Co., 1978), p. 110.

3. William K. Frankena, *Ethics* (Englewood Cliffs, NJ: Prentice-Hall, 1963), pp. 5-6.

4. Ibid., p. 7.

5. Ibid., pp. 7-8.

6. Maguire, *Moral Choice*, p. 73.

7. Walter M. Abbott, S.J., ed., *The Documents of Vatican II* (New York: America Press, 1966), pp. 213-214.

8. W. J. Ross, ed., *The Works of Aristotle* (Oxford: Clarendon Press, 1925), Vol. IX, *Ethica Nicomachea*, Bk. I, 1 in H. Richard Niebuhr, *The Responsible Self* (New York: Harper & Row, 1963), p. 49. Niebuhr considers Aristotle's *Ethics* "the most influential book in the West in this field."

9. Thomas Aquinas, *Summa Theologica*, I-II, Q. I, Resp., translated by J. Rickaby, S. J., *Aquinas Ethicus* (London: Burns and Oates, 1896), Vol. I, in Niebuhr, *Responsible Self*, p. 49.

10. Niebuhr, *Responsible Self*, p. 49.

11. Ibid., p. 52.

12. Ibid., p. 130.

13. Ibid., pp. 56-57.

14. Ibid., p. 55.

15. Ibid.

16. Ibid., p. 63.

17. Ibid., pp. 123-124. It is interesting to note how Niebuhr's presentation of the moral life parallels Fowler's Stages Five and Six and Kohlberg's postconventional Stage Six.

18. Ibid., p. 125.

19. National Conference of Catholic Bishops, *To Live in Christ Jesus* (Washington, D.C.: United States Catholic Conference, 1976), p. 5.

20. Ibid.

21. Niebuhr, *Responsible Self*, p. 143.

22. Ibid., p. 142.

23. Ibid., p. 145.

24. Ibid., p. 126.

25. See Sean Fagan, S.M., *Has Sin Changed?* (Wilmington, DE: Michael Glazier, 1977), pp. 124-127.

26. Abbott, *Vatican II Documents*, p. 681.

27. Thomas Aquinas, *Summa Theologica*, I-II, 19.5, quoted in "A Catholic View of Conscience" by Josef Ruden in *Conscience: Theological and Psychological Perspective*, edited by C. Ellis Nelson (New York: Newman Press, 1973), p. 109. See also Timothy E. O'Connell, *Principles for a Catholic Morality* (New York: Seabury Press, 1978), p. 93.

28. Fagan, *Has Sin Changed?*, p. 114.

29. Ibid., pp. 114-115.

30. *To Live in Christ Jesus*, p. 5. The bishops refer us to Luke 6:43-45.

31. Louis Monden, S.J., *Sin, Liberty and Law* (Kansas City: Sheed, Andrews and McMeel, 1965), p. 31.

32. O'Connell, *Principles*, p. 64.

33. See E. Mark Stern and Burt G. Marino, *Psychotheology* (New York:

Paulist Press, 1970), chapter 2, especially pp. 27-28. See also Niebuhr, *Responsible Self*, chapter 4, "Responsibility in Absolute Dependence."

34. *National Catechetical Directory*, p. 55 (#98).

35. Ibid.

36. O'Connell, *Principles*, p. 89.

37. Maguire, *Moral Choice*, 72.

38. O'Connell, *Principles*, p. 90.

39. Ibid.

40. Ibid., p. 91.

41. Ibid.

42. Ibid., pp. 91-92.

43. Ibid., p. 93. This distinction that objective wrong may not necessarily be moral evil is parallel to the distinction Aquinas makes between vincible and invincible ignorance. If one has gathered all the pertinent information possible, the ignorance eventuating in objective wrongdoing is invincible; therefore, it is not morally evil.

44. *To Live in Christ Jesus*, p. 10.

45. Ibid., p. 10.

46. See *To Live in Christ Jesus*, p. 10 (sections entitled "Conscience" and "The Church"). I have evolved this schema over the years, thanks to readings too numerous to mention, although the most recent is Maguire's *The Moral Choice* (see especially p. 115 for his diagram); and thanks to lectures, the most informative of which were those by Bernard Häring, Jerald Coleman, and Dennis Regan. Christians who are not Catholic can also use this schema by substituting their own tradition's teachings for the Catholic ones listed.

47. Maguire, *Moral Choice*, p. 122.

48. Abbott, *Vatican II Documents*, p. 244.

49. *To Live in Christ Jesus*, p. 12.

50. O'Connell, *Principles*, pp. 93-97, especially p. 95.

51. T. W. Adorno, Else Frenkel-Brunswik, D. J. Levenson, and R. N. Sanford, *The Authoritarian Personality* (New York: Harper, 1950).

52. *To Live in Christ Jesus*, p. 3.

53. For examples, see Fagan, *Has Sin Changed?*, chapter 5.

54. Lawrence Kohlberg, "Moral Development" in *International Encyclopedia of the Social Sciences*, Vol. X (New York: Crowell, Collier, and Macmillan, 1968), pp. 489-491. As with any human invention, aspects of Kohlberg's theory do not stand up under critical scrutiny. See Suzanne De Benedittis, "Styles of Moral Education: An Ethical Analysis" (doctoral dissertation, School of Religion, University of Southern California, 1977), pp. 254-274, for an extended critique of the strengths and weaknesses of the theory and concomitant educational practice.

55. See Peter Scharf, ed., *Readings in Moral Education* (Minneapolis: Winston Press, 1978), p. 308, for more extended outline.

56. Lawrence Kohlberg, "Stage and Sequence: The Cognitive-Developmental Approach to Socialization," in *Handbook of Socialization Theory and Research*, edited by D. A. Goslin (Chicago: Rand McNally, 1969), p. 352.

57. For an extended comparison of social and moral cognitive development, see Robert L. Selman, "Social-Cognitive Understanding: A Guide to Educational and Clinical Practice," in *Moral Development and Behavior*, edited by Thomas Lickona (New York: Holt, Rinehart & Winston, 1976), pp. 299-316.

58. See Herbert D. Saltzstein, "Social Influence and Moral Development: A Perspective on the Role of Parents and Peers," in Lickona, *Moral Development*, pp. 253-265, especially p. 262 on the critical importance of role-taking opportunities for moral development.

59. John W. Glaser, "Conscience and Superego: A Key Distinction," in *Theological Studies*, 32 (1971): 38, reprinted in Nelson, *Conscience*, p. 169.

60. Ibid., in Nelson, *Conscience*, pp. 175-176.

61. Ibid., p. 175.

62. John C. Gibbs, "Kohlberg's States of Moral Judgment: A Constructive Critique," *Harvard Educational Review*, 47, 2 (1977): 43-61.

63. See Stephen Rowntree, S.J., "Faith and Justice, and Kohlberg," in Scharf, *Readings*, pp. 230-247.

64. Lawrence Kohlberg, "Continuities in Childhood and Adult Moral Development Revisited" in Kohlberg, *Collected Papers on Moral Development and Moral Education* (Cambridge, MA: Laboratory of Human Development, Harvard University, 1973). Also in *Life-Span Developmental Psychology, Personality and Socialization,* edited by Paul B. Baltes and K. Warner Schae (New York: Academic Press, 1973), p. 45.

65. Lawrence Kohlberg and Carol Gilligan, "The adolescent as a philosopher: The discovery of the self in a postconventional world," *Daedalus,* 100 (Fall 1971): 1065.

66. Robert C. Leslie, *Sharing Groups in the Church: An Invitation to Involvement* (Nashville: Abingdon Press, 1971), pp. 92-115. It has been this author's experience that students alienated from traditional approaches to Scripture have found this approach so sustaining that they have formed their own sharing groups on campus and have continued them, or formed new ones, after graduation.

67. Thomas H. Groome, "The Crossroads: A Story of Christian Education by Shared Praxis," *Lumen Vitae,* 32 (1977):58. For an extended treatment of this process see Thomas H. Groome, *Christian Religious Education: Sharing Our Story and Vision* (San Francisco: Harper & Row, 1980).

68. Ibid., p. 68. See also Reuel L. Howe, *The Miracle of Dialogue* (New York: Seabury Press, 1963), for an exposition of the principles of dialogue and how this process is essential for growing to full personhood. *Peer Counseling in the Church* by Paul M. Miller (Scottdale, PA: Herald Press, 1978) also treats the subject of listening to enable the other to get in touch with his or her own depths and so facilitate healing. Gene and Barbara Stanford, *Learning Discussion Skills Through Games* (New York: Citation Press, 1969), present ten essential communication skills for working in groups and a sequence of activities to develop these group skills.

69. In addition to these books, of special interest to teachers are *Growing Up Moral: Dilemmas for the Intermediate Grades* by Peter Scharf, William McCoy, and Diane Ross (Minneapolis: Winston Press, 1979) and *Moral Education: A Handbook for Teachers* by Robert T. Hall (Minneapolis: Winston Press, 1979). Hall's book provides insights and practical strategies for helping adolescents to become more caring, thoughtful, and responsible persons. *Interact for Moral Growth,* by Sister Mary Peter Traviss, provides an in-service teacher education program on filmstrips and cassettes. It is available from Winston Press (430 Oak Grove, Minneapolis, MN 55403). The Winston catalog lists many other titles dealing directly with, or treating areas related to, more education; religion and values education are their focus.

70.   Barry K. Beyer, "Conducting Moral Discussions in the Classroom," *Social Education* 40 (1976): 199.

71.   George Gallup, *The Unchurched American* (to be published) in *Show Christ to the World: A Look at Evangelization for the People of the Archdiocese of Los Angeles* (Commission on Evangelization, 1440 West Imperial Highway, Los Angeles, CA 90047), pp. 38-39.

4. ON THE DEVELOPMENT OF VIRTUES: CATECHESIS FOR AFFECTIVE CHRISTIAN COMMUNITY

It is not by the intellect alone that we know. There are reasons of the heart that have their own "logic," or psychodynamics, and that affect our beliefs and actions. This chapter first looks at the effect of the faith community through the power of its symbols and worship in the religious socialization of the individual. Then it describes Erikson's contributions on the role of the community in forming virtuous, or morally strong, people. Because Erikson's work helps us understand both how society forms individuals who in turn form society—that is, the next generation—and how basic moods, or deep affections, and virtues are formed within the individual, this chapter details only his first four stages and their religious implications, suggesting approaches when appropriate. The remaining stages are presented in the next chapter. This chapter concludes with the presentation of a youth ministry program that models a holistic catechesis with an emphasis on the affective domain.

Discussion of moral questions is necessary for the development of mature moral reasoning. Morality, however, is not realized merely by talking or engaging in philosophical discussions. Morality is actualized as life-style. One's life-style is the expression of one's faith, since one's faith is made evident in one's everyday life and daily activities. And the actual expression of one's faith in everyday life exemplifies and constitutes one's moral stance.[1]

A Christian's faith manifests its vitality in the joyful doing of truth. In this biblical sense, then, morality is knowing—that is, experiencing and doing—what is just and loving and true. In this sense morality is more than a matter of reason and logic alone. That the discursive intellect is needed but is of itself insufficient to comprehend the ways of the Lord is evident throughout the Scriptures. The point of recognition in the story of the disciples on their way to Emmaus (Luke 24:13-35) illustrates how the heart or affections apprehend truth that transcends intellectual discourse. The story also represents a sacramental way of knowing.

COMMUNITY AND WORSHIP

As a social (not an individualistic or privatistic) religion, Christianity calls for a community way of life. Without community its sacraments or public worship would be idolatrous. Hence the emphasis on the building of community if our corporate faith is to culminate in communal worship. The bishops' pastoral *To Teach as Jesus Did* stresses this point. It states that through Baptism the Christian becomes a member of that community whose core is a common faith, hope and love; hence community is not simply a concept to be taught, but a reality to be lived.[2] In the section on "Liturgy and Catechesis," the National Catechetical Directory also attests to the essential need for community in order to worship. "Faith brings *the community* together to worship: and in worship faith is renewed."[3] Our bishops explain:

> Christian fellowship grows in personal relationships of friendship, trust and love infused with a vision of men and women as children of God redeemed by Christ. It is fostered especially by the Eucharist which is at once sign of community and cause of its growth. From a Christian perspective, *integral personal growth, even growth in grace and the spiritual life, is not possible without integral social life.* To understand this is a high form of learning; to foster such understanding is a crucial task of education.[4]

In a report prepared for the 1977 Synod of Bishops on the state of catechesis, the communal and affective function of catechesis is reiterated. Catechesis is described as "leading to conversion (change of heart), to commitment, to knowledge and love of the scriptures, to worship, participation in the sacraments, prayer, to service of others (becoming stewards of the world, agents for change in society and prophets of the kingdom.)"[5] Catechesis is seen as flowing from the faith of the community and the catechist, a "re-echoing" in one another of our vital personal commitment to God in Christ through the Spirit. In existential terms:

Catechesis is to help Catholics relate the meanings and values of faith to their experience of life, particularly its more profound moments of guilt, separation, reconciliation, concern, commitment, love, etc. It invites and guides persons into the joy of a new life in Christ, a life of openness and healing. In addition, it assists Catholics to internalize the meanings and values of faith as they encounter the major challenges of human growth, from childhood to old age.[6]

RELIGIOUS SOCIALIZATION. The work of Erik H. Erikson helps us understand how the community catechizes and how the parish dynamic itself is the source from which religion is "caught" much more than taught. John Westerhoff's distinctions between schooling, religious education, and intentional religious socialization put Erikson's research in context. In *Generation to Generation* he says: "Religious socialization is a process consisting of lifelong formal and informal mechanisms, through which persons sustain and transmit their faith (world view, value system) and life-style."[7] He continues (in a sentence which summarizes the theme of the book): "This is accomplished through participation in the life of a tradition-bearing community with its rites, rituals, myths, symbols, expressions of belief, attitudes and values, organizational patterns, and activities."[8] He defines religious education as "those deliberate systematic and sustained efforts of a community of faith which intentionally aim at enabling persons and groups to evolve particular ways of thinking, feeling, and acting."[9]

Westerhoff cautions that too often education becomes narrowly defined as schooling, referring almost exclusively to printed curricula, confirmation classes, adult education programs, and the like. Unconsciously this concentration on religious education as schooling tends to remove from the learner's purview "social interaction and social organization—the rites, rituals, symbols, myths, organizational patterns, activities, and other social and cultural aspects of the church's life."[10] To avoid confining religious education to schooling alone, to the cognitive domain, and thereby cutting out its heart, Westerhoff urges a holistic educational approach which he terms intentional religious socialization.

Westerhoff describes three primary means of intentional religious socialization (or holistic religious education). First, he asks the faith community to *create meaningful rites, rituals, and ceremonials.* These embody our faith and symbolically support and transmit its meaning and vision. Second, he notes that living faith demands experience, and so he counsels the faith community to establish opportunities to *experience and reflect* upon its faith and thereby to personalize theology by evolving an integrated set of answers to questions that arise about present-day Christian personal life and the world. And third, he points to the need for *planned action* around personal and social issues which emerge from the faith community's desire to actualize and live out its beliefs and values.[11]

CHRISTIAN COMMUNITY: EDUCATION AND WORSHIP. The Catholic bishops stressed these same needs when they described the educational mission of the Church, in *To Teach as Jesus Did,* as "an integrated ministry embracing three interlocking dimensions: the message revealed by God (*didache*) which the Church proclaims: fellowship in the life of the Holy Spirit (*koinonia*); service to Christian community and the entire human commmunity (*diakonia*)."[12] In detailing these three interlocking and equally important dimensions of catechesis, the bishops remind us that as God's plan unfolds in our individual lives we grow in the awareness that as God's children we cannot live in isolation from others, that from the moment of Baptism we become members of a new and larger family, the Christian community, since we are joined to others in a common faith, hope, and love.

This community is based not on force or accident of geographic location or even on deeper ties of ethnic origin, but on the life of the Spirit which unites its members in a unique fellowship so intimate that Paul likens it to a body of which each individual is a part and Jesus Himself is the Head. In this community one person's problem is everyone's victory. Never before and never since the coming of Jesus Christ has anyone proposed such a community.[13]

Through education, the bishops tell us, Christians "must be moved to build community in all areas of life; they can do this best if they have *learned the meaning of community by experiencing it.*"[14] In the same vein, the National Catechetical Directory describes the Church as a community of believers (referring us to Acts 2:44). It defines the Christian community as one "based on the willingness of all community members, as good stewards, to accept responsibility, individually and corporately, for the way each lives, uses his or her time, talent, and treasure, and responds to the needs and rights of others (Cf. Gal 6,2)."[15]

In describing the mobility characteristic of life in the United States, the Directory says that ". . . Church leaders can no longer take for granted a sense of community; often they must instead work to develop and sustain it," and that "Many people have had little experience of parish community and must be gradually prepared for it."[16]

These two Church documents complement each other. The former stresses the building of community; the Directory, coming later, focuses on the worshiping community. The progression makes sense if it is understood that there has to be a community before one can have communal worship. Worship and community are essential for each other's vitality, just as ebb and flow are for tides. A commune or community will come unglued and disintegrate—that is, lose its integrity—if it has no transcendent point of reference which its rituals, rites, stories, and sacraments symbolize in a way which makes its essence significant. So too a worshiping community needs the immanent reality of the everyday experiences of its members living the kind of community which their rituals signify in order to preserve the potency of the symbols, to keep them life-inspiring, to protect the sacred signs from becoming vapid, ethereal or unreal—a condition theologically referred to as idolatry.

RITUALS, SYMBOLS, AND WORSHIP

In writing about "The Rituals of Jesus, the anti-Ritualist," James Burtchaell describes how rituals reveal the meaning of our lives and provide us with intense moments of meaning and opportunities to display the powerful forces that shape the way we live. "It is by ritual that we embody why we live and celebrate what we believe. Ritual releases meaning. Better put: it craves meaning, and can possess it only from other kinds of human activity. It cannot supply meaning, it only reveals it."[17]

Just as sexual intercourse is ritual expression of the love a husband and wife have for each other, symbolizing the substance of their everyday care and service, so too ritual is verified by service, as in turn service is quickened by ritual. Burtchaell goes on to say that the actual business of two persons becoming one in love is the exchange of service. A man who loves his wife senses when she has a headache without having to be told, cares for the runny noses of their children without being asked to, allows for her growth in career, and wipes the ring out of the bathtub. It is in all these ways that he is making love happen, that he is growing in love with his wife—the ecstatic vision of which he celebrates in bed with her.

So too our sacramental rituals are never self-ratifying nor self-sufficient. Their celebration gives us insight into our lives, and drives us to live up to the vision symbolized in their celebration. Rituals are not mere expressions of beliefs and values. They work both from the inside out and from the outside in, expressing what lies within us and also shaping us in response. A true ritual, like the sacraments, "effects what it signifies is already in effect. Where ritual is not ratified by service, there we have hypocrisy, sham, and magic. Where service is not given meaning by ritual, there we have drift and drudgery and an end of human civilization."[18] Susanne Langer makes the same point when she explains how the fabric of meaning in life comes from our metaphysical symbols, which in turn must spring from reality.

SYMBOLIZATION. Langer writes in *Philosophy in a New Key* that the essential act of thought is symbolization—that is, the symbolic representation of what we perceive as reality. Symbol-making is prior to and essential for thinking. Hence education in faith and morals calls for making symbols meaningful so that we can understand the reality about which we reason. Since all thinking begins with the senses as they take in experience, our moral meanings are informed by the wisdom of our bodies. These meanings are stored within us and shape our realities physically and psychologically or spiritually.

Langer states that "symbolization is preratiocinative, but not pre-rational. It is the starting point of all intellection in the human sense, and is more general than thinking, fancying, or taking action."[19] Dissociating herself from behaviorists or determinists, she compares the human brain not to a transmitter (as a transmitter does a fairly good job) but to a tremendously powerful transformer. In so doing, Langer affirms the transcendental freedom or creativity that is at the core of being human, that is expressed by means of our imagination in ritual, art, laughter, weeping, speech, superstition, and scientific genius. She states that the current of experience that passes through the brain "undergoes a change of character, not through the agency of the sense by which the perception entered, but by virtue of a primary use which is made of it immediately: it is sucked into the stream of symbols which constitutes a human mind."[20]

In concluding her study, Langer notes that just as we have to adapt all our biological activities to given limitations, so too do we have to adapt our peculiarly human mental functions— that is our symbolic functions. "The mind, like all other organs, can draw its sustenance only from the surrounding world; our metaphysical symbols must spring from reality. Such adaptation always requires time, habit, tradition, and intimate knowledge of a way of life."[21] She cautions that if the field of our unconscious symbolic orientation is suddenly plowed up by tremendous changes in the external world and in the social order, we lose our hold on life, as we lose our convictions and with them our effectual purposes. "In modern civilization there are two great threats to mental security: *the new mode of living*, which has made the old nature-symbols alien to our minds, and the *new mode of working*, which makes personal activity meaningless, unacceptable to the hungry imagination."[22]

Commenting that most of us never see the goods we produce as we stand on assembly lines repeating a million identical movements in a succession of hours, days, and years, Langer says this sort of activity is too poor, too empty, for even the most ingenious mind to invest it with symbolic content, so that work is no longer a sphere of ritual. So too has social mobility destroyed another anchoring point for the human mind. "Most people have no home that is a symbol of their childhood, not even a definite memory of one place to serve that purpose. Many no longer know the language that was once their mother-tongue. All old symbols are gone, and thousands of average lives offer no new materials to a creative imagination."[23] Although technical progress has offset physical deprivation's tyrannical grip on the workaday life of modern man and woman,

such progress in effect leads to a more devastating starvation—
that of the spirit. Langer continues: "The withdrawal of all
natural means for expressing the unity of personal life is a major
cause of the distraction, irreligion, and unrest that mark the
proletariat of all countries."[24] She concludes that technical
progress is putting the human being's freedom of spirit in
jeopardy. But there is a way out of this culturally suicidal
dilemma: the transformative power of the sacraments.

SACRAMENTS. A highly charged form of ritual, a sacrament
overtly is usually a homely, familiar action that is essentially
realistic and vital, such as washing, eating, drinking. Its intent is
not to entertain but to achieve a certain morale. Rituals and
sacraments are part of our ceaseless quest for conception and
orientation; they embody dawning notions of power and will, of
death and victory. They give active and impressive form to our
demonic fears and to our ideals. According to Langer, "Ritual is
the most primitive reflection of serious thought, a slow deposit,
as it were, of people's imaginative insight into life. That is why it
is intrinsically solemn, even though some rites of rejoicing may
degenerate into mere excitement, debauchery, and license."[25]
Through its ceremonials, religion draws all of nature into the
domain of ritual. And there is "a type of ceremonial that runs
the whole gamut from the most savage to the most civilized piety,
from blind compulsive behavior, through magical conjuring, to
the heights of conscious expression: that is the Sacrament."[26]
    Catholic theology affirms this phenomenology of
sacraments, attesting that the sacraments as we know them raise
our morale to the heights of conscious expression. In the section
entitled "The sacraments/mysteries as symbol," the National
Catechetical Directory states:
        The mystery of Christ is continued in the Church . . .
    in a specific way through the signs that Christ instituted,
    which signify the gift of grace and produce it, and are
    properly called sacraments.
        The Word of God is the full manifestation of the
    Father; thus He may be called a symbol, an icon, an image
    of the Father. Created through the Word, the world is in its
    very reality a symbol of its creator.
        Because they have been created by His Word and in
    His image, *human beings have the greatest capacity for*

symbolizing God. Jesus Christ, the Word incarnate, was the perfect symbol or sacrament of God on earth. The community of faith, which strives to follow Christ's example and live by His teachings, is the symbol or sacrament of His continued presence among us.

The sacraments, symbolic actions which effect what they symbolize, celebrate the coming of the Spirit at special moments in the life of the community of faith and its members, and express the Church's faith and interaction with Christ. The Church celebrates the mysteries of God's presence through word, bread, wine, water, oil, and the actions of the ordained ministers and the people.[27]

VITALITY OF SYMBOLS AND SACRAMENTS. In line with Langer's philosophy, Berard L. Marthaler, in "Handing on the Symbols of Faith," states that "symbols have the capacity to translate vague feelings into meaningful experience, confused impulses into purposeful activity and puzzlement into understanding."[28] He notes that symbols have a dynamism of their own that at once expresses and creates culture and tradition, that they are the means by which concrete, social forms of religious faith are perpetuated or transformed. "As Lonergan says, 'community is not just an aggregate of individuals within a frontier, for that overlooks its formal constituent, which is the common meaning.' Common meaning is a product of shared experience, complimentary [sic] points of view, social and personal values and goals communicated by symbols which are mutually understood."[29]

In *Dynamics of Faith*, Paul Tillich states that our "ultimate concern must be expressed symbolically, because symbolic language alone is able to express the ultimate."[30] He also asserts that symbols cannot be produced intentionally, but grow out of the individual and collective unconscious. They function by resonating this aspect of our being. Thus symbols cannot be invented. "Like living beings, they grow and they die. They grow when the situation is ripe for them, and they die when the situation changes."[31] He explains: "Symbols do not grow because people are longing for them, and they do not die because of scientific or practical criticism. *They die because they can no longer produce response in the group where they originally found expression.*"[32]

Applying the foregoing statements to the vitality of the sacraments, we must ask how we symbolize God to one another as a community of faith. Is our sacramental symbol system signifying a liberation of the spirit of man and woman? Or have the sacraments lost their relevance? To answer these questions we have to examine the prior reality of which the sacraments are signs. Burtchaell explains:

> Sacraments are a celebration of faith. They are not the events by which we are rescued, and emerge from our sins, and are transformed into loving men. This we do by the daily exchanges of life with our brothers. In fact, worship is an interlude in the actual business of salvation. It deals in symbol, not in substance. In the Eucharist no concrete, substantial sharing of bread, and of all the supports of life that bread represents, is given from man to man. What is shared is a token bread. And it is only in the real order of work and sacrifice that men are transformed. Yet this interlude is a most necessary one. It is the pause we need to glimpse the inwardness and the purpose and the eternal worth of what we do when we work.[33]

Comparing the Eucharist to sexual union between spouses, Burtchaell shows how these sacred moments are interludes in the real business of love, are ecstatic expressions of the everyday love of one for another; so too, it is not in the church building that we make love, are saved, or emerge from selfishness into charity. "The sanctuary is not the place set aside for us to encounter God (whom we are unremittingly reminded to seek in our neighbor), but the sacred place where we draw aside momentarily to rediscover and refresh our faith that it is in serving our neighbor that we cleave to God."[34] He goes on to say that the sacrament catches the congregation's conscience, revealing to them that in their everyday, secular, humane occupations, eternity is at stake. "The specific purpose of worship is not to save, but to reveal that there is a God who is at all times saving. Sacraments are not meant to draw one's attention away from his secular pursuits, as from a distraction. On the contrary, what they celebrate is the salvific power of common activities performed with uncommon generosity."[35] In the words of the "Constitution on the Sacred Liturgy" (*Sacrosanctum Concilium*), "The liturgy is thus the outstanding means by which the faithful can express in their lives, and manifest to others, the mystery of Christ and the real nature of the true Church."[36] In a response to this document Jaroslav Pelikan reiterates that "worship is the metabolism of the Christian life. In the liturgy through the Word of God and the sacraments, the Church receives the grace of God by which she lives; in the liturgy, through prayer and sacrificial action, she offers herself to God for His service in the world."[37]

SACRAMENTS AND SOCIAL LIFE. "The Church Today" (*Lumen Gentium*) explains service in the world by clarifying what help the Church strives to give to human activity through Christians. It cautions that those who think that religion consists in acts of worship alone and in the discharge of certain moral obligations, and who would imagine that they can plunge themselves into earthly affairs in such a way as to imply that these are altogether divorced from the religious life, have missed the point of their proper vocation and are shirking their earthly responsibilities. "This split between the faith which many profess and their daily lives deserves to be counted among the more serious errors of our age."[38] Exhorting that there be no false dichotomy between professional and social activities on the one part, and our religious life on the other, the document warns that "the Christian who neglects his temporal duties neglects his duties toward his neighbor and even God, and jeopardizes his eternal salvation."[39] But "In the exercise of all their earthly activities, they can thereby gather their humane, domestic, professional, social, and technical enterprises into one vital synthesis with religious values, under whose supreme direction all things are harmonized unto God's glory."[40]

ERIKSON'S CONTRIBUTION TO UNDERSTANDING COMMUNITY BUILDING THROUGH VIRTUES DEVELOPMENT

For a personalist understanding of the dynamics of social life, of how we enable one another to live virtuously or to suffer the sins of our forebears, we must move from a theological to a psychological plane. The work of Erik Erikson on the development of personality helps us see how grace builds on nature as we strive to engage in a catechesis of the heart, one which fosters affective Christian community.

In bidding farewell to his community Jesus made very clear their distinguishing characteristic. "I give you a new commandment: love one another; just as I have loved you, you also must love one another. By this love you have for one another, everyone will know that you are my disciples" (John 13:34-35).

How do we enable one another to love? What ego-strengths, or virtues, are needed? How can they be developed so that Christians can live wholeheartedly in response to this invitation to divine affiliation? To address these questions we need to understand the dynamics of personality development.

A psychologist who is also a moralist, Erikson has shed light on these questions by providing insights into the meaning of life for the individual and for society. Having himself resolved an identity crisis in undergoing his own journey of faith, Erikson is one of the leading figures in the field of psychoanalysis and human development. He has not only worked clinically but has also studied the process of growing up in a variety of cultural and social settings. His insights on the role of culture and society in the formation of personality are pertinent for understanding the development of Christian community.

Just as cognitive dissonance, or creative tension, is necessary for the development of moral reasoning, so conflicts or crises, according to Erikson, are the substance out of which virtues grow. He presents human growth as the process of inner and outer conflicts which the vital personality weathers, "re-emerging from each crisis with an increased sense of inner unity, with an increase of good judgment, and an increase in the capacity 'to do well' according to his own standards and to the standards of those who are significant to him."[41] The healthy personality is one which actively masters the environment by means of a certain unity and ability to perceive the world and self correctly.

Erikson believes that anything that grows has a ground plan out of which the parts arise. Each part has a critical time of special ascendancy, until all parts have arisen to form a functioning whole. This critical time is both a risk and an opportunity for greater growth and integration of personality. It is a crucial period of increased vulnerability and heightened potential. If resolved positively, each crisis becomes the source of personal virtue and generational strength; if not, of maladjustment. The resolution of these crises constitutes the manner in which an individual becomes uniquely himself or herself. The personality develops according to steps predetermined in the human organism's readiness to go forward and to interact with a widening radius of significant individuals and situations. Chart 6 presents the essence of Erikson's eight major stepping stones, or stages, in personality development.[42]

Erikson describes three interrelated processes as taking place

Chart 6
ERIKSON'S STAGES OF PSYCHOSOCIAL DEVELOPMENT

Psychosocial Stage	Bipolar Emotional Crisis A sense of ⟷ A sense of	Virtue
	versus	
A. Infancy (oral-sensory)	basic trust ⟷ mistrust	hope
B. Early childhood (oral-musculature)	autonomy ⟷ shame doubt	will power
C. Play age (genital-locomotor)	initiative ⟷ guilt	purpose
D. School age (latency)	industry ⟷ inferiority	competence
E. Adolescence (puberty)	identity ⟷ role confusion	faithfulness
F. Young adulthood	intimacy ⟷ isolation	love
G. Adulthood	generativity ⟷ self-absorption	care
H. Maturity (old age)	integrity ⟷ disgust despair	wisdom

simultaneously within each individual. They are (1) biological or physiological development, (2) psychological response to what is going on within the organism and how it is interpreted by others, so that there is (3) a social organization by the individual, in which he or she establishes basic orientations to society or the world. An example of these interrelated processes would be (1) a child who feels rage at someone treating her unfairly, but (2) her parents tell her that little girls must never fight and that she should not feel that way. She may well internalize their prohibition, so that (3) she is outwardly meek to all but inwardly will suffer and later show symptoms, such as depression, ulcers, or other ailments, since her social organization, her response to the world, is blocking an emotional energy flow.

During the first four stages the child is in the womb of society. His or her personality is being formed in response to the actions of the socializing agents, primarily of the mother (or surrogate), other family members, including the father, the school, the church, and any other significant others or institutions directly affecting the child's life. In adolescence, the crises of childhood are relived with an acute consciousness as the individual tests society and is tempered and tested by it. In the remaining three stages of the life cycle, the individual who has emerged as an adult is now part of the social fabric, forming or deforming the younger generation.

Erikson presents the ethical implications of his psychoanalytic theory in *Insight and Responsibility*. Therein he defines virtues as ego strengths that are inherent in the individual life cycle and in the sequence of generations. Virtues are active qualities which animate us, giving us the spirit to live fully. They are developed from stage to stage and from generation to generation. Without the basic strengths of the virtues, both the person and society are weakened. Without virtues morality becomes mere moralism, and ethics becomes feeble goodness. "Man's psychosocial survival is safeguarded only by vital virtues which develop in the interplay of successive and overlapping generations, living together in organized settings."[43]

Erikson's theory about how we develop virtues and personal characteristics is accepted as having important implications for catechesis. We will look at the first four developmental crises and note their catechetical implications.

FAITH AS TRUST OR MISTRUST

The earliest and most indispensable virtue for a faithful life, according to Erikson, is hope. "Hope is the enduring belief in the attainability of fervent wishes, in spite of the dark urges and rages which mark the beginning of existence."[44] Hope, he says, is nourished by an adult faith which pervades patterns of child-care. As a sense of basic trust that life is good, hope is the most fundamental prerequisite of mental and religious vitality. The life-giving strength of hope, which is a pervasive attitude toward oneself and the world, is derived from the experiences of the first year of life. This essential trustfulness toward others, as well as a fundamental sense of one's own trustworthiness, becomes a basic mood, the cornerstone of one's personality, pervading all areas of one's life and thereby affecting the basic mood of others.

Depending on the resolution of crises confronted in the first year of life, an individual develops a mood of basic trust or basic mistrust. The optimist and the pessimist, the Pollyanna and the paranoid, the fearless and the fearful, exemplify their bottom-line faith or basic belief that life is to be trusted or mistrusted. Two equally commmitted Christians exemplify their faith as basic trust or basic mistrust as one thumbs through Scripture focusing on God as merciful, forgiving, tending his people, while the other sees God as wrathful, seeking revenge, punishing and condemning sinners.

EMERGENCE OF THE BASIC MOOD. How do these opposing world-views emerge? A description of the infant's kinesthetic, or bodily, learning process shows how our predisposition to trust or mistrust comes about. The following scenarios enable us to see what we may be passing on to others. (In actuality most of us were probably nurtured in between the extremes depicted.) Imagine two infants. One is hungry, cries but a few moments, is fed, burped to prevent colic, diapered regularly. She is cuddled often, held securely, and, as her gurgles indicate, is experiencing good feelings. Although she cannot think yet, messages about the world are being encoded in her brain and throughout her body. If she could talk, the infant might well say, "Indeed! It is good for me to be here." For even as she develops teeth and accidentally bites the mother's breast in being fed, there is patience on the parent's part. The prevailing mood and the interaction between mother and child is teaching her about human existence in a manner that goes to the core of her being, and it is establishing a pattern for the child to learn how to get needs satisfied throughout life without hurting others.[45]

Imagine the other infant. He is hungry and cries and cries and cries and, eventually, is fed. But the crying resumes, now due to colic and the little one's discomfort with a wet diaper that is producing a rash. Eventually he is attended to. Later he is hurriedly held and then jerked away from the warmth of the mother's breast for biting too hard; this infant too is learning—a harsh lesson about life, a lifelong lesson (unless there is graceful or therapeutic intervention) that life is harsh and existence is painful. If this child could speak he might well ask if this existence is worth the anguish.

If we watch the lives of these two infants unfold, their stories will most likely proclaim their respective, and deeply ingrained, messages. And not only their own offspring but all those with whom they come in contact will be tinged with their messages of basic hope or of basic fear or mistrust of life.

RELIGIOUS IMPLICATIONS. Were it not for religion, in its original sense, there would be no hope for the hopeless. Erikson names religion as the institution which throughout history has striven to verify basic trust in life. "Religion, it seems, is the oldest and has been the most lasting institution to serve the ritual restoration of a sense of trust in the form of faith while offering a tangible formula for a sense of evil against which it promises to arm and defend man."[46] More simply, Erikson is reminding us that as a community of faith, our vocation is to call forth hope in one another. If we relate this to the insights of Niebuhr, Fowler, and Kohlberg as explicated in earlier chapters, we can begin to see how we can be sacraments to one another, enabling one another to grow beyond our moral myopia so that grace can indeed transform our fallen nature.

The new Rite of Christian Initiation of Adults inspires us with manifold possibilities for the healing and reconciliation so many hunger for. In communicating hope by our life-style, the community of faith indeed becomes sacramental if it signs death to fear and to old, mistrustful ways of being and brings in a new way of life through a Baptism it breathes and lives daily. *Such a community witnesses by its life-style* that its sacraments are not merely verbal rituals, magical rites, or formal obligations. The sacraments of such a faith community evidence a celebration of shared meaning, of embodied hope that indeed a God who is Love is alive and dwelling among us!

Just as the mother's manner even more than her words evidences her basic mood of trust or mistrust, and in turn shapes her child's attitude toward life, so too are we as individuals in a community we call Holy Mother the Church daily doing the same to one another. Thus, for example, the rite of Reconciliation in a hopeful community is not a hopelessly recurring laundering, or a denigrating experience to be avoided. Reconciliation is a reckoning—an exchange of our hopelessness for God's trust in us. Engaged in this manner, a new way of life can grow, engendering renewal within the individual and the community as each comes to recognize their faith as a basic sense of trust and relatedness to everyone in the universe. Thus the hopeful can truly cooperate with the Holy Spirit to renew the face of the earth. Mere poetry? For the hopeless, maybe. For those serious about a therapeutic or salvific faith community, Erikson provides data to support the view that an expansive way of life within a generous immediate group brings about healing.[47]

FAITH AS FREELY WILLED OR AS SHAME AND DOUBT

If hope is instilled, then free will, which is the basis for the acceptance of law and necessity, can emerge. Free will, autonomy, or will power is the "unbroken determination to exercise free choice as well as self-restraint, in spite of the unavoidable experience of shame and doubt in infancy."[48] Erikson cautions that to will does not mean to be wilful. Rather it is to gain gradually the power of increased judgment and decision in the application of our drives.

During the second and third year of life the child is being toilet-trained. At this time individual coordination and social guidance need to become cooperative agents as the individual learns to control wilfulness and to offer and exchange good will.

Poor training instead leads to deep shame and compulsive doubt in later life, to feelings of anger at the power of others.

EMERGENCE OF FREE WILL. At this stage there are rapid gains in muscular maturation and the ability to control the eliminative sphincters. The child has to learn when to "hold on" and when to "let go." The manner in which the parents work with the child to control eliminative body functions teaches the individual not only a biological lesson, but a critical psychological one as well, because the child is in effect becoming imbued with a sense of automony, of selfhood, or with feelings of worthlessness, anger, shame, and doubt. The child is learning affectively whether or not God is basically good, kindly, accepting, and forgiving, whether personal worth is considered apart from one's mistakes and misdeeds, and whether moral authority comes from both within oneself and from above.[49]

The following scenarios will illustrate how the still-highly-dependent child is beginning to experience an autonomous will or shame and doubt. A little one (whose fragile sense of trust in her parents is developing) starts to eliminate on the kitchen floor. Firmly, but tolerantly, the parent says, "No! No! Hold it. Good girl. Let's go to the bathroom, and then we have to clean up the mess in the kitchen." Another child begins to do the same and is greeted by his parent with a harsh "You bad boy! Haven't I told you to hold it until we get to the bathroom? Good boys always do what their mommies say. You never listen. You're so bad! You'll never learn. I'm going to have to punish you [whacking him]. I'll *make* you learn, and you won't forget it."

Both children are learning lessons which they will be hard put to forget, lessons which will affect them as adults, as they strive to make sense of law and necessity. One is learning self-control, that it is forgivable to have an accident, and that it carries consequences, such as cleaning up. She is learning that it is much better to regulate herself, to know when to retain and when to eliminate, and that there is a particular pleasureableness attached to this process. When this crisis repeats itself in adolescence with respect to genital self-control, she will have a healthier basis on which to develop a positive sexuality.

But the other child is getting a confusing message about his body. Relieving himself (as we all know) feels naturally good. But he is being told that he is bad. This contradictory message produces a secondary mistrust called doubt. And he is also being filled with shame. Shame is the feeling of being completely exposed and conscious of being looked at, of being "caught with one's pants down," as Erikson puts it. It is expressed in an impulse to bury one's face or to sink, right then and there, into the ground. "Shaming exploits an increasing sense of being small, which paradoxically develops as the child stands up and as his awareness permits him to note the relative measures of size and power."[50]

Erikson cautions that too much shaming can lead to shamelessness since "there is a limit to a child's and an adult's individual endurance in the face of demands which force him to consider himself, his body, his needs, and his wishes as evil and dirty, and to believe in the infallibility of those who pass such judgment."[51] Turning things around, the individual becomes oblivious to the opinions of others and considers their existence evil as he or she seizes the opportunity to do whatever feels good when the authority figures are gone or when the individual can leave them.

IMPLICATIONS FOR RELIGION. Too much shaming may well account for many Catholics leaving the Church. In *Catholic Schools in a Declining Church*, Andrew Greeley and his colleagues state: "The decline in Catholic religiousness...is in part the result of a joint decline in the acceptance of the pope as a leader in the church and acceptance of the church's sexual ethic."[52] The authors suggest that "people first disagree with the church's sexual teaching, reject the authority of the leader who reaffirms that teaching, and then become estranged from other aspects of the church's teaching and practice."[53] Official teachings, like our parents' messages, may be well-intended. Yet depending on their content and delivery, their outcome can be a strengthening of the freedom to do good, or an increase in shame and doubt, or even the loss of faith in authority. *The Unchurched American*, a monumental study issued by Gallup Poll and underwritten by a coalition of 31 Catholic and Protestant groups, has some provocative findings in this regard.

In it an overwhelming majority of both the churched and unchurched agree that "an individual should arrive at his or her own religious beliefs independently of any church or synagogue."[54] Whereas the churched and the unchurched differ most sharply on matters of personal freedom, both groups have the following criticism of organized religion. They regard most churches and synagogues as having lost the real spiritual purpose of religion, as being too concerned with organizational rather than spiritual issues. They do not see organized religion as effective in helping people find meaning in life.

Yet the vast majority of the unchurched are not atheists, unbelievers, or anti-Christian. In fact they hold traditional religious beliefs such as praying to God, wanting religious education for their children, believing that Christ is God, that he rose from the dead, and that there is an afterlife. Over thirty percent of the religiously inactive said they would return if they could find a pastor or church community with whom they could openly discuss religious doubts and personal spiritual needs.[55]

In *Young Man Luther*, Erikson indicates the role religion can play as one goes through the crisis of developing autonomy or shame and doubt. He shows how religion can be a force empowering the person to act by giving the individual a reason to exist.

IMPLICATIONS FOR RELIGIOUS EDUCATION. To develop a mature faith, free will is necessary, since faith demands a strong will to live and to overcome the obstacles to fullness of life. Organized religion, when it is mindful of the individual, offers the balance needed to develop both personal autonomy and adherence to external law and order. Just as the rudiments of conscience, that is, the beginnings of free will, are awakened within the individual, so too must they be awakened within the community of faith if we are to grow from being "the children of God" to becoming "the People of God." The Church leaders and all of us engaged in catechesis need patient understanding that enables us to master the art of knowing what and when to hold on and what and when to let go, to distinguish between the essentials and the cultural accidentals in our tradition.

Retaining and eliminating are basic human operations. Each operation can express either a hostile or a benign intention. Thus retaining or letting go of something or someone expresses an individual's or a community's patterns of affirmation or rejection.[56] For example, letting go an incompetent teacher can reflect affirmation or rejection of that human being—depending on the principal's intention. If the principal summarily dismisses the incompetent teacher, the teacher will probably feel rejected (and perhaps become defensive, react in a self-destructive or retaliatory manner, and engender a negative cycle.). On the other hand, if the principal has the moral courage to dialogue, to let the teacher know that the evidence shows that his charism is not in teaching, and that although she has to let him go, she appreciates his efforts and is willing to help him find something more suited to his God-given gifts, her benign intention is evident—that is, to direct competent education without destroying or rejecting a human being in the process.

So too if religious educators treat individuals as animals whose wills must be broken and trained or whose bad habits must be eliminated, or even as machines to be set and tuned, they are violating the learner and impeding the growth of virtue. The *intent* with which we catechize can lead to a religious socialization that is hostile and retentive. This is exemplified in a catechesis in which the past is held onto in a cruel, destructive-retaining manner which restrains the development of others; it is passed on when those so socialized, in turn, become the catechists for the next generation. Such a religious socialization stands in opposition to a catechesis which strives to develop a pattern of caring, of holding on to traditions and beliefs which are cherished as vital and dear.

So too, letting go can become an inimical letting loose of destructive forces, of "excommunicating" or ostracizing those who differ from us by verbally or physically expelling them from our midst. However, if it is taught as patience, as divine detachment that is tolerant of differences, letting go becomes graceful as we learn to let things pass and with divine benignity allow the sun to shine on all as we let others be by respecting their autonomy.

How is autonomy achieved? "Just as the sense of trust is a reflection of the parents' sturdy and realistic faith, so is the sense of autonomy a reflection of the parents' dignity as individuals."[57] To generalize about the community of faith as educator: No matter how simple or how sophisticated the religious education program may be, the catechized are sensing our motivation as freely willed or as shame- and doubt-filled, and they are imbibing our spirit. Erikson cautions that "no matter what we *do* in detail, the child will *feel* primarily what we live by, what makes us loving, cooperative, and firm beings, and what makes us hateful, anxious, and divided in ourselves."[58] He concludes: "The question is always whether we remain the masters of the rules by which we want to make things more manageable (not more complicated) or whether the rules master the ruler. But it often happens, in the individual as well as in group life, that the letter of the rules kills the spirit which created them."[59]

In our catechesis we must be continually aware of the spirit, mood, or attitude being conveyed. Is it an autonomy grounded in hope? Is it the freedom of the sons and daughters of God? Or is the message felt by the receiver one that instills shame and doubt? Is the community of faith strengthening trust and stimulating the growth of inner freedom and personal responsibility? Is it encouraging mature, or immature, relationships with authority? Only a community trusting the Holy Spirit and willing to grow in the virtues basic to a mature Christianity will risk such an examination of its consciousness and be willing to speak to these questions in a manner which makes its faith evident.

FAITH AND CONSCIENCE FORMATION

In each of the stages or developmental crises, it is becoming evident that the adults, as they form the younger generation, pass on to them, for better or worse, what they themselves have inherited. In the third major crisis in human development the child's conscience is formed as "the consistent inner voice which delineates permissible action and thought."[60] If properly developed, one's conscience exhibits a sense of purpose or initiative. Purpose is the temporal perspective giving direction and focus to concerted striving. It comes from the example of the family and puts ideals into action. The virtue or ego-strength of purpose results from the child's play which is fueled by fantasy and tempered by guilt.

Morally restrained yet ethically active, purpose is defined as "the courage to envisage and pursue valued goals uninhibited by the defeat of infantile fantasies, by guilt and by the foiling fear of punishment."[61] In *Identity, Youth and Crisis*, Erikson describes how sexual desire and energy gets diverted from the parents who first awakened the child's tenderness. It is turned first toward a fantasy-filled future and then to more and more realizable goals or purposes.

EMERGENCE OF CONSCIENTIOUSNESS AND PURPOSE IN LIFE. At this stage, which is critical in the development of initiative and/or guilt, the child begins to find out what kind of person he or she is going to be. The little one identifies with the parents, playing with the idea of how it would be to be them— wanting to be like the parent who appears very powerful, very beautiful, and fantastically dangerous. What brings on this crisis of ambition and independence is the development of locomotion, language, and imagination. No longer crawling or stumbling along, the youngster now moves around more freely, intruding into others' space, intruding into others' ears with words, and intruding into the unknown with a consuming curiosity. Continually asking why, the child cannot avoid becoming frightened by the dreams and scenes he or she has imagined. From this ever-expanding imagination, which calls for tempering rather than punishing, come nightmares, imaginary friends or pets, and the fabrications that for adults would be called lies.

This is the phallic stage of infant sexuality in which genital excitability and infantile sexual curiosity are aroused. Often this rudimentary genitality is not particularly noticeable. If ignored the energy goes into a latency period, coming to the fore again in adolescence and adulthood. However, if there is preoccupation with sexual concerns on the parents' part, such as punishing the youngster for fondling his genitals, a castration complex can ensue. That is the intensified fear of losing, or on the part of the girl child that she has lost, the male genital as punishment for secretly pleasurable fantasies and deeds. Such a fear governs initiative and leads to the formation of conscience.

Psychoanalysis verifies the simple conclusion that boys attach their first genital affection to the maternal adults who have otherwise given comfort to their bodies and that they develop their first sexual rivalry against the persons who are the sexual owners of those maternal persons. The little girl, in turn, becomes attached to her father and other important men and jealous of her mother, a development which may cause her much anxiety, for it seems to block her retreat to that self-same mother, while it makes the mother's disapproval ever so much more magically dangerous because unconsciously "deserved."[62]

Fantasizing the self as wed to one parent and fearing this discovery by the other, the child moves from jealous rage to a rivalry climaxing in guilt and failure, since the youngster can never be the equal of the adult. From the fear of being found out, the child begins to hear an inner voice—observing, guiding, punishing. This is the beginning of conscience. More properly speaking, it is the superego and the ego-ideal which are being formed as the child internalizes the commands and admonitions of the one parent out of attachment and a wish to please the admired one, and of the other out of appeasement or fear of being punished if ever the fantasy were found out.

DEFORMATION OF CONSCIENCE. As detailed in the previous chapter, the child's conscience (the superego) is primitive, cruel, and uncompromising. Yet the very power of symbolization or fantasy that led the child into this consciousness can also serve to liberate it. However, when a child overly inhibits fantasies and demonstrates an obedience even more literal than that demanded by the parents, the youngster is not exemplifying virtue. Instead, deep resentments are being conceived. For the child is beginning to feel that life is a matter of artibrary power and so resents the parents for seemingly trying to get away with the very transgressions that were intolerable in himself or herself. Deep conflicts then ensue as suspicion and evasion emanate from this uncompromising conscience which cannot envision alternatives. In such a person morality becomes synonymous with vindictiveness and the suppression of others.[63]

The potential powerhouse of destructive drives which can be aroused (and temporarily buried at this stage) will come out in later life if the opportunity provokes it. The self-righteous guardian of morality, whether in the form of a vindictive censor or of an hysterical preacher or of a self-restrictive ascetic more absorbed in containing the flesh than in praising its Creator, may well be the outcome of conscience malformed. The situation, however, is not hopeless. Erikson emphasizes that there is little in these inner developments which cannot be turned to constructive and peaceful purposes if we learn to understand the conflicts and anxieties of childhood and their importance for future generations. "But if we should choose to overlook or belittle the phenomena of childhood, along with the best and the worst of our childhood dreams, we shall have failed to recognize one of the eternal sources of human anxiety and strife."[64]

Erikson goes on to note how these conflicts over initiative or purpose in life which come from a malformed conscience keep the individual from living up to inner capacities and powers of imagination and feeling. Such conflicts become evident in psychosomatic diseases, including sexual impotence and frigidity. They also manifest themselves in over-compensation, wherein the individual is continually "going at it" with seemingly tireless energy yet is inwardly depressed and depleted from striving to derive self-worth and equality from ceaseless displays of initiative. The social cost of this aggressive idealism is the insensitive exploitation of the weakness of others, a blindly prevailing dominance or chauvinism.

IMPLICATIONS FOR RELIGIOUS EDUCATION. Misguided conscience formation can be averted by fostering a healthy initiative which minimizes a crippling sense of guilt. Erikson points out that by playfully doing things together with the child, the parent can guide the youngster into a more realistic self-identification. By encouraging the child to get up and go, rather than discouraging him or her with reprimands and rebukes, the parent is enabling the two to become companions instead of rivals. The child is experiencing equality in worth, even though the parent and child are unequal in size.

Taking Erikson's insights to heart as religious educators—whether we be parents or professional catechists—forces us to probe into our own purpose in life. Are we doing whatever we do out of compulsion and guilt? Or is it from a heart that is loving, free, and willing to give of itself? On the one hand, we cannot give what we do not have. What eventually comes through is the truth of our being—a feeling of fullness or emptiness of life. Therefore, words alone, no matter how masterfully spoken, will not communicate life if they are not lived. In fact, if spoken under stress or duress, our words will deplete the life energy of those who listen.[65]

On the other hand, as Christ exhorted, we must not hide our light under a bushel basket. We need to exemplify our gifts for one another's edification (literally, the building of a temple or holy place). In behavioral terms, Erikson explains the importance of modeling for identity development. "Adults by their own example and by stories they tell of the big life and of what to them is the great past, offer children of this age an eagerly absorbed *ethos of action* in the form of ideal types."[66]

What Erikson is saying about the youngster correlates well with descriptions of individuals at Fowler's Stages Two and Three and Kohlberg's Stage Three. By recounting stories of saints and heroes, of people who have gone before us and whose lives have made a difference because of their goodness, and by living in a congruent manner, we are filling our children with spirit, inspiring their imaginations, energizing them to live this sacred calling to love.[67]

NURTURANCE AND WORSHIP. In place of dreadful visions the youngsters' burgeoning fantasies are thereby becoming saturated with stories symbolizing hope. And as they see their parents, sitters, or caretakers bring joy and forgiveness to one another, the new generation *feel* themselves enjoyed and forgiven, and they begin to assimilate the same attitudinal stance toward others. For in their role-taking, as they dress up and prance and dance like their elders, our children are formed and will in turn form forthcoming generations.[68]

In this playful way our children are being introduced to the sacred work of the People of God, to the liturgy or worship, which is symbolization of the highest order.[69] Our rituals are not practical things; rather, they express who we believe ourselves to be. Our rituals symbolize our reality. Illuminating, signing, pointing out the practices of our everyday lives, our rituals invest them with coherence and meaning. In turn, our worship is the recognition and adoration of the worth-ship of God who is Love. As such, our worship culminates in like action, so that we as adults too are role-taking, are "putting on Christ." As it was with our Brother, the firstborn among many, God's work becomes our work.

Erikson notes that rituals with vested celebrants dramatize, in a ceremonial present, noble purposes reflected from a glorified past and projected onto a larger and always more perfect future. In this manner they sanction initiative and assuage guilt by submission to a higher authority.[70] Thus where rituals have lost their meaning, it may be that the symbol has lost its power to communicate, but not because it is no longer potent to point us to the sacred and to help us transcend the dense ordinariness and opaqueness of our limited vision.

It may be that we have eyes that refuse to see, and ears that will not hear the marvels the Lord has prepared for those who love.[71] It may well be that we have become so grown-up that we have lost the playfulness of little children, that we have lost our imagination, the gift which enables us to see the sacred immanent in the everyday affairs of life, to hear the Lord calling us to care for all, for the rich and the poor, for mother earth and for her helpless issue: the air and the water, the animals and plant life, the *anawim* all over the universe crying out for justice. Or it can be that we do hear but that we fear because we cannot appreciate our call to universal community. And so we relegate our responsibility to poetry and prayer and live our lives as individuals bound by fear.

GRASS-ROOTS COMMUNITIES. This sacred task calling for universal concern cannot be performed alone. We need the support of one another. Especially in fractured families there is need for a healing family—for a community of faith. This extended family can provide a variety of role models for the young ones. These alternative models enable them to grow beyond the limits of their parents and so break the cycle of those limitations being perpetuated from generation to generation. In Erikson's words, "Only a combination of early prevention and alleviation of hatred and guilt in the growing being, and the consequent handling of hatred in the free collaboration of people who feel *equal in worth although different in kind or function or age*, permits a peaceful cultivation of initiative, a truly free sense of enterprise."[72]

As the *comunidades de base*, the grass-roots communities of the Third World, have shown, greater good accrues to all both within and beyond the community of faith. Individual deficiencies can be obliterated, or at least compensated, by the strengths of the others in a worshiping community which has hearths wherein each comes to know the other by name. And the nuclear family is redeemed as the children have many *comadres* and *compadres* (godparents or co-mothers and co-fathers) to turn to.

In such a community, conscience formation becomes once again a communal responsibility and no longer a private, family onus. In such an extended family, for example, baby-sitting not only becomes a gratuitous exchange but a moment of grace for all. By providing this service for parents and children, by acting as surrogates, celibates and singles are in turn fulfilling their parenting needs or their need to be needed. All gain as the lives, the histories, and mysteries of these people of God become strengthened through each one's helping to form the other's ego-ideal simply by the example of their own life-style.

In a supportive community which downplays weaknesses by nurturing one another's strengths simply by caring for one another, the younger generation is provided with healing from the rich diversity of role models by whom they are affirmed and with whom they can identify and so assuage the oedipal conflict or guilt.[73] In a caring Christian community, the child's world expands as he no longer needs to be tied to Mommy's apron strings, nor she to being Daddy's little girl. In a grass-roots community the emotional intensity of this crisis would be diffused as the youngster is freed to explore and identify with parents of other children, or with a teacher or deacon or anyone else representing vocations which the child can imaginatively "try on."

This extended family, the grass-roots community of faith, need not be domiciled under the same roof, but the members do need to come together to play and to pray, to build relationships of celebration and of service. The invitation to the single person, single parent, widower, divorcee, elderly, and others on the fringes of parish society to become part of a cross-age, mixed grass-roots community evidences faith that God is at work in all and through all, building his Mystical Body. Similarly, the encouragement of like-minded support groups, e.g., of senior citizens or single parents, will provide a warp and woof that can only serve to strengthen the spiritual and social fabric.

In this regard, the new Rite of Christian Initiation of

Adults, with its manifold possibilities for strengthening both worship and community, is a timely invitation for us all to explore. Aidan Kavanagh concludes that

> Clearly, the document is concretely specific on who a Christian is. He is not merely a set of abstract, yet imponderable good intentions that are essentially incommunicable and subjectively sovereign. Rather, a Christian is a person of faith in Jesus Christ dead and risen among his faithful people. This faith is no mere noetic thing but *a way of living together; it is the bond which establishes that reciprocal mutuality of relationships* we call communion, and it is this communion which constitutes the ecclesial real presence of Jesus Christ in the world of grace, faith, hope, charity, and character.[74]

Kavanagh cannot imagine religious education, theological training, and even the practical day-to-day running of dioceses and parishes to be possible without taking this present document as their starting points. "For what it contains is not merely some more ceremonial changes for use *ad libitum*. Its core is an ecclesiology of rich existential concreteness and disciplinary clarity arising out of the best that two thousand years of Christian tradition has to offer."[75]

FAITH AND GOOD WORKS

Essential to true community is cooperation, or working together. The willingness to collaborate with others, which undergirds community, is the virtue which results from the positive resolution of the crisis between industry and inferiority which marks this stage of human development. At this time, called the latency period by Freud, the more aggressive drives are dormant. (They are in a lull before the storm of puberty, in which they re-emerge in new combinations.)

Now the child's energies shift from the inwardness of the imaginary to the outward world. The child's energies are focused on making things work, on how they are made, what they do, how they operate. A sense of industry is developing as the child strives to be useful, wanting to make things or do them well, even perfectly. If this crisis is successfully resolved, the virtue of competence emerges.

In the United States, children are entering school at this age. And as they learn academic and social skills, they are learning to be failures or successes. Exposed to structured interpersonal relationships and made to work in groups, children quickly learn what is expected and what is not permitted. They learn which behaviors call forth praise and which blame and what cannot be tolerated in a social situation. They learn to win recognition by producing things, by achieving high grades, by success in arts and crafts, athletics, and the like. Some also learn that recognition can be achieved by misconduct, since that is the only way they gain attention.

EMERGENCE OF INDUSTRY OR INFERIORITY. The school-age youngster is learning both how to fit into society and what skills or tools are necessary for survival. At this stage it is crucial that the child have good teachers who are healthy and relaxed, who feel trusted and respected by the community. Such teachers have the charism to recognize special efforts and encourage special gifts. They know how to alternate work and play, games and study. As they give each child due attention, they are able to handle those for whom school is more a matter of endurance than of joy.

Good teachers inspire even the slower students by bringing out less-obvious talents and abilities in each; insensitive teachers instill inferiority, at times, even in the bright. Erikson advises: "The development of a sense of inferiority, the feeling that one will never be 'any good,' is a danger which can be minimized by a teacher who knows how to emphasize what a child *can* do."[76] He also cautions that children can become workaholics by identifying too strenuously with an overly work-oriented teacher or by becoming teacher's pet, and that because of the manner in which they are schooled, many may never learn to enjoy work and to take pride in doing at least one kind of thing well.

IMPLICATIONS FOR RELIGIOUS EDUCATION. The following scenarios put Erikson's insights in context for formal religious education classes for children. In one setting the youngsters are welcomed by older children, and in their classes the older children are greeted by adolescents who serve as teaching assistants. Each child is known by name and greeted affirmatively—in a manner that bespeaks interest, that says, "It is good that you have come. This is indeed a reunion, and this community has cause to celebrate." Whether the assistants decorate name cards or make prayer cards or other such surprises periodically, such reinforcers will not only help keep attendance steady but will also strengthen the belief that each of us is gifted, that we are gifts to one another, and that we have the God-given power to grace one another as God is continually doing to us.

Since each of us has preferred modes of learning, a variety of approaches should be used. For example, the teacher may commence the lesson by hushing the group to create the mood in which to tell a story. Or group dramatization, creative projects, or written activities may be used to engage the children in a manner appropriate to their level of development as they learn through the mood generated and the activities performed to live as Jesus invites us to live.

As older students help the younger ones whenever they are called on to do so, the older students develop feelings of being productive and worthwhile, and the whole group learns the reciprocity essential for a caring community. The younger ones, too, feel good as they are encouraged in their efforts. Given this nurturing attention, they cannot help but admire their mentors, sensing that they themselves can serve this way some day soon. Just as the little ones bring home completed tasks and can tell of their triumphs (for with a little help from their friends they were able to do work that may have been too taxing if done alone), so do their mentors. Annually in such a program, there is a Catechists' Recognition Day in which the parish community is invited to fete all those who have actively assisted in this ministry, whether in the classroom, in the office, on field trips, in being responsible for media, driving, or doing any of the tasks that tap the talents of each and make for rewarding intentional religious socialization.

Is such a program possible? Or is it too idealistic? It cannot of course be done alone. A communal effort is needed. That is, there need to be initially at least two or three people foolish enough to believe that if they gather together in the Lord's name and open themselves, the Holy Spirit will show them the way. The alternative, too frequently resorted to, is engaging in this ministry as if it were nothing more than programming persons

for patterned performances—a process which in effect violates
their mystery while it abuses salvation history. Too frequently in
religious education programs the Word of God is taken so
literally and cognitively that from their earliest years the children
are schooled in a manner heavily dependent on reading,
recitation, and writing. Having had too much too soon, when
they *are* developmentally ready for a deeper cognition of the
faith, many chalk it off with "I've had all that already. Catechism
is for kids."

NEGATIVE RELIGIOUS SOCIALIZATION. The Scripture
shows that the Lord enjoys reaching us by means of reverie or
dreams.[77] Yet in the traditional program the child engaged in
reverie is scolded for not paying attention. At the same time, the
child who has a quick recall is rewarded for a wonderful memory,
since recitation of the right words is equated with living their
truth. The tyke who cannot master verbal content is not
examined on desire or aspiration but instead is told, "You can't
make your first Communion until you can recite these prayers."
Or some other message is given which equates faith with
knowledge.[78]

Memorization of simple truths and common prayers is
necessary for a common expression of faith and as a centering
point to turn to in troubling times. But a child who is put
down for what may well be a lack of parents' time or interest is
being burdened with inferiority, mistakenly sensing "I must be
dumb because the other kids can say them, but I can't." If
enough significant persons reinforce this message, the child
"learns" that he or she is stupid or bad and begins to act
accordingly. And so begins a cycle of improper behavior which
calls forth negative labels which in turn generate more
misbehavior that dams the individual's potential and burdens all
with the social costs of talents misspent. For what can any
community expect of people who from early childhood have
been socialized to believe they are bad or stupid, immoral,
wretched, or perverse?

WORK AND PLAY, SERVE AND PRAY. In contrast, where a
sense of industry prevails, where the catechized are involved in
doing things beside and with others, competence can develop.

Essential for education in faith and morals, competence is "the free exercise of dexterity and intelligence in the completion of serious tasks unimpaired by an infantile sense of inferiority. This is the lasting basis for co-operative participation in productive adult life."[79]

It must be noted that competence is not compulsion. Although faith without good works is dead, it is not good works which justify us. It is God's grace. Work is a production, bringing a certain amount of pleasure and worth when it is a calling forth of our natural resources, our unique talents or charisms. Work is neither a punishment nor a ticket to heaven.

Our gift to humanity as Catholics may well be to exorcise ourselves of the Protestant work ethic and to reinstate the rhythm of working and playing, which is the basis for serving and praying. This spirit is still beautifully expressed in our ethnic festas and fiestas, and it was the Church's intent in its original panoply of holy days.[80] Restoration of the Sabbath as a day to engage wholly in the opposite of our everyday fare, a day of true leisure, will not only free us from undue care which evidences itself in neurosis and fear but will also make ready the way for a deepening of our spirit because a quiet mind and rested spirit enable us to hear the Lord in prayer.

On a mundane yet equally important level, Erikson warns that if there is not a balance of work and play, the child may become entirely dependent on prescribed duties and develop an unshakable and costly self-restraint "with which he may later make his own life and other people's lives miserable, and in fact spoil his own children's natural desire to learn and to work."[81]

FAITH AND ADOLESCENCE

Because our technology and economy have forced us to extend schooling so that there is more and more time spent before beginning one's career or formal vocation, adolescence has become a distinct and critical period between childhood and adulthood. This period is like a crucible in which the faith community's beliefs are tested. The testing of beliefs continues through one's youth. Youth is the term which distinguishes the millions of post-adolescents in the advanced nations of the world who "have not settled the questions whose answers once defined adulthood; questions of relationship to the existing society, questions of vocation, questions of social role and life-style."[82]

The adolescent begins to define his or her identity with the onset of puberty, with its rapid genital maturation and physiological changes. In puberty there is a quantum leap in consciousness from concrete thinking to critically reflective reasoning. A frightening sense of the fragility of life and a hidden fear of the imminence of death also prevails, especially in light of the adolescent's growing consciousness of a desperate situation threatening all with nuclear annihilation.

Erikson points out that given their very weak sense of personal identity, adolescents tend to overidentify with heroes, cliques, and crowds. They become remarkably clannish, intolerant, and cruel in their exclusion of others whom they consider different, whether because of skin color, cultural background, tastes, or talents. Often entirely petty aspects of dress and gesture arbitrarily demarcate the in-group from the out-group. By forming cliques and stereotyping themselves, their ideals, and their enemies, adolescents temporarily help one another gain an identity.[83] Youth is more settled in identity, yet unsettled regarding society.

Kenneth Keniston differentiates adolescence from youth by noting that "in adolescence, young men and women tend to accept their society's definitions of them as rebels, truants, conformists, athletes or achievers. But in youth, the relationship between socially assigned labels and the real self becomes more problematic, and constitutes a focus of central concern."[84] This happens because in youth there is an increased awareness of conflict, or disparity, between one's identity, values, and integrity and the resources and demands of society. "The adolescent is struggling to define who he is; the youth begins to sense who he is and thus to recognize the possibility of conflict and disparity between his emerging selfhood and his social order."[85]

Three needs are characteristic of both adolescents and youth as they go through the identity crisis: (1) the need for devotion, or a cause to dedicate oneself to, (2) the need to repudiate, that is, to stand against the identity given by one's parents in the attempt to form one's own, and (3) the need for a moratorium in which this future identity can incubate and come to be.[86]

EMERGENCE OF IDENTITY. During the identity crisis, the four childhood crises are re-experienced in a more conscious and pressing manner. Erikson states that delinquent and psychotic incidents are not uncommon where there has been strong doubt about one's ethnic or sexual identity. Adolescents bewildered by roles forced on them run away in one form or another. Some run outwardly, leaving schools and jobs, staying out all night, or literally running away from home. Others run inwardly, into drugs, bizarre behavior, and inaccessible moods. Their greatest need and often only salvation is the refusal of older friends, advisors, parents, and judiciary personnel to type them as delinquent. They need forgiveness in the form of people reaching out to help them find a positive identity. Sadly, as Erikson remarks, "Many a youth, finding that the authorities expect him to be 'a bum' or 'a queer,' or 'off the beam,' perversely obliges by becoming just that."[87]

For the community of faith, the painful turmoil of adolescence may in effect be a divine turbulence inviting both the individual and the community to express its full humane potential. Where one or a number of the earlier crises may not have been adequately resolved, the opportunity is now given to the community to extend healing to the individual and so enable all to grow in virtue. If the adolescent identity crisis is adequately resolved, then trust, free will, a sense of purpose in life, and competence will be exhibited and highlighted by fidelity.

THE VIRTUE OF FIDELITY. Fidelity, or faithfulness, is the positive outcome of adolescence. Erikson defines fidelity as "the ability to sustain loyalties freely pledged in spite of the inevitable contradictions of value systems. It is the cornerstone of identity and receives inspiration from confirming ideologies and affirming companions."[88]

Just as in the earliest stage of development there is a critical need for trust in others in order to come to trust oneself, the world, and all in it, so too in adolescence one looks fervently for people and ideas to have faith in. Adolescents need people or a cause to which to devote themselves, in whose service it would seem worthwhile to prove their own trustworthiness to themselves and to all. And so adolescents search for truth both within themselves and in others, in confirming adults and in affirming peers. To bolster their striving to be loyal, the individuals in crisis look for a high sense of duty, truthfulness, sincerity and conviction, genuineness or authenticity, and fairness in others. And they tend to become vociferous in condemning the hypocrisy of others, especially since they are inwardly critical of themselves for not yet being able to live up to the highest ideals.

IDEOLOGY AND RELIGION. Religion can address these idealistic needs of the adolescent. Other ideologies do too. Erikson notes that both religion and other ideologies counteract a threatening sense of alienation with positive ritual and affirmative dogma and with a rigorous and cruel ban on the unorthodox in their own ranks or in foreign enemies. Ideologies do this by presenting themselves as historical perspectives on which to fasten individual faith and collective confidence.[89]

For Erikson an ideological system is any coherent body of shared images, ideas, and ideals. Whether it is based on a formulated dogma, on an implicit or a highly structured world view, on a political or scientific creed, or on a simple "way of life," an ideology provides its participants a coherent overall orientation in time and space, in means and ends. As simplified conceptions of what is to come, ideologies also serve as rationalizations of what has come about and provide meaningful combinations of the oldest and the newest in a group's ideals.

Religion and other ideologies provide the adolescent with the necessary conditions for further individual maturation. They provide the solidarity linking common identities in joint living, acting, and creating. In Erikson's words, the system of ideas which a community presents to its young in the explicit or implicit form of an ideology offers youth:

1. a simplified perspective of the future which encompasses all foreseeable time and thus counteracts individual "time confusion";
2. some strongly felt correspondence between the inner world of ideals and evils and the social world with its goals and dangers;
3. an opportunity for exhibiting some uniformity of appearance and behavior counteracting individual identity-consciousness;

4. inducement to a collective experimentation with roles and techniques which help overcome a sense of inhibition and personal guilt;
5. introduction into the ethos of the prevailing technology and thus into sanctioned and regulated competition;
6. a geographic-historical world image as a framework for the young individual's budding identity;
7. a rationale for a sexual way of life compatible with a convincing system of principles; and
8. submission to leaders who as superhuman figures or "big brothers" are above the ambivalence of the parent-child relation.[90]

Erikson cautions that without some such ideological commitment youth suffers a confusion of values which is dangerous for both self and society.

IMPLICATIONS FOR RELIGIOUS SOCIALIZATION. At the same time that they need a cause to be devoted to, adolescents fear making foolish, all-too-trusting commitments and so, paradoxically, express the need for faith by means of loud and cynical mistrust. There is a similar fear in respect to free will. Adolescents look for opportunities to exercise free assent, but at the same time they are mortally afraid of being forced into activities in which they will be exposed to ridicule and self-doubt. This phenomenon leads to the paradox of their choosing to act shamelessly in the eyes of elders rather than be forced into activities which would be shameful in the eyes of peers, as the drop in Sunday Mass attendance illustrates.

In *Five Cries of Youth*, Merton Strommen records the feelings of self-hatred and alienation that many adolescents suffer. He describes how the majority of adolescents perceive themselves as psychological orphans, evidencing frustration that springs from living in an atmosphere of parental hatred and distrust stemming from family disunity, disinterest, or divorce. Others decry the hypocrisy and prejudice within the home and the Church. They denounce the lack of social justice and disrespect for the dignity of others. While some exhibit boredom with life and make it clear that they consider religion meaningless, others practice their faith only nominally. A minority of youth experience joy deriving from a sense of personal identity and mission that centers in the person of Jesus.[91]

In "A Report on Contemporary Catholic Teen-Agers," Andrew Greeley emphasizes that a New Breed is emerging which may have a different religious consciousness because it had a different religious formation. The new religious consciousness found in a high proportion of 13- to 17-year-olds is "a story of God that emphasizes the tender, loving intensity of the relationship between humans and God and the action-filled, pleasurable, delightful life He has prepared for those who related to Her/Him as a mother and a lover."[92] This change apparently stems from Vatican Council II and is transmitted by passionately loving spouses, devout mothers, and sympathetic parish priests, according to Greeley, who reports that sixty-seven percent of the New Breed go to Mass every week and that fifty-five percent receive Communion. Although their personal devotion may sag a little during the alienation interlude of youth, Greeley says that in comparison with a generation ago, the New Breed have become "more socially committed, more demanding of Church leadership, more conservative, but no less liberal, more devout and more open to the possibility of a career of service to the church."[93]

CATECHESIS FOR ADOLESCENCE. The community of faith seeking to develop this New Breed of Catholics is challenged to present them with catechists who exhibit love, calmness, openness, flexibility, and encouragement. The critically-reflective adolescents are longing to find people and ideals worthy of their fidelity as they critically test whether those surrounding them are worth staking their lives on.

The alarming increase of suicides among adolescents tells the tragic response some are giving to that haunting question. Strommen reports that of the many feelings associated with suicidal behavior, the most characteristic are feelings of isolation and withdrawal, which are compounded for adolescents living in conflicting home situations. Strommen states that "suicide and attempted suicide are best seen as the culmination of progressive family disorganization and social maladjustment."[94]

A communal approach—that is, a team united in a holistic catechesis calling for the exercise of a variety of charisms—is essential if we are to intervene effectively where the family is disintegrating. A holistic, or team, approach also bolsters supportive families in their efforts toward the religious socialization of their children and themselves too.

A communal approach provides the shelter of a supportive group in which teenagers, although still within their families, can yet outgrow the limitations of those families. Such a parish environment provides adolescents and youth a safe arena in which to enjoy their moratorium as they test out family-imposed religious, social, sexual, and other oughts and shoulds in a context of devoted, mature, caring, and joyous adults—role-models of who they are called to be.

QUALITIES OF EFFECTIVE YOUTH MINISTERS.
Strommen found that leaders who were successful in reaching out to youth were deeply committed, desiring to share their faith to influence youth in directions consonant with the Christian way of life. Concern, love, and a profound respect for the autonomy of youth made these leaders keenly sensitive to techniques, so that the medium or approaches used would not, in effect, contradict their message. "Thus, they did not speak of evangelizing youth, controlling their environment, supervising their behavior, preaching the gospel to them, or other tactics that might be interpreted as applying pressure."[95]

Strommen details the skills exhibited by those church workers who were found to be effective in reaching out to youth. Their skills include: (1) the ability to build relationships, (2) being genuine, (3) being available, (4) showing interest, (5) being skilled at empathic communication, and (6) leading.[96] Correlating Strommen's research with Erikson's, it becomes evident how trust, initiative, free will, and competence can be fostered as we enable our adolescents and youth to mature in fidelity or faithfulness.

To build relationships that model faithfulness, the catechist has to be willing to get to know the adolescents' home life, school life, and circle of friends by exhibiting more than superficial concern for them. Showing courtesy by participating with the adolescents as an equal in the various activities, a sensitive minister also shows appreciation for jobs well done and so reinforces their sense of competence. Helping when called on, the minister inspires trust by sharing experiences and feelings about life.

A youth worker's genuineness is evidenced by being adult
and speaking from his or her own heart, avoiding either
theological or adolescent jargon, except when such a response is
fitting. An honest and open catechist demonstrates autonomy
and witnesses the freedom of adult conscience by speaking out in
the name of justice and fairness, even when those in power do
not prefer hearing truth. Accepting and dealing with his or her
own hang-ups, the youth minister admits not knowing all the
answers, yet will openly state convictions without expecting
everyone else to assent. In this manner the minister is also
respecting the autonomy of those being catechized.

Being available means going to teen events when adults are
welcome, spending time with teens and their friends, working
and playing with them in various activities, taking them to
"away" games, and inviting them over for dinner at times. To be
at ease with the adolescent, it is essential to know each by name.
Interest is shown by learning about their world, being able to
understand and speak their language, by listening to their music,
respecting their symbols, such as beads or long hair, punk or
disco dress, and the like. Making phone calls or sending
individuals letters commending their accomplishments not only
affirms youths' initiative or sense of purpose; such gestures also
enable deeper communication to take place. Empathic
communication involves letting youth know you understand, or
telling them that although you do not understand you are
willing to listen to their story. It means intense and interested
listening. Listening. And more listening. And it means personal
counseling.

As a leader the catechist functions to discover and employ
each teenager's talents and interests. By providing a host of
options and by encouraging committed participation, the
minister is enabling the catechized to develop competence and to
explore the variety of possible life purposes that they can make
uniquely their own. By involving youth in planning, decision-
making, and executing all catechetical activities, the catechist
demonstrates trustworthiness and respect for human dignity as
the adolescents are initiated into realizing their adult capabilites.

SUCCESSFUL YOUTH MINISTRY: AN APPROACH.
Although ideal, the approach to catechesis which I have

described is becoming real in parishes where it is no longer isolated and no longer rests solely upon individuals. As is becoming evident, success comes from calling forth the charisms of each, and making of all a team, a community striving to mature in faith as it assists younger members to mature through the coordination of the interlocking dimensions of understanding the message, building community, and rendering service— inspired and signified by participation in liturgy.

The following story by Joanne K. Frazer, with the accompanying Chart 7, is quoted at length because it lucidly illustrates the theology and theory that have been presented here.[97]

. . . Spurred on by implementation of a new model (see Chart 7), a true interrelatedness has been developing among our programs.

There are 350 to 400 participants making our retreats yearly (we have five or six a year), and many are delighted to be called to work on "Dining for the Poor," parish gardening, or orphanage-visitation service teams.

Candidates for sacrament reception are encouraged to become part of the larger youth community by attending the retreats and getting involved in service projects.

Ongoing education (catechesis) programs lead from and back to retreats. Many of the thirty-five to fifty attending each class have made the weekend experience, and they convince the others of its worth. The ongoing education classes have been established by retreat team personnel (young people and adults) because they recognized the need for continuing spiritual growth of the youth.

When a "Today's Catholic" speaker series was planned, the Youth Night leaders were happy to have it begin with their regular monthly session.

When looking for experts to speak on social justice, ongoing education people asked the service coordinators to use their expertise and contacts to set up a meaningful presentation.

In athletics, instead of pitting existing areas against each other, the teens are drawn from the whole parish for sports teams, with parents as referees and the teens themselves as coaches. Many people are attracted into the youth community

Chart 7
A MODEL FOR YOUTH MINISTRY

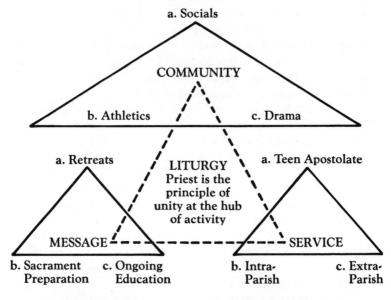

a. Socials

COMMUNITY

b. Athletics   c. Drama

a. Retreats   a. Teen Apostolate

LITURGY
Priest is the
principle of
unity at the hub
of activity

MESSAGE   SERVICE

b. Sacrament   c. Ongoing   b. Intra-   c. Extra-
Preparation   Education   Parish   Parish

COMMUNITY
a. *Socials*
   Dances
   Beach outings
   Snow trips
   Roller skating
b. *Athletics* (coed teams)
   Baseball
   Basketball
   Volleyball
   Football
c. *Drama*
   Summer production
   Acting lessons
   Dance lessons

SERVICE
a. *Teen apostolate*
b. *Intra-parish*
   Parish gardening
   "Dining for the poor"
   Hungerthon
   Christmas Basket
   Donut Sales

Home helpers/visitors
c. *Extra-parish*
   Maryvale visits
   Los Niños trips

MESSAGE
a. *Retreats*
   Turning Points
   (juniors/seniors)
   Awakening
   (freshmen/sophomores)
b. *Ongoing education*
   Bible Sharing
   Youth Night
   "Today's Catholic" Series
   Mini-courses
   Rel. Ed. Congress
c. *Sacrament Preparation*
   Classes for
      Baptism
      Reconciliation
      Eucharist
      Confirmation

that have never been seen in the Message or Service areas. Depending on the sport, there are up to 200 youth participating in any one season.

When it came time this year for Christmas food baskets, Pat, who is in charge of Intra-Parish Service, called each program chairman for help in collecting food, money, and gifts for the youth ministry family assignment. She received all the help needed.

The young people from all areas get involved in socials with very little coaxing from the adult leaders. They themselves spread the word.

For us, it's finally coming together. But the evolution took several years and lots of growing pains.

Taking the problem areas one at a time, here's how we progressed despite our dilemmas.

1. Programs suspicious of each other. Although it's easy to see that lack of understanding and absence of unity were the source of the problem, solving it was not so easy. About four years ago, we were near virtual collapse in youth activity—CCD was struggling and nothing else was really working. A small group of us (youth and adults) started a mini-retreat series that met every four to six weeks; we named it Awakening. When CCD folded, Awakening became the only thing (except sacrament preparation) for parish high school students. But even with the absence of any other activity, Awakening never was a tremendous success in terms of numbers—thirty-five to fifty each time. But to give Awakening we had to have meetings to plan them. We had to have a team. And that has become the long-term value of Awakening mini-retreats—it was our first real venture into team. The adults and youth were equals; and with prayer, much struggling, and even real anger, we grew together. This team usually consisted of about six adults and twelve to fifteen youth.

We had used the word "team" before, but our understanding of it had been "committee." In discovering that it is much more than that, we found ourselves ministering to each other and calling forth gifts and talents that we were unaware of in ourselves. We were becoming community, and as we developed, we were better able to comprehend how to build a larger community of teens.

Much of what is happening now had as its roots that early awareness of, and struggling to develop, team. As we deepened our asssociation with youth (by working with them) we came to see the importance of all youth activities.

2. Adults didn't last long. We had a paid youth minister, Tim, for about a year, and other teams began to form. A retreat for juniors and seniors started, followed by one for freshmen and sophomores. We found that it was easier to invite adults to work with youth by including them on existing teams. This did a couple of things. They personally did not feel responsible for the success or failure of an event. And affirmation flows freely when a team is functioning properly, so adults found real support on the team. Even when an activity failed, there was company in misery! An evaluation was held, and the whole program benefited by what was learned. Another plus was when our present associate pastor in charge of youth, Father Ferraro, came to St. John Vianney. He has a gift for calling forth people to work with youth, and they respond to him. This has added to our program the athletics and social areas and new teen apostolate team.

As an additional aid to those adults already involved, Father Ferraro recognized the need to continue having an office just for youth ministry staffed by clerical workers. This has also greatly helped to raise parish consciousness to the special needs of youth.

3. Youth complaining. It helps to know that adolescents always complain. But as youth are included on teams, they come to own the program. A program that's less than top-notch can fly if the young people giving it are enthusiastic and feel a degree of responsibility for its success. If an activity is threatened by errant behavior (e.g., disorderly conduct, drugs) team youth often step in to solve the situation.

The young people still gripe, especially when a new program is starting up. Their complaints must be heard and must become part of the struggle.

4. Understanding "Youth Ministry." Many of the people now leading various areas started in the early teams. So our understanding of youth ministry has expanded as we saw new needs and as people from existing teams stepped out to begin or enrich programs.

The unity and camaraderie developed earlier carries over and translates into a sense of integratedness and relatedness to each other. So our understanding of youth ministry has come from our own growth, our own evolution.

I said at the beginning that we have made it. That's a monumental overstatement, of course. The farther we come, the more obvious our shortcomings become. In our acceptance of one another and of our programs, we really fall far short of the ideal. Working with teams is often frustrating and always time-consuming.

To move forward, we need to take many more steps. Our new core team will need to be expanded to include young people. Although the core team adults have all worked with youth for some time, they need the continual input of youth. We must build prayer experiences into our core team sessions so that we can become the community we strive for in our programs. We must also continue to clarify our function as a core team.

The constant invitation to become involved must be open to all potential leaders. And as more come into youth ministry we must instill in them the value of all youth activities so that our interrelatedness will continue.

As youth ministry grows and we come to understand ourselves more, we must attempt to become a more integral part of the total parish.

We need a paid youth minister so that we can "free" our priests to serve the youth and all parishioners through their liturgical and sacramental ministries.

Although the program described happens to be in an affluent parish, similar opportunities for renewal through youth ministry are available beyond suburbia. A dynamic example exists in a barrio in Los Angeles. In the midst of tragedies emanating from youth-gang rivalry, members are being converted, reforming themselves, and forming a vibrant community of faith.[98] In this case the same dedication inheres in working-class parents and others who with a priest as leader again make it clear that God's grace is available to all who choose to channel it.

POSSIBILITIES FOR A RENEWED CONCEPTION OF RELIGIOUS COMMUNITY. Strommen concludes *Five Cries of Youth* by drawing attention to "at least two imperatives in a youth ministry—*mutuality* and *mission*. Youth of all subcultures want the warmth of an accepting group which is *mutuality*. They need activities which give them a sense of purpose, that is, *mission*. Within these two polarities, there is powerful need for *educational experiences* for youth and adults that open minds, develop skills, clarify values, and encourage commitment."[99]

In ministry marked by mutuality and mission, not only is the basic human need for community addressed, but the sociological function of religious life is too, as these emergent programs are witnessing. For their very existence symbolizes or makes significant a holier, more wholesome way of life. If we can accept a broadened conceptualization of the religious life, a reading of the various decrees of Vatican Council II may provide provocative and new insights.[100]

By renewing itself, such a parish community would essentially live the elements of biblical morality as each member responds to the baptismal challenge, living a discipleship evident to all.[101] Although functions would remain intact, former hierarchical distinctions would pale as each contributes according to God-given charism rather than rank. In a renewed community, the commitment may be a promise of simplicity of life-style or a vow to humanity to symbolize the actuality of the sharing of one's unique gifts for the benefit of all. Those who are professsed religious would not be set apart nor continually transferred, for they serve as the core, with skills and example, kindling all to share their charisms in like manner.

Thus the apparent alienation of adolescents and youth, evident in abusive drinking, drugs, sex, and violence, can be a challenge to make our baptismal promises and sacramental prayer come alive and serve as a centering point for the moral rejuvenation of all who are willing to work together within and beyond the parish as a team or community of faith. As with major historical movements and the foundation of religious orders, youthful idealism with its concomitant zeal is required of all. And so, youth's problems and youth's honesty can keep our systems and our faith from becoming dead weights. "Adolescence is thus a vital regenerator in the process of social evolution, for youth can offer its loyalties and energies both to the conservation of that which continues to feel true and to the revolutionary corrrection of that which has lost its regenerative significance."[102]

NOTES

1. See Alfred Schutz, *On Phenomenology and Social Relations*, edited by Helmut R. Wagner (Chicago: University of Chicago Press, 1970), pp. 25-30.

2. National Conference of Catholic Bishops, *To Teach as Jesus Did*, (Washington, D.C.: United States Catholic Conference Publications Office, 1973), pp. 6-7 (#22, 23).

3. National Conference of Catholic Bishops, *Sharing the Light of Faith: National Catechetical Directory for Catholics of the United States* (Washington, D.C.: United States Catholic Conference, 1979), p. 66 (#112). Italics added.

4. *To Teach as Jesus Did*, p. 7 (#24). Italics added.

5. "The State of Catechesis: Report to Synod Secretariat," *Origins*, 6 (April 21, 1977):706.

6. Ibid.

7. John H. Westerhoff III and Gwen Kennedy Neville, *Generation to Generation* (Philadelphia: United Church Press, 1974), p. 41.

8. Ibid.

9. Ibid.

10. Ibid., p. 42.

11. Ibid., p. 83.

12. *To Teach as Jesus Did*, p. 4 (#14).

13. Ibid., pp. 6-7 (#22).

14. Ibid., p. 7 (#23). Italics added.

15. *National Catechetical Directory*, p. 39 (#70).

16. Ibid., p. 11 (#21) and p. 127 (#209).

17. James Tunstead Burtchaell, C.S.C., *Philemon's Problem: The Daily Dilemma of the Christian* (Chicago: ACTA Foundation, 1973), p. 130.

18. Ibid., pp. 132-133.

19. Susanne K. Langer, *Philosophy in a New Key* (Cambridge, MA: Harvard University Press, 1957), p. 42.

20. Ibid.

21. Ibid., p. 291.

22. Ibid.

23. Ibid., p. 292. See also Emile Durkheim, *Suicide, A Study in Sociology*, translated by George Simpson (Glencoe, IL: Free Press, 1951).

24. Langer, *Philosophy*, p. 292.

25. Ibid., pp. 157-158.

26. Ibid., p. 159.

27. *National Catechetical Directory*, p. 66 (#114). Italics added.

28. Berard L. Marthaler, O.F.M. Conv., "Handing on the Symbols of Faith," *Chicago Studies* 19 (Spring 1980):26.

29. Ibid., pp. 25-26.

30. Paul Tillich, *Dynamics of Faith* (New York: Harper & Row, 1959), p. 41.

31. Ibid., p. 43.

32. Ibid. Italics added.

33. Burtchaell, *Philemon's Problem*, p. 139.

34. Ibid.

35. Ibid., p. 140.

36. Walter M. Abbott, S.J., ed., *The Documents of Vatican II* (New York: America Press, 1966), p. 137.

37. Jaroslav Pelikan, "A Response," in Abbott, *Vatican II Documents*, p. 179.

38. Abbott, *Vatican II Documents*, p. 243.

39. Ibid.

40. Ibid.

41. Erik H. Erikson, *Identity, Youth and Crisis* (New York: W.W. Norton & Co., 1968), p. 92.

42. See Erik H. Erikson, ed., *Adulthood* (New York: W.W. Norton & Co., 1978), p. 25, and Richard M. Lerner, *Concepts and Theories of Human Development*, (Reading, MA: Addison-Wesley, 1976), pp. 196-209.

43. Erik H. Erikson, *Insight and Responsibility* (New York: W.W. Norton & Co., 1964), p. 114.

44. Ibid., p. 118.

45. Note that although Erikson goes beyond Freud, his description of the childhood stages is based on Freud's oral, anal, genital, and latency stages respectively. Compare Erik H. Erikson, *Childhood and Society* (New York: W. W. Norton & Co., 1964). For mother and father as referents for the child's image of God, see John J. Gleason, Jr., *Growing Up to God* (Nashville: Abingdon Press, 1975), pp. 30-33.

46. Erikson, *Identity, Youth and Crisis*, p. 106.

47. Ibid., p. 325, note #3.

48. Erikson, *Insight and Responsibility*, p. 119.

49. Gleason, *Growing Up to God*, pp. 39-40, gives further details regarding this crisis in the child's religious development.

50. Erik H. Erikson, "Identity and the Life Cycle," *Psychological Issues*, Vol. I (New York: International Universities Press, 1955), p. 69.

51. Erikson, *Identity, Youth and Crisis*, p. 111.

52. Andrew M. Greeley, William C. McCready, and Kathleen McCourt, *Catholic Schools in a Declining Church* (Kansas City: Sheed and Ward, 1976), p. 129, as cited in Jackson W. Carroll, Douglas W. Johnson, and Martin E. Marty, *Religion in America: 1950 to the Present* (San Francisco: Harper & Row, 1979), p. 42.

53. Carroll et. al., *Religion in America*. The trend is summed up with a cartoon caption from Oliphant, *The Washington Star*, November 15, 1976, in which a group of bishops, having reaffirmed the pope's teaching in the encyclical, are standing in the door of a church. One says to the others: "Well, we've solved the birth control problem, the abortion problem and the sex problem—now, what do you suggest we do about the attendance problem?"

54. George Gallup, *The Unchurched American* (to be published), cited in *Show Christ to the World: A Look at Evangelization for the People of the Archdiocese of Los Angeles* (Commision on Evangelization, 1440 West Imperial Highway, Los Angeles, CA 90047), p. 39. The unchurched, Catholic as well as non-Catholic, are defined as "those who say they do not belong to any church, synagogue or temple, or those who claim membership but have not voluntarily worshiped in the church, synagogue or temple of their choice for six months or more, not counting funerals, weddings, Christmas, Easter or the High Holy days."
    By this definition, forty-one percent of all Americans over the age of eighteen, that is sixty-one million adults, are unchurched. Eleven million Catholics, or eighteen percent of all Catholics over the age of eighteen, fall into this category.

55. Ibid. Note that the faith and moral education processes detailed in the preceding chapters speak directly to this expressed need.

56. See Erikson, *Identity, Youth and Crisis*, p. 109.

57. Erikson, *Psychological Issues*, p. 72.

58. Ibid., p. 71. Italics added.

59. Ibid., p. 73.

60. Erikson, *Insight and Responsibility*, p. 122.

61. Ibid.

62. Erikson, *Psychological Issues*, p. 73. See also Freud on the oedipal conflict and electra complex.

63. See Erikson, *Identity, Youth and Crisis*, pp. 118-120.

64. Ibid., p. 120.

65. John Diamond, M.D., *Your Body Doesn't Lie* (New York: Warner Books, 1979), pp. 108-112.

66. Erikson, *Identity, Youth and Crisis*, p. 120.

67. See Diamond, *Your Body Doesn't Lie*, chapter 7, "The People Around You."

68. Derek Wright, *The Psychology of Moral Behaviour* (Middlesex, England: Penguin Books, 1971), pp. 42-43, and chapter 6, "Altruism," especially pp. 148-151.

69. See Abbott, *Vatican II Documents*, pp.137-138 (#1-3), and Erik H. Erikson, *Toys and Reason, Stages in the Ritualization of Experience* (New York: W. W. Norton & Co., 1977).

70. Erikson, *Identity, Youth and Crisis*, p. 121. See also Erik H. Erikson, *Young Man Luther* (New York: W. W. Norton & Co., 1958).

71. Compare Matthew 13:13-17, Isaiah 6:10 and 50:4. A meditative reading of these passages illustrates the power of symbolization.

72. Erikson, *Psychological Issues*, p. 82.

73. See Gleason, *Growing up to God*.

74. Aidan Kavanagh, O.S.B., "Christian Initiation of Adults: The Rites" in *Made, Not Born* by the Murphy Center for Liturgical Research (Notre Dame: University of Notre Dame Press, 1976), pp. 132-133. Italics added.

75. Ibid., p. 133.

76. Erikson, *Identity, Youth and Crisis*, p. 125.

77. See *The New World Dictionary—Concordance to the New American Bible* (New York: World Publishing, 1979), p. 139: "Among all ancient peoples dreams were considered favorite means that God used to communicate with men." See also Morton Kelsey, *Dreams: A Way to Listen to God* (New York: Paulist Press, 1978), chapter 5, "Dreams in the Bible."

78. It is an interesting phenomenon that in the Roman rite a child has to have some understanding of the sacrament in order to receive the Eucharist or Confirmation yet needs absolutely no understanding of anything in order to be baptized, even though all three are sacraments of initiation.

79. Erikson, *Identity, Youth and Crisis*, p. 126.

80. Harvey Cox, *Feast of Fools* (Cambridge, MA: Harvard University Press, 1969) and Brian P. Hall, *Value Clarification as Learning Process: A Sourcebook* (New York: Paulist Press, 1973), pp. 164-175 on festival, guilt, and celebration.

81. Erikson, *Psychological Issues*, p. 83.

82. Kenneth Keniston, "The Struggle of Conscience in Youth," in C. Ellis Nelson, ed., *Conscience: Theological and Psychological Perspective* (New York: Newman Press, 1973), p. 333.

83. Erikson, *Psychological Issues*, p. 92.

84. Keniston, "Struggle of Conscience," p. 335.

85. Ibid., p. 336.

86. See Erikson, *Young Man Luther*, for a biographical exemplification of these three needs.

87. Erikson, *Psychological Issues*, p. 92.

88. Erikson, *Insight and Responsibility*, p. 125.

89. Ibid., p. 127.

90. Erikson, *Identity, Youth and Crisis*, pp. 187-188. It is interesting to compare Erikson's notation on the function of ideology with Fowler's Stage Four, which I termed religion as ideological certainty (because at this stage, religion serves the very purposes Erikson describes).

91. See Merton P. Strommen, *Five Cries of Youth* (New York: Harper & Row, 1974). Compare also "Religion" entry in *America, Gallup Opinion Index 1977-78*, Report #145 (Princeton, NJ: American Institute of Public Opinion), pp. 3-4.

92. Andrew M. Greeley, "A Post-Vatican II New Breed? A Report on Contemporary Catholic Teen-Agers," *America*, 142 (June 28, 1980):535.

93. Ibid., p. 536.

94. Strommen, *Five Cries*, p. 46.

95. Ibid., p. 188.

96. Ibid., pp. 119-120.

97. Joanne K. Frazer, "Evolution of Youth Ministry, St. John Vianney's Story," Parts I and II in *Response*, the official publication of the Office of Religious Education (CCD), Archdiocese of Los Angeles, vol. 8, #7-8 (February and March 1980). Ms. Frazer points out that the DRE at St. John Vianney, Sister Joann Heinritz, developed the model for youth ministry (Chart 7). It is an adaptation of Thomas A. Downs, "A Model of Youth Ministry," *PACE* 5: Approaches B (1974), St. Mary's College Press, Winona, MN 55987.

98. I am referring to the work of Reverend Tom Fitzpatrick, who formed Los Hermanos Unidos at St. Gertrude's in Bell Gardens, California.

99. Strommen, *Five Cries*, p. 126.

100. I am thinking particularly of the following decrees for a creative-meditative reading, that is, a reading of each in a kaleidoscopic manner, gently turning titles and topics around, allowing the Spirit to surface with renewing inspiration: *Perfectae Caritatis*, on the appropriate adaptation and renewal of the religious life; *Apostolicam Actuositatem*, on the apostolate of the laity; *Presbyterorum Ordinis*, on the ministry and life of priests; and *Ad Gentes*, on the Church's missionary activity. Germane to this reflection is Edward W. O'Rourke (Bishop of Peoria), *Living Like a King: A Plea and a Plan for the Simple Life* (Springfield, IL: Templegate Publishers, 1979), especially pp. 81-84.

101. Timothy E. O'Connell, *Principles for a Catholic Morality* (New York: Seabury Press, 1978), chapter 3, "Elements of a Biblical Morality."

102. Erikson, *Identity, Youth and Crisis*, p. 134.

5. ON THE DEVELOPMENT OF WHOLENESS: CATECHESIS FOR HEALING AND HOLINESS

This chapter describes stages and crises in adult development—specifically, learning to live in love, facing mid-life challenges, and growing in wisdom. The chapter then focuses on the need for both spirituality and social service in order to mature, to experience holiness or wholeness. The chapter concludes by showing how both the spiritual and the physical aspects of our being can be cultivated to bring about integrity of life or healing within ourselves and to our world.

A Navajo medicine man was asked for a definition of what is human. "Indicating the figure of a cross, he said that a person was most human where the (vertical) connection between the ground of creation and the Great Spirit met the (horizontal) one between the individual and all other human beings."[1] José Comblin, a Catholic theologian, speaks in a similar manner in *The Meaning of Mission.* He stresses that the evangelists are very clear on the point of Jesus seeking out his Father and returning to him, but only after he has spoken to human beings. "Therein lies the proper relationship between movement towards God on the one hand and movement towards human beings on the other. The mission starts out from God, but it cannot return to God until it has passed through the midst of human beings."[2] God is the ultimate origin and end of the Gospel mission, but God does not compete for our love as we go about our social mission, for God is not self-seeking. The unconditional or selfless love of God for all creation is the very principle that makes the Christian perspective radically different from that of any other religion: that love of God and love of neighbor are one and the same. "Any real attempt to separate those two loves will destroy Christianity."[3]

The same theme is reiterated in the National Catechetical Directory. The conclusion of the chapter on the worshiping community states that the faith community grows in its sense of unity and awareness of the Church's mission to the world as it gathers to thank the Father in Christ through the Holy Spirit. "The liturgy, heart of the Church's life, leads its members to seek justice, charity and peace."[4]

Even more clearly, within the section on "Specifics in the teaching of morality," the Directory lists not only the Ten Commandments but also the Sermon on the Mount, especially the Beatitudes, and Christ's discourse at the Last Supper.[5] In describing the guidance given by moral law, the Directory stresses that created goods and loves are God's gifts. They tell us about their giver and his will for humanity. "Those who value Christ will value all that is truly human and be reminded by it of his call.... True morality, then, is not something imposed from without; rather it is the way people accept their humanity as restored to them in Christ."[6] It explains that "human beings rejoice in friends, in being alive, in being treated as persons rather than things, in knowing the truth. In doing so they are rejoicing in being themselves—images of God called to be His children. Truth and life, love and peace, justice and friendship go into what it means to be human."[7] Interestingly, what the Gospel has preached through its history is once again espoused theologically and is being discovered as sound psychology: that we are whole when we can embrace both God as Pure Spirit and our neighbor and ourself as found in the community of all creation, and that this wholeness or holiness calls for extending our self outwardly in service and inwardly in prayer.

EARLY ADULTHOOD AND AFFECTIVITY

How does one develop a full humanity? Erikson posits the lifelong process of identity formation. It involves simultaneous reflection and observation leading to an ever-deepening commitment of life; it is evidenced in the virtues of love and care and wisdom. Erikson emphasizes that for the "maintenance of the world" the virtues as psychosocial strengths require active adaptation rather than passive adjustment. Whereas in childhood the self comes into society and is shaped by the communal culture, as the cycle progresses into adolescence the individual begins to develop an ethical view, a grasp of what life can mean. When former environments become inner equipment, the progression has come full circle, since the formerly passive self has now become the social world shaping new generations. This cannot be effected by mere servitude and compliance. "It means rather a continuous reciprocal facilitation of social and psychological development and of larger and smaller institutions and—where such facilitation has become impossible—radical changes in social mores and institutions."[8] Erikson concludes that if individuals do not find affirmation and confirmation in personal rituals (such as the things we daily do at home) as well as in the rituals of society (such as going to work), then both individual generational cycles will show symptoms of pathology that point to specific needs for social change. These symptoms are evident in the high incidence of nervous breakdowns, divorce, unemployment, and the like.

In *Insight and Responsibility*, Erikson stresses how living communally is a moral necessity. Our "psychosocial survival is safeguarded only by vital virtues which develop in the interplay of successive and overlapping generations, living together in organized settings. Here, living together means more than incidental proximity. It means that the individual's life-stages are 'interliving,' cogwheeling with the stages of others which move him along as he moves them."[9]

Providentially, renewed parishes can become communities enabling healing and moral maturity. The United States Catholic Conference defines the parish as "a multiplicity of small and varied Christian communities, each having a unique role but called to a unity which makes the parish community whole. Parish leadership (priest, religious, and laity) are responsible for calling forth that unity while encouraging a variety."[10] The Symposium on the Parish and the Educational Mission of the Church continues: "Substantively, however, the parish must view itself as a growth system including an educational process. It is *not* just a dispenser of services. The parish community consists of a group of people learning: growing toward incarnation—a deepening conversion."[11] In *Christian Life Patterns*, the Whiteheads draw from Erikson's work implications for parishes that are serious in their commitment to adult religious education. They suggest the creation and reintegration of rituals to help adults negotiate life's passages in a manner that enables them to grow in virtue.

INTIMACY OR ISOLATION. The task of young adulthood is
to grow in intimacy and mutuality. If the individual develops
intimacy, then love emanates; if not, the individual tends toward
isolation. Intimacy, according to Erikson, is the "capacity to
commit oneself to concrete affiliations and partnerships and to
develop the ethical strength to abide by such commitments, even
though they may call for significant sacrifice and compromise."[12]
To risk true intimacy (which involves a fusion of identities) the
individuals must know their own personal preferences, strengths
and limits, interests and abilities. Otherwise the challenge to give
one's gifts, which is love, becomes overwhelming and leads to
distancing or isolating oneself from others.

The resolution of this tension of giving of oneself in order
to become more truly oneself is the challenge posed to the newly-
found young adult identity. Erikson attests that "the strength of
any one stage is tested by the necessity to transcend it in such a
way that the individual can take chances in the next stage with
what is most vulnerably precious in the previous one."[13] Risk
situations can evoke and strengthen intimacy as they call for self-
disclosure and empathy, caution and selectivity. Such situations
include close friendships, group solidarity as in religious life or
the military, sexual love, relationship inspiring encounters that
allow for self-revelation, and intuitions from within oneself.
Hence intimacy is not necessarily genitality or romance, nor are
the latter necessarily intimate.

By taking a chance with one's identity and risking self-
revelation in a mutual openness and psychological availability,
one's personality grows richer, deeper, stronger.[14] The inflexible,
however, confusing strength with rigidity, avoid encounters that
facilitate self-revelation and remain untouched and impoverished.
Unsure of their identity, they shy away from interpersonal
intimacy, retreating into self-centeredness, at times acting
aggressively or promiscuously, but without true fusion with
another's self-revelation or real abandonment of their own egos.
Distancing themselves from others, ready to repudiate, isolate,
and even destroy those forces or people who threaten their shaky
identity, such individuals lacking in love may actually be
successful in their outward life and yet continually feel empty
within. They experience a deep sense of isolation. They never

feel really comfortable with themselves and are always uncomfortable with others.[15]

Without true intimacy, which comes from a positive identity or an open sense of self, "love" can become a joint selfishness in the service of some territory, be it bed or home, parish or church, village or country. That such distorted love characterizes many affiliations and associations is one reason for clannish adherence to styles, rules, and customs which people defend as if their lives depended on them, when indeed they do not. What depends on them is the ego's coherence, or certainty of orientation; ". . . and it is for this reason that ego-panic can make man 'go blind' with a rage which induces him, in the righteous defense of a shared identity, to sink to levels of sadism for which there seem to be no parallels in the animal world."[16] Examples of this are the rage with which some self-righteous are ready to "kill a queer," the sadistic readiness with which others will inspire dread of life, or encourage the use of both nuclear power and weapons for our supposed welfare.

LOVE AND MUTUALITY. Characteristic of intimacy is an awareness of oneself and of the other with a concomitant strength which enables one to share deeply with another. It is accompanied by a sense of self that is adequate to the demands of mutuality and to the possibility of failure, and it is flexible and creative in response to the individuality of the other.[17] Mutuality is "a relationship in which partners depend on each other for the development of their respective strengths."[18] It is a commitment to love and can be described by the prayer of St. Francis: "Grant that I not so much seek to be consoled as to console; to be understood, as to understand; to be loved as to love; for it is in giving that we receive. . . ." Erikson draws out the psychological truth of these words, stating that only the individual who approaches encounters in an active and giving attitude, rather than in a demanding or dependent one, can make of them all that they can become.

Although in our culture the social paradigm for the achievement of intimacy is marriage, intimacy can take many forms. It can range from friendship with others to befriending the depths of oneself. It can be intellectual, athletic, spiritual, sexual, vocational, recreational, or familial. The different kinds of intimacy and its levels are not necessarily shared with all, nor enjoyed exclusively with only one other. Hence an individual may be enriched by sharing sexual intimacy with a spouse, spiritual intimacy with a prayer group of which the spouse may or may not be a part, household (task-related) intimacy with a maid, and so on.

The Whiteheads note, however, that marriage stands as an archetype of intimacy—that is, of the mutual regulation of complicated patterns. "But heterosexual marriage is not the only context for the resolution of the challenge of intimacy. Erikson and other psychologists note that a homosexual relationship can be a context for the resolution of the intimacy crisis as well as a sign of this resolution."[19] What is at issue in the polarity between intimacy and isolation is the emergence of love. So too, celibacy lived responsibly will bring forth a communality or intimacy expressing love. Erikson defines the virtue of love as "mutuality of devotion forever subduing the antagonisms inherent in divided function."[20]

IMPLICATIONS FOR RELIGIOUS SOCIALIZATION. Given that the challenge of adulthood is to grow in love, and given that love calls for self-awareness and self-acceptance, for the recognition of where we stand on the continuum between intimacy and isolation, catechesis has to be affective. Morton Kelsey dedicates a chapter to "Education in Love" in his proposal for effective communication of our Christian religion, *Can Christians Be Educated?* Consonant with Erikson, he states that emotional maturity begins when a person puts away childishness and becomes an adult, when one wants to give love rather than just receive it. "Indeed until one can give love and understanding and consolation without any strings attached, *without expecting anything in return*, one is only part of the whole person he was intended to be. No matter how physically or intellectually grown up, he is still simply an immature, emotional child."[21] Kelsey refers to his own life experience as evidence that as we give up our desire to be consoled and understood and loved, we die to our old self and something new begins to live in us; we lose our lives in order to gain them.

Stating that the only way one learns to love is by

experiencing loving concern or unconditional acceptance, Kelsey notes that ideally this is what the Church is for. Yet until the Church becomes a community filled with the compassion, understanding, and the love of Christ, many must often find understanding and unconditional acceptance in psychological counseling. And yet ironically even in very practical, profit-conscious work situations unconditional love can be given. Kelsey cites the example of a businessman who, when his company was floundering, in desperation turned to prayer. From his depths an answer emerged that there was only one way for the company to become solidly successful: "Create the conditions whereby each individual could develop to the maximum of his potential within the opportunities at hand."[22] The industrialist felt that the way to create such an atmosphere was to apply as many of Christ's teachings to the practical concerns of his business as possible. Kelsey believes that the following rules which the man devised for that purpose can readily be applied to the operation of our religious education programs, committees, neighborhoods, everywhere:

> Serve those whom you expect to serve you. Consider no man inferior, but recognize his limitations. Lead men by action and example. Be humble in your accomplishments. Teach and be taught. Attack unfairness from any quarter. Believe that your fellowman must prosper if you are to prosper. Seek the truth no matter who may get hurt. Pray for God's guidance when you must make a decision affecting the life and future of any person. Make your own decisions based on your own best judgment only after careful consideration has been given to *all* the facts. Forgive honest mistakes where the person making the mistakes is honestly self-critical. If he is not self-critical, he must learn to be or he can never successfully supervise others or develop to his best abilities.[23]

AFFECTIVE RELIGIOUS EDUCATION. Over and over again we see that affirmation, that is, unconditional love, is the distinctive sign of Christianity. In great people from Jesus to Francis of Assisi to Mother Teresa of Calcutta we recognize that our essential call is to live in love. Yet too often we remain content to rationalize the concept, so that the essence of maturity in faith, which is to live and love wholeheartedly, remains unrealized. Since we cannot give what we do not live, we need healing. Therapy and encounter groups are means to enable growth in Christian living; learning to love oneself, neighbor, stranger, and enemy in order to love God is a present-day necessity.

Daily we can all reach out in many simple ways that build one another's self-esteem.[24] Retreats and workshops, especially Engaged Encounter and Marriage Encounter, can focus on the many faces and styles of loving to assist in interpersonal relationships and offset debilitating expectations.[25] Just as engagement and marriage are opportunities for growth in intimacy, so too are divorce and homosexuality. All four are crises providing the community of faith an opportunity to symbolize its ministry. Just as we have a sacrament for those marrying, so too we need rites to minister to those whose marriages have died although the partners survive. The Whiteheads challenge our compassion towards the divorcing.

> The ministerial challenge concerns how they will survive: whether they will have the opportunity to learn from failure, to find—with the help of a community and loved ones—new strengths hidden within this (often) traumatic loss, to discover in the midst of this crisis graces that invite them to go on, to love again, to continue to trust. Such growth can occur if a community can move beyond simply being scandalized by change and give itself both to the effort to witness to its ideals and to care effectively for those who are in crisis.[26]

The effects of a rite designed for those whose marriage has died will help healing to occur by incorporating the wounded and the grieving within the Christian community. The Whiteheads state that by structuring times in which the divorcing may speak of their grief and mourn their loss with trusted others, they are enabled to make a religious passage beyond isolation, self-hatred, and blame.

Pragmatically the present situation in the United States and the prominence of single-parent families pose a pressing need for such a ministry as many Catholics find themselves deserted or divorcing, much to their own dismay. Experiences of the faith community's support assist the divorcing to become reconciled with himself or herself as a now-different self, as one no longer married to so-and-so, and to become aware of strengths and limits, hopes and needs, and so to be reconciled with God in a new relationship, forgiven and graced with a new maturity and a cautious hope for the future. As the divorcing become reconciled to the truth of life's experience, they recognize that although a marriage may have died, life goes on, and that the Christian can move on to a new life healed. Wounded but wiser, the divorcing are encouraged to remain open to intimacy and so to renew themselves and thereby make more vital contributions to the faith community.[27]

So too the community of faith which professes love is called to accept its homosexual members to help them live lives of Christian fecundity. At issue is the need for every adult to come to self-realization, acceptance of what God has given, and a life that is mature and fulfilling.

The challenge is the development of rites of passage through which the Church can assist its members, gay and straight, to make the transitions that are required for development as mature Christians. Religious communities that refuse to explore, concretely and openly, the challenges of gay Christian life are refusing to assist the religious growth of their gay members. In so doing, they deny the larger community the benefit of the religious gifts and insights with which its gay members have been graced.[28]

Noting that discussions and debates will continue as to the meaning, origins, and morality of homosexuality, the Whiteheads counsel that exhortations to orthodoxy are less instructive for a believing community than the patient witness of orthopraxy— that is, the mature, wholesome lives of gay Christians.

In regard to homosexuality, divorce, death, or any other issue, the critical question posed to the faith community is how it will respond to those in crisis. Since it is certainly unlike Christ to ignore or blame those heavily burdened for their situation, love's challenge remains. Thus the faith community must develop rites and create a hospitable environment so that in a context of care and challenge, each of its members can become healed, a more whole person capable of intimacy, generativity, and ultimately integrity, more traditionally termed holiness or sanctity.

MID-LIFE GENERATIVE CARE VERSUS STAGNATING DESPAIR

The next choice facing the adult who has experienced love is to generate or to stagnate. Although parenting is for many the prime generative encounter, it is not the only form of generativity. The perpetuation of humanity calls for generative ingenuity of all kinds. Thus Erikson defines generativity as "the interest in establishing and guiding the next generation, although there are people who, from misfortune or because of special and genuine gifts in other directions, do not apply this drive to offspring but to other forms of altruistic concern and of creativity."[29] On the other hand, when an adult fails altogether to enrich others, a regression to pseudo-intimacy takes place, often with a pervading sense of depression and interpersonal impoverishment. Individuals who are not generative often begin to indulge themselves as if they were their own child or pet, as their nurturing energies turn in on themselves.

ON CARING. Individuals who avoid self-absorption in fulfilling the human need to be needed develop the virtue of care. In caring we recognize the other as gift. Caring is the existential way of thanking Life for all that we have received. Milton Mayeroff explains that "in caring as helping the other grow, I experience what I care for (a person, an ideal, an idea) as an extension of myself and at the same time as something separate from me that I respect in its own right."[30] He points out that the only sense in which one can ever be said to be at home in this world is not through dominating or explaining or appreciating but through caring and being cared for. Through caring one finds out what life means for oneself. Thus it is through caring and being cared for that one no longer feels "out of it" or unfit and comes to recognize one's own special place in God's providence.

"Caring, as helping another grow and actualize himself, is a process, a way of relating to someone, that involves development, in the same way that friendship can only emerge in time through mutual trust and a deepening and qualitative transformation of

the relationship."[31] Similar to Erich Fromm's explication of the
art of loving as implying care, responsibility, respect, and
knowledge, is Mayeroff's explanation that caring involves these
and patience, honesty, trust, humility, hope and courage.[32] Thus
through caring we find the fullness of our potentiality as moral
beings, for caring leads to self-actualization.

Mayeroff explains the reciprocity involved in caring.
"Besides the other's need for me if it [person or project, e.g.,
music, art, woodwork, cooking] is to grow, I need the other to
care for if I am to be myself. . . . *I do not try to help the other grow
in order to actualize myself, but by helping the other grow I do
actualize myself.*[33] Just as a student needs a teacher, so the teacher
needs students; a writer needs ideas to be creative just as much as
ideas need a writer to be born or expressed. So too parents need
their children but do not own them. As Gibran poetizes, "Your
children are not your children. . . . They come through you but
not from you, and though they are with you yet they belong not
to you."[34]

CARING AND CATECHESIS. In the same vein, in *Reaching
Out*, Henri Nouwen writes of parents and children, teachers and
students, healers and patients, and all of us. He states that the
second movement in our spiritual development is from hostility
to hospitality, from being competitive and overpowering to being
hospitable, amiable, creating an open space in our hearts and in
our lives wherein the other can be at home, can find a hearth or
a hospice as a place from which to create his or her own hearth.
Hence "Children are not properties to own and rule over, but
gifts to cherish and care for. Our children are our most
important guests, who enter into our home, ask for careful
attention, stay for a while and then leave to follow their own
way."[35]

Nouwen describes teaching from the point of view of
Christian spirituality. "When we look at teaching in terms of
hospitality, we can say that the teacher is called upon to create
for his students a free and fearless space where mental and
emotional development can take place."[36] A reverent or
respectful teacher does not impose prefabricated answers but
provides the environment for questions to come to consciousness
and without dogmatic rigidity encourages the learners to face the

questions seriously and personally, allowing truth to be revealed and affirming its discovery.

Especially in religious education, revelation and affirmation are of great importance. The fact that so many students do not care for religious instruction is largely related to the fact that their own life experience is hardly touched. There are just as many ways to be a Christian as there are Christians, and it seems that more important than the imposition of any doctrine or precoded idea is to offer the students the place where they can reveal their great human potentials to love, to give, and to create, and where they can find the affirmation that gives them the courage to continue their search without fear.[37]

Rather than using what is cared for to satisfy one's own needs, the mature adult paradoxically finds these needs met by coming to know the uniqueness and inherent needs of the dependent. In response to dependence one comes to realize his or her own dependability. As mentioned earlier in Erikson's terms, there is an intergenerational cogwheeling. Individuals become dependable or mature when they realize that others need to count on them for suppport. Care, like the other virtues, is developed by the individual in community.

LIFE-STRUCTURES. Caring distinguishes the relationship of a mentor to protege. In *The Seasons of a Man's Life*, a major study extending our understanding of adult individual-social development, the authors describe five components as especially significant: (1) forming and modifying a dream; (2) forming and modifying an occupation; (3) love, marriage, and family; (4) forming mentoring relationships; and (5) forming mutual friendships.[38] Chart 8, reprinted from Rita Weathersby, "Life Stages and Learning Interests," is a summary of adult life phases or life-structures—that is, the pattern or design of our lives at any given time.

Levinson characterizes adulthood as an ongoing process of initiation, stabilization, and then termination of a series of age-linked phases or structures (with no one phase necessarily better or more developed than another). As we leave our childhood family, we create our own dream which we seek to live out, and so go through periods of stability and change as we strive to fulfill our aspirations, at times modifying and even changing our dream. Hence we see a young adult whose dream is of raising a family attracting a spouse whose dream is similar. Another whose dream is to live a professed religious life is attracted to a community whose dreams serve to reinforce this vision. And as the individuals mature, their dreams are fulfilled or crumble, and new ones take their place. In poetic terms, our reality is the tapestry or fabric woven from the stuff of our dreams as life unfolds for each of us through a sequence of alternating periods or seasons.

A relatively stable period of fulfilling a dream or building a structure ordinarily lasts six to eight years. It is followed by a transitional period which terminates a structure that has become inadequate or been completed and initiates a new one. As a boundary between two periods of greater stability, a transition generally lasts four to five years. "The major developmental tasks of a structure-building period are to make crucial choices, to create a structure around them, to enrich the structure and pursue one's goals within it. . . . In a transitional period the major tasks are to reappraise the existing structure, explore new possibilities in self and world, and work toward choices that provide a basis for a new structure."[39]

Thus when the dream of raising a family or living a professed religious life is being fulfilled, a new dream is in the offing. If the dream corresponds with that of one's spouse or community, then both grow more deeply together. If, however, because of lack of communication or for any other reason, the individuals' dreams and thus their lives take different directions, separation and divorce or leaving the convent or priesthood often ensue. Dialogue, or depth communication, and the restoration or creation of a common dream that both commit themselves to can effect a reconciliation.

MID-LIFE AND SPIRITUAL AWAKENING. From what has been described we can begin to see adulthood's complexity and the dire need for a lifelong catechesis to help us realize our dreams. As Carl Jung has shown seminally, and present-day psychologists, theologians, and medical doctors are stressing more and more, our dreams provide a store to maintain health or bring about a cure. The seeds of a new creation lie fertile, or

Chart 8
WEATHERSBY'S BRIEF CHARACTERIZATION OF ADULT LIFE PHASES

Life Phase	Major Psychic Tasks	Marker Events	Characteristic Stance
Leaving the Family (16 or 18 to 20-24)	Separate self from family; reduce dependence on familial support and authority; develop new home base; regard self as an adult.	Leave home, new roles and more autonomous living arrangements; college, travel, army, job. Initial decisions about what to study, career, love affairs.	A balance between "being in" and "moving out" of the family.
Getting into the Adult World (early 20's to 27-29)	Explore available possibilities of adult world to arrive at initial vision of oneself as an adult. Fashion an initial life structure; develop the capacity for intimacy, create a dream; find a mentor.	Provisional commitment to occupation and first stages of a career; being hired; first job; adjusting to work world; quitting, being fired; unemployment; moving; marriage; decision to have a child; child goes to school; purchase of a home; community activities; organizational roles.	"Doing what one should." Living and building for the future; transiency is an alternative track.
Age 30 Transition (late 20's; early 30's)	Reexamine life structure and present commitments; make desired changes, particularly to incorporate deeper strivings put aside in the 20's.	Change occupation or directions within an occupation; go back to school; love affair; separation; divorce, first marriage; re-marriage.	"What is life all about now that I'm doing what I should? What do I want out of life?"

Settling Down (early 30's)	Make deeper commitments; invest more of self in work, family and valued interests; for men and career women, become a junior member of one's occupational tribe; set a timetable for shaping one's life vision into concrete long-term goals; parenting.	Death of parents; pursue work, family activities, and interests; children old enough for mother to return to school.	Concern to establish order and stability in life, and with "making it," with setting long-range goals and meeting them.
Becoming One's Own Person (35-39; or 39-42)	Become serious member of occupational group; prune dependent ties to boss, critics, colleagues, spouse, mentor. Seek independence & affirmation by society in most valued role. For woman whose first career is in the home, a growing comfort with family responsibilities and independence to seek valued interests and activities.	Crucial promotion, recognition; break with mentor.	Suspended animation; waiting for the confirmatory event; time becomes finite and worrisome.

Life Phase	Major Psychic Tasks	Marker Events	Characteristic Stance
Mid-Life Transition (early 40's)	Create a better fit between life structure and self, resolve experience of disparity between inner sense of the benefits of living within a particular structure and what else one wants in life.	Change in activities from realization that life ambitions might not develop; change of career; remarriage; empty nest, a second career for women whose first career was in the home; loss of fertility; death of friend, sibling or child.	Awareness of bodily decline, aging, own mortality; emergence of feminine aspects of self for men, masculine aspects for women.
Restabilization (a three-year period around 45)	Enjoy one's choices and life style.	Become a mentor, share knowledge and skills with younger friends and associates, contribute to the next generation, develop new interests or hobbies; occupational die is cast for men.	
Transition into the 50's (late 40's to mid-50's)	Another reexamination of the fit between life structure and self; need for redirection, a whole new beginning for some.	Last chance for women to have a career, or vigorously pursue a deferred life goal or interests—family crises, diminished home duties, change in husband's job status.	An imperative to change so that deferred goals can be accomplished.—"It is perhaps late, but there are things I would like to do in the last half of my life."

Restabilization, Mellowing and Flowering (late 50's, early 60's)	Accomplishing important goals in the time left to live.	New opportunities related to career and valued interests; personally defined accomplishments.	A mellowing of feelings and relationships, spouse is increasingly important, greater comfort with self.
Life Review, Finishing Up (60's and beyond)	Accepting what has transpired in life as having worth and meaning; valuing one's self and one's choices.	Retirement of self and spouse; aging; death of friends, spouse, and self.	Review of accomplishments; eagerness to share everyday human joys and sorrows; family is important; death is a new presence.

remain dormant, within the gifts called imagination, intuition, fantasy, visions, dreams, and reverie. And our response to the call of the Spirit within us is manifested in our body, in our physical health, and in our emotional state of being.[40]

Levinson credits Jung with giving the idea of a mid-life transition its first modern formulation. Jung distinguished the first half of life from the second half, which begins around age forty. At this time redirection of energy becomes critical as individuals move from more exterior to interior concerns. Referring to mid-life as the afternoon, Jung warns: "The significance of the morning undoubtedly lies in the development of the individual, our entrenchment in the outer world, the propagation of our kind and the care of our children. This is the obvious purpose of nature. But...whoever carries over into the afternoon the law of the morning...must pay for doing so with damage to his soul."[41] He asserts that money-making, social existence, family, and posterity are natural, but not the end or goal of human purposiveness. "The afternoon of human life must also have a significance of its own and cannot be merely a pitiful appendage to life's morning."[42]

Jung states that nervous breakdowns and all sorts of catastrophes in marriages are very common at this turning point because we embark upon the second half of life unprepared. Just as the position of the sun shifts, so too what is true in the morning may well be a lie by evening. He makes a plea for institutional religion to become the "colleges" where forty-year-olds can prepare themselves for their coming life and its demands. "Our religions were always such schools in the past, but how many people regard them as such today? How many of us older persons have really been brought up in such a school and prepared for the second half of life, for old age, death, and eternity?"[43] At the end of *Modern Man in Search of a Soul*, he asserts that among all his patients over age thirty-five, "There has not been one whose problem in the last resort was not that of finding a religious outlook on life."[44] Jung goes on to say that every one of them fell ill because he or she had lost what living religions have to give and that none was really healed who did not regain a religious outlook.

Striving to live the American dream, striving to live life scientifically, with no interiority, but instead with mechanical efficiency, in blind conformity or critical compliance to a heady religion or other set of rules, employs but one part of human potentiality. As stated at the beginning of this book, taking one part of our psyche for the whole of what we are called to be results in an unbalanced personality. Most of us are blind to how delicately we have been created to live in harmony with ourselves and other selves whether they be people, tuna, air, water, land, trees, or bees. The imbalance becomes manifest in bodily disease and in social maladies.

The psychiatrist Roberto Assagioli has developed a therapy which, in Catholic terms, can be described primarily as meditative prayer designed to enable the ailing to hear the voice of the Spirit within and so reclaim lost energies. Responsive to the wisdom of the Higher Self, the blind can see and captives of whatever malady can be set free.[45]

Assagioli is like the cognitive developmentalists, Kohlberg, Fowler, and Piaget, in this. Tension—that is, cognitive dissonance or disequilibrium—is healthy if it forces one to grow, to integrate even more of life's complexity. Failure of nerve to allow for life's fuller expression eventuates in regression, a repression of energies, hence dis-ease. In scientific terminology, Assagioli states that mid-life crises, ailments, and other disrupting events in our forties and fifties are really blessings in disguise, a "call from above" forcing opportunities for us to become all that we have been called to be, by balancing out our lives and personalities.[46]

CATECHETICAL IMPLICATIONS AND APPROACHES

In Catholicism we refer to the fullness of who we are called to be as sanctity, or holiness of life. Its achievement calls for a lifelong journey, a purification of the egotistic self, illumination as to the Way, and comtemplation of the Self in all. In Jungian psychology, this phenomenon is termed individuation. It is a lifelong developmental process through which a person becomes more and more the unique individual he or she is created to be.

WILLING TO LIVE WHOLLY. The theme of becoming all that we are called to be is treated in *The Act of Will* by Roberto Assagioli. He differentiates six functions of the psyche (see

Diagram 5). Assagioli gives prominence to the centrality of the will for one to come to fullness of life—that is, to live in harmony transpersonally, in union with the Universal Self, or God, as we term this mystery.

Diagram 5
ASSAGIOLI'S FUNCTIONS OF THE PSYCHE

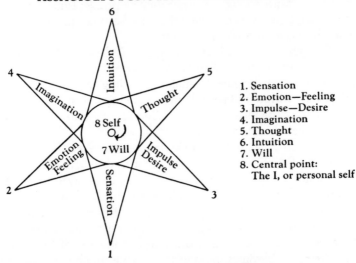

1. Sensation
2. Emotion—Feeling
3. Impulse—Desire
4. Imagination
5. Thought
6. Intuition
7. Will
8. Central point:
   The I, or personal self

ASSAGIOLI'S LEVELS OF CONSCIOUSNESS

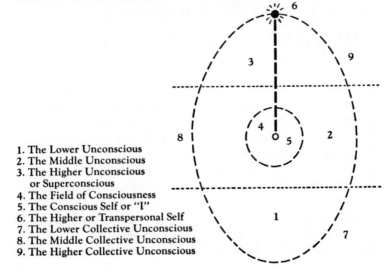

1. The Lower Unconscious
2. The Middle Unconscious
3. The Higher Unconscious
   or Superconscious
4. The Field of Consciousness
5. The Conscious Self or "I"
6. The Higher or Transpersonal Self
7. The Lower Collective Unconscious
8. The Middle Collective Unconscious
9. The Higher Collective Unconscious

Distinguishing several levels of consciousness (Diagram 5), Assagioli specifies activities in both *The Act of Will* and in *Psychosynthesis* that can be used by all eager for spiritual development. These techniques work to bring about a synthesis of personality by means of the development of a joyous will that is skillful, strong, and aligned with God's will, so that in all things the individual is living in response to the divine call. Among the other activities designed to bring out insights to enable an individual to live to his or her full potential with a fully developed, balanced personality and to unify the individual with the Universal Will are visualization, creative imagining, reflective and receptive meditation, transmutation and sublimation of wayward energies. In addition to daily meditation, journal-keeping is very helpful. Much more than a log or daily diary, a journal helps to chart the journey of the soul by reflection on where one has already been so that life is not spent in endless repetition of stifling cycles that keep the soul from spiritual maturation.[47]

Stressing that we do not lose our individuality when we align ourselves with God's will to live in universal harmony, Assagioli notes that even in states of mystical ecstasy, *satori*, cosmic consciousness, and the like, a sense of individuality is not lost. Individuality is necessary for one to experience universality. Thus to "merge into the whole," to become as a "drop in the sea," or to annihilate oneself in prayer is to evade the responsibility posed by God-given individuality. Jung comments on this burden, or gift, of our individual uniqueness. He frowns on the notion of imitating Christ by blindly copying his life, yet he acknowledges: "It is no easy matter to live a life that is modelled on Christ's, but it is unspeakably harder to live one's own life as truly as Christ lived his."[48] To describe how we are created to be at one with God, which is to live wholly, Assagioli quotes Radhakrishnam. "The peculiar privilege of the human self is that he can consciously join and work for the whole and embody in his own life the purpose of the whole....The two elements of selfhood: uniqueness (each-ness), and universality (all-ness), grow together until at last the most unique becomes the most universal."[49]

ACTUALIZATION THROUGH FULFILLING NEEDS. The characteristics which the humanistic psychologist Abraham Maslow attributes to self-actualizing persons correspond with those emphasized by his colleagues, Jung and Assagioli, and with those found in Catholic theology as a way that can open individuals to sanctity or to the realization of their full potentiality.

From his study of healthy people, Maslow tells us that they have sufficiently gratified their basic needs for safety, belongingness, affection, respect, and self-esteem, so they are no longer motivated by these. What impels them now is a spiritual hunger to actualize their potentials, their talents, and to fulfill their vocation or mission in life. This hunger is marked by an unceasing trend toward unity, integration, or synergy. Clinically observed characteristics of the most healthy people, of those who are realizing their God-given gifts or potency, include:

1. Superior perception of reality.
2. Increased acceptance of self, of others, of nature.
3. Increased spontaneity.
4. Increased problem-centering.
5. Increased detachment and desire for privacy.
6. Increased automony and resistance to enculturation.
7. Greater freshness of appreciation and richness of emotional reaction.
8. Higher frequency of peak-experiences.
9. Increased identification with the human species.
10. Changed [that is, improved] interpersonal relations.
11. More democratic character structure.
12. Greatly increased creativeness.
13. Certain changes in the value system [is/ought meld].[50]

Diagram 6 presents Maslow's hierachy of needs, the process of growth in consciousness that one goes through in moving from the primarily physical sensations, to emotionality and affectivity, to mentality, and finally toward spirituality. For an individual to progress, each higher level has to possess a certain attractiveness that far outweighs fear or other dangers.

The fear of one's own greatness can, however, lead to a repression of the sublime, so that an individual can achieve self-actualization but then stop short of aligning his or her life with transcending values. Maslow refers to this evasion of one's destiny as the Jonah Complex, the running away from the ultimate responsibilities we are called on to face. "It is certainly possible for most of us to be greater than we are in actuality. We all have unused potentialities or not fully developed ones. It is certainly true that many of us evade our constitutionally suggested vocations."[51]

Diagram 6
MASLOW'S SELF-ACTUALIZATION AND THE HIERARCHY OF NEEDS

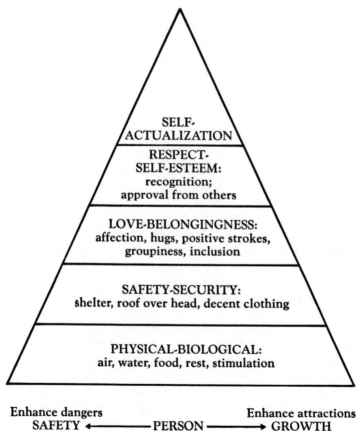

SELF-ACTUALIZATION

RESPECT-SELF-ESTEEM:
recognition;
approval from others

LOVE-BELONGINGNESS:
affection, hugs, positive strokes,
groupiness, inclusion

SAFETY-SECURITY:
shelter, roof over head, decent clothing

PHYSICAL-BIOLOGICAL:
air, water, food, rest, stimulation

Enhance dangers   Enhance attractions
   SAFETY ←———— PERSON ————→ GROWTH
Minimize attractions   Minimize dangers

By fearing the farthest reaches of human nature and so hemming ourselves in with everyday reasonableness, sound human judgment, and commonplace, average and normal matter-of-facts, we bring upon ourselves spiritual suffering for keeping ourselves from experiencing the fullness of life we are invited to experience. It is the same as the phenomenon of deprivation which causes suffering or sickness when by being denied or denying ourselves physical needs, such as food or rest, we end up ill or ailing or physically deformed, as pictures of starving children with bloated bellies patently portray. Jung asserts that "a psycho-neurosis must be understood as the suffering of a human being who has not discovered what life means for him. But all creativeness in the realm of the spirit as well as every psychic advance of man arises from a state of mental suffering, and it is spiritual stagnation, psychic sterility, which causes this [mental suffering]."[52] Just as we need medicine for ailing bodies, so we need spirituality for sickness of the soul.

Maslow, Jung, and Assagioli's psychologies are consonant with Catholic theology in their belief in the basic goodness of human nature—that is, that the healthy human organism hungers for ever-greater goods which tend to become more spiritual and less material as one evolves into higher consciousness. And like Catholic theology they do not deny the bodily, since obviously the majority of human beings cannot become all they are called to be unless physical necessities, such as food, clothing, shelter, and rest, are adequately met.

This psychology grounds our personal and social moral responsibility to feed the hungry, clothe the cold, house the homeless, and the rest. For how can anyone praise the Almighty when his or her consciousness is cursing life's bitterness? And by a sadder twist of irony, those who oppress are also suffering emptiness and self-inflicted spiritual distress! Perhaps the cup of cold water given in Christ's name is an insightful way to proclaim that whatever people give forth, whether it be good things or evil, one hundred percent more of the same is what they can expect in return. Thus for a balanced spirituality there is the need to provide, for oneself and all others, some level of physical security, frolicking and fun, and opportunities to grow wholeheartedly.

CONTEMPLATION AND ACTION. This same respect for the bodily is found in mystical theology. Describing mysticism as a journey of love, William Johnston explains that the existential love of God of which he speaks is not purely spiritual. "It has its roots in matter; it has its roots in the body; it does not reject physical or emotional or erotic love but simply goes beyond them, further and further beyond.[53]

Cognizant of bodily needs, contemplative prayer leads to a healing care for the earth, to committed involvement in action evidencing justice and mercy, in works that make available the hierarchy of goods to all the earth's inhabitants to aid them to actualize their potentials to the fullest so that each of us and all the earth can sing a new song and tell of the wonders of its Maker. In Charismatic Renewal and Social Action, a dialogue between Cardinal Suenens and Dom Helder Camara, Catholics are reminded that we are called before God to be "co-creators," "co-redemptors," "co-sanctifying" the earth by being at the service of man and woman as apostles of Christ in the heart of the city.

The authors urge us to avoid the imbalances of being too spiritual or too material—that is, to be leery of a pietism evident in a disembodied Christianity, and wary of a materialism found in a Christianity lacking the spirit of Jesus. Materialism or pietism by itself produces misshapen men and women who take seriously only one dimension of life to the detriment of the other. The Christian, as symbolized by the cross, rejoins both the vertical and the horizontal dimensions of life. Cardinal Suenens tells us that "to be Christian means to be 'tuned in' to both Jesus Christ and the world's events; to be open to God in one's very openness to the world; to be at once a man of prayer and a man of action, faithful to Jesus Christ, the only begotten Son of God and the brother of all men."[54]

The Cardinal emphasizes that "the service of men and the contemplation of God are intimately united. For us, the desertion of the world in the name of God is just as unacceptable as the neglect of God in the name of temporal commitments. The false, disembodied mysticism cannot give way to a political faith that has lost its Christian resonance."[55]

CATECHETICAL IMPLICATIONS. In a manner consonant with Jungian psychology these churchmen demonstrate respect for different types of approach to life's fullness. Some take the path extending from God to man and woman; others go from humanity to God. Wise catechists will begin with individuals' preferred ways. Whether one's penchant be toward the more spiritual, such as a holy hour or retreat, or toward the temporal, such as assisting battered children or visiting the people of the street, effective catechesis leads the person to a balanced fullness that comes with the development of the other side of the personality. Such a catechesis will restore more of life's energy to the individual and to society.

A holistic catechesis will redress imbalances in the Church that are causing debilitating stress. The empty piety that causes youth and others to accuse the Church of hypocrisy would be dissipated as Christian prayer makes itself manifest in a tender care for the world evidenced in firm and just and loving action. Where lack of care makes for a vacuum in the social sphere, lack of prayer creates problems in the individual's interior, which in turn affects the outward sphere.

Thus the socially committed Christian needs to drink deeply of spirituality if the good to be accomplished is to result in more than just another kind of chauvinistic score. Joseph Chilton Pearce, author of *Crack in the Cosmic Egg*, recently addressed the limits of our rationality, so manifest in our technology. He showed that by employing this mode alone, for every problem solved we have created more—hence the futility of continuing to try to solve the world's problems solely by using rationality. Unreservedly he urged a (non-religious) conference of three thousand doctors, health professionals, and educators to engage in daily meditation and to cultivate a healthy spirituality.[56]

The need to look inward and develop the interior life, especially for those most engrossed in life's busyness, is signalled by the incidence of burn-out and stress-related illness. These ills attest to the numbers who, in all earnestness, are too busy about too many things, and in one essential are found wanting. The overworked coordinator, the overburdened religious educator, campus minister, the priest in charge of social justice will eventually drop their critically needed form of ministry if they expend their energy too actively.

GRATITUDE AND STRESS. The biologist Hans Selye, in his research in *The Stress of Life*, presents an important lesson. People in all practical walks of life "also need the pure enjoyment of impractical pleasures to live a balanced life."[57] Defining stress as "the rate of wear and tear in the body,"[58] Selye presents biological evidence that aging is physiological, not a matter of chronology. Aging is the expenditure of adaptive vital energy to the point where an essential part wears out before the rest and so wrecks the health or wholeness of the body.

With humans, as with tires on a car, *even* wear gives longest wear. The more we can vary our actions, the less any one part suffers from attrition. Selye and others demonstrate empirically that to equalize stress throughout our being calls for frequent shifting over of work from one part to the other. What monastic theology has exhorted as a disciplined life, allowing time for work and for prayer, for recreation, aesthetics, and physical care, science is beginning to tell us is a necessity for well-being.

In addition to balancing what current psychology describes as right-lobe and left-lobe activities (formerly given various names, such as the Dionysian and the Apollonian, the feminine and the masculine), Selye's study of physiology culminates in philosophic insights about morality. He presents natural laws of conduct regarding the fight between altruistic and egotistic tendencies which accounts for most of the stress in interpersonal relations. Acknowledging that the most ancient and essential characteristic of life is egotism—that is, to shift for oneself or die—Selye presents a way to transform this necessity into altruism: through gratitude. It is through gratitude that one turns the original sin of selfishness into a grace without curtailing the ego's self-preserving impulses. The negative counterpart of gratitude is not ingratitude but rather the need for revenge.

For Selye, too, life has an ultimate aim. Our final goal is not to avoid stress, but to express ourselves as fully as possible, according to our own lights.[59] And in the final analysis "Gratitude and revenge are the most important factors governing our actions in everyday life; upon them also chiefly depend our peace of mind, our feelings of security or insecurity, of fulfillment or frustration, in short, the extent to which we can make a success of life."[60] Selye argues that any harmony or discord in our social relations is due to our nervous system. "It governs all our major decisions and attitudes toward each other through one type among its many products: the emotions. (Some unobservant people also attribute a major importance to logic in social relations, but they are mistaken; as far as I can see, here logic plays hardly any role at all.)"[61]

Selye regards revenge as a grotesque distortion of the urge to teach others not to hurt us. Revenge is "the awakening in another person of the wish that I should not prosper, because of what I have done to him. It is the most important threat to security (homeostatis)."[62] Revenge hurts both the giver and receiver of its fruits as it reproduces what it sows.

Gratitude also tends to incite still more gratitude. It is "the awakening in another person of the wish that I should prosper, because of what I have done for him. It is perhaps the most characteristically human way of assuring security (homeostasis)."[63] Respecting the need for self-preservation, altruism, or gratitude as the active cultivation of one's charisms or graces for the good of all "takes away the motive for a clash between selfish and selfless tendencies, because, by inspiring the feeling of gratitude, I have induced another person to share with me my natural wish for my own well-being."[64]

In a manner that resonates with our theology, which says that gratitude is the gracious acceptance of God's beneficence, the giving thanks by living our gifts fully, Selye concludes that gratitude provides a common denominator for the most diverse ways of self-expression. With effects that are positive for all and lasting too, inspiring gratitude by our good works is more reliable than wealth, force, or any show of power to assure security and peace of mind.

WISDOM AS INTEGRITY OF LIFE VS. DEPRESSION AND DESPAIR

Psychology and biology are beginning to verify empirically the truth of moral teachings that all great religions have announced repeatedly. To live altruistically, to render service not just to socially accepted neighbors or our friends but to all humanity, is what we are about as human or humane beings. Loving self and all others as oneself is how we live in Love wholeheartedly.

In Christianity we stress response to our vocation, or God's call. In the words of St. Paul, faith comes through hearing.

Christianity, then, presupposes that some form of external summons is necessary. The summons does come from outside, and only in that sense can we say that salvation comes from outside us, but it is someone outside calling to the individual. That is precisely how Christianity differs from self-enclosed systems and ideologies. It is grounded on the summons of one human being issued to another human being, and that summons takes the form of service; love of neighbor is the service that embodies the summons. Thus Christian salvation does not spring from human beings who are open to others, and the whole process is initiated by Christ himself. Christian salvation begins with one person's act of love for another person. Self-reflection will never bring us to salvation. Someone must approach us and summon us, to awaken the humanity that lies dormant within us.[65]

From this explication by Comblin, as from Church documents themselves, it is evident that evangelization, or the calling of the unchurched, and the new Rite of Christian Initiation of Adults, call for our own ongoing conversion to our humanity, to love seeking expression from within us. The mid-life identity crisis, in which we find ourselves surrounded with goods and values that are no longer meaningful, may well be nature calling us once more to restore a childlike faith clothed in works of love that is mature.

THE FAITH THAT DOES JUSTICE. Biblical scholarship is making clear the essential unity of faith in God and the doing of justice daily, in all our communities—in our associations with people and the land. John R. Donahue quotes the scholars and illustrates how "engagement in the quest for justice is no more 'secular' than the engagement of Yahweh in the history of his people or the incarnation of Jesus into the world of human suffering."[66] He concludes that the Bible gives us a mandate and a testament, that in our doing of justice we are recovering the roots of the biblical tradition and are seeking to create a dwelling place for the word of God in human history.

Stating that the Bible as a whole is the history of the revelation of God's righteousness, Donahue cites von Rad to describe the genesis and importance of justice: "There is absolutely no concept in the Old Testament with so central a significance for all relationships of human life as that of a *sᵉdāqāh* [justice/righteousness]."[67] A biblical understanding of justice is protean and many-faceted, applying to a wide variety of things. For example, Exodus 21-23 presents justice legally by describing ordinances regulating communal life and by prescribing cultic regulations and restitutions for injury done to person or property. "The justice of Yahweh is not in contrast to other covenant qualities such as steadfast love (*hesed*), mercy (*rahᵃmin*), or faithfulness (*ᵉmunah*) but in many texts, is virtually equated with them."[68] The biblical idea of justice describes fidelity to the demands of a relationship.

In contrast to modern individualism, for the Israelite to live is to be united with others in a social context either by bonds of family or by covenant relationships. (A present-day parallel evidencing the strength and solidarity that comes from closeness to the earth, enjoyment of family, and a spirited sociality can be seen in the United Farmworker Movement.) For the Hebrews, Yahweh, lawgiver and Lord of the covenant, is a just God whose saving deeds are the doing of justice—that is, the restoration of community welfare when it has been threatened. "Laws are just not because they conform to an external norm or constitution, but because they create harmony within the community. Acting justly consists in avoiding violence and fraud and other actions which destroy communal life and in pursuing that which sustains the life of the community."[69]

In both Old and New Testaments, sin is social isolation. "Sin is not simply bad moral action, but a power which affects all life. It makes man live for himself, is deceit (Romans 7:11) and cuts him off from God and neighbor."[70] Sin is the desire and tendency to live for oneself alone in a world of religious and social isolation.

Donahue, in doing a biblical exegesis of justice, notes how injustice breaks faithfulness and so brings out basic mistrust which destroys community. "Since human life is a life with others, mutual trust is destroyed by a *single* lie, and mistrust—and thereby sin—is established; by a *single* deed of violence defensive violence is called forth and law as organized violence is made to serve the interest of individuals, etc."[71] The sad conclusion is a world of selfish solitariness, with each insisting on his or her individual rights and fighting for an existence in which life becomes a struggle of all against all even when the battle is involuntarily fought. This biblical exegesis is eminently apparent today. It is corroborated by Erikson's research which has been reviewed here, and illustrated by Niebuhr as the myth of death: a morality that refuses to assume responsibility, that refuses to respond to the Universal, Loving Will.

CONVERSION AS CHANGING THE INDIVIDUAL AND SOCIETY. In spite of these conditions in which individuals and the world suffer from overwhelming need, a lover of wisdom cultivates integrity of life and not despair. The parables of Jesus pithily portray what the courage of conversion signals.

Nathan Mitchell, in speaking of "Ethics and Earthiness: Elements in Liturgical Spirituality," states how the structure of the parables and of conversion are the same. Both involve a *finding*, a *losing*, and a *choosing*. And they catch us. If we let ourselves get captivated by the treasure (by a wisdom that in the eyes of a rational world is folly), we are given a new consciousness in return. A new or renewed way of life is found or discovered about which not much in sensible or logical terms can be said, as eyes have not seen nor have ears heard of a future staked on God's own. When the gift—the treasure or the pearl of great price—is discovered, something radical is done, according to Mitchell. There is a letting go, a loosening or losing of old ways, such as selling all that one has. Something decisive and risky is ventured, so that one's whole future depends on the find.[72]

The parallel between the parables, conversion, and Levinson's description of transitions in life-structures is noteworthy. It raises a crucial question, for as Levinson indicates later, newer life-structures are not necessarily better than former ones. In scriptural terms, how is one to know that he or she has indeed found the pearl of great price and not a foil? Levinson speaks about the dream. This is based on Jungian psychology which holds that, properly understood, our dreams guide us to discern the good.

In *Dreams: A Way to Listen to God*, Morton Kelsey develops this theme. Reviewing the place of the dream in our spiritual development, he quotes Tertullian. "Is it not known to all the people that the dream is the most usual way that God reveals himself to man?"[73] Stating that dreams and visions are among the New Testament list of the gifts of the Holy Spirit, Kelsey asserts that dreams do not determine the future but rather show what *may* occur. They indicate the good that can be actualized and the evil to be avoided. Dreams never lead astray if taken symbolically. That is, if we learn to read the language of symbolism, if we learn to decipher the levels of meaning a dream contains, our dreams become our guides. For dreams attempt to show us the way to develop wholeness, to bring together all parts of our personality.[74] The question remaining is whether we have the courage to let go the securities that shackle us in order to follow our dreams or aspirations.

There is another way for us to see the treasures the Lord has hidden so transparently. Selye states that stress without distress means living graciously; gracious living calls for a turning from everyday business and returning to do what is not ordinary for us. Thus if we but open our souls we can see the extraordinary graces abounding in our everyday reality. God's graces are not some supernatural pie in the sky to be savored by and by. What is extraordinary is the ordinary that calls for our redemptive glance.

God's Kingdom comes crashing into our everyday reality. For some it is a stumbling-stone to be treated with disdain, as they vainly strive to evade the "hound of heaven," their neighbor in need, and vainly strive to forge a self-encased identity. For others the discovery of their ability to minister to those in need is like finding a pearl of great price. It helps relieve anxiety, mid-life despair, neuroses, and other physical pains that accumulate when one lives life imbalanced and vainly. The incrashing of the Kingdom is to be found all around us in the cries of people on Skid Row, the migrant farmers, those who labor in the slavery of the garment industry, minority and youth prostituted in the streets and by the lure of ROTC, others who in fear register for a draft which does not make clear how mongering death preserves a nation's liberty. Carcinogens color our food and are in the fabric of the clothes we wear. Excrements exhaust the sea, pollutants the air; poisons and hungry people are everywhere. And the social malady shows up in personal ills, physical and mental.

The oppressed are broken from without, while the bourgeois and wealthy suffer within themselves the same despair as the victims they curse. Even worse, they oppress themselves with anomie, politely termed a "mild depression," as they refuse life its full expression. Instead they are seeking life's meaning in fashion, in drink or in work, in pills and exotic escapades while they hope for ecstasy and perpetual security in the stock market or in the extremes of sexuality as shown in promiscuity or in self-righteous, sterile purity.

It is evident that God who is Love did not intend this as the way for life to be. Can the "death of God" today be forms of theology, psychology, philosophy, economics, and all the rest that seek to suppress ongoing revelation of how we can be living to the fullest a life of justice, peace, and liberty? And among the ministers of immorality perhaps are those who catechize with wafers and waffled words bespeaking mystic magicking, for fear of tasting heartily the stuff of life and drinking deeply of the cup which signifies death to narrow interests bent upon oneself. For the Christian, faith and morality symbolized in the Cross and its quadernity is a letting go of worldly logic esteemed as the only way to know. In this loosening of the divisive grip of rationality, one can be born anew and find the wisdom of God's reality.

RENEWAL AND CHANGE OF HEART. Nathan Mitchell concludes his address on "Ethics and Earthiness" by indicating that the revitalization of Christian liturgy will come through a sense of justice made manifest in politics and in the rough-and-tumble world of needy people. Revitalization will not come about through books and bells. The community of faith, he states, will collapse unless it nourishes the larger community. Our body and the stories embedded in memory make us who we are. In this way we possess the Word and are possessed by it. What is the Word, the heritage often glossed over and little understood, Mitchell tells us, but the table ministry of Jesus? The table ministry is a point of controversy and conflict, for it symbolizes solidarity and communion with the misfit and the oppressed, not just with those properly dressed. As Christians we can either disclaim who we are by pretending Christ's life was tidy and pretty and so stay stifled in our malaise, suffering individual and social disintegration for hardhearted ways; or we can proclaim the story that is ingrained not only in our brain but in the very marrow of our bones—that faith and Gospel morality makes us see God's Kingdom where and when we least expect to see it.

Mitchell states that this *revelation* of who we can be calls for a *revolution* in our behavior or life-style, a revelation which comes from the *resolution* of the crisis or situation we find ourselves in. The parables actually portray the situation found today. From this understanding that Christ's parables call for a moral revolution, we know that education in faith and morals leading to a renewed Catholic Christian community is not a cosmetic facade. Such a catechesis calls for a fundamental option made individually and a fundamental stance of the faith community to embark on a pilgrimage or journey, to engage in catechesis as ongoing process educating the head and the heart and the hands and the spirit of one and all in a process that is lifelong.

If catechesis is understood parabolically, catechesis invites us to risk, to think unthinkable thoughts, Mitchell explains. A courageous catechesis will provoke heartfelt decision. The dead will be left to nurse the dead as the saved go about saving the saved with words that entomb. Those who risk a rising from their deadening ways to choosing life are thereby made active participants in an ongoing story, disclosing to themselves and all they touch something new and real. Present-day discontent within ourselves and in the churches can also be the sign of a divine ferment.

DISCERNING THE SPIRIT. Meister Eckhart has said that "the supreme purpose of God is He will not rest content until His Son is born in us."[75] Specifically, how does one become a Christ-bearer to a world overwhelmed in needs when one is needy too? How does one refrain from the immorality of sinning against the neighbor and the stranger by ignoring their pleas and at the same time not sin against oneself by becoming overburdened with their cries of misery? A terse response lies in humility and prayer, individually and within the community.

Henri Nouwen poignantly portrays how humility and prayer are the ground in which we discover that the seemingly heavy task of ministry is in fact the easy yoke and the light burden of our Lord. Nouwen puts prayer at the center of ministry. "Without prayer, ministry quickly degenerates into a busy life in which our own needs for acceptance and affection start to dominate our actions and being busy becomes a way of convincing ourselves of our importance."[76] He continues:

> For the ministry to be a vital event in the midst of our contemporary society, it is of crucial importance that the minister be burning with love for the Lord. This requires a deep commitment to contemplative prayer in which we enter into our closet and spend "useless time" with our Lord and Him alone. In the solitude of this closet we will slowly rediscover our first love and recognize the voice calling us again and again to selfless service. Our prayer with others, whether it be devotional or sacramental, can only be real prayer when it is warmed by the furnace of our cell, where we present ourselves in all our powerlessness and vulnerability to the Lord.
>
> There is more, however. To live in the name of Jesus Christ also leads us into close communion with our people. In the silence of our prayer we will soon experience the presence of all those to whom we are called to minister. We cannot encounter our Lord without encountering Him as the Lord of the poor, the oppressed, the lonely, the forgotten and the despised. Thus we come to realize that prayer never excludes anyone. On the contrary, it creates that unlimited space where all who are in need can be led into the healing presence of the Lord.[77]

In prayer, then, we slowly come to sense "the all-embracing love of God and realize that in that mysterious, virginal point where our heart and God's heart speak to each other community finds its root."[78] Through contemplative prayer, or meditation, we are shown how God's will can become our own. To discern that it is the Holy Spirit leading the way, one needs to test the emotions prevailing in our life. A sense of delight within our prayer, continued by a joyful satisfaction as we engage in action in spite of its minutiae and drudgery, is a test that our particular ministry is a true response to the particulars of who we are called to be.[79]

PRAYER AND PHYSICAL CARE. Centering prayer, meditation, and contemplation are essential for religious education. Interestingly, medicine and holistic education are starting to stress how basic such prayer is to our physical well-being, to the relief of stress, and to the transformation of negative emotional states. Herbert Benson, author of *The Relaxation Response*, in an address to the medical and educational professions, showed that every great religion has known a wisdom which science is now confirming empirically: the body's need for prayer.[80]

The *Upanishads* or Hindu Scriptures, the *Cabala* of Judaism, as well as Christianity, Mohammedanism, Zen Buddhism, Shintoism, Taoism, Confucianism, the new England nature mystics and poetic transcendentalists, Shamanism with its chanting, Judaism's davening, and Catholicism's rosary all have a common need—the need for meditative prayer. This need can be generalized as the setting aside of ten to twenty minutes once or twice a day in a way that breaks the train of everyday thinking. Benson's research has now quantified the physiological manifestation of the wisdom in these prayers. Whether through transcendental meditation (TM) or the more traditional forms of meditative prayer, there is an increase and intensity of alpha and theta waves which compose the relaxation response. As opposed to the fight or flight response which is the basis of stress, the relaxation that comes from meditation lowers blood pressure and gastrointestinal wear and can offset arteriosclerosis, heart attacks, and the other diseases of civilization.[81]

Basic to each form of prayer are (1) posture: sit quietly with eyes closed; (2) repetition of a word or sound, a phrase or prayer; and (3) passive disregard of other thoughts that wander in. M. Basil Pennington, a Trappist monk, has written three simple rules for those eager to begin to meditate.

Rule One: At the beginning of the prayer we take a minute or two to quiet down and then move in faith to God dwelling in our depths; and at the end of the prayer we take several minutes to come out, mentally praying the "Our Father" (or some other prayer).

Rule Two: After resting for a bit in the center in faith-full love, we take up a single, simple word that expresses this response and begin to let it repeat itself within.

Rule Three: Whenever in the course of the prayer we become aware of anything else, we simply return to the prayer word.[82]

A SIMPLE PRAYER. In "The Dark Night Ongoing Surrender Survival Kit," Kent Hoffman describes the Jesus Prayer, a form of prayer going back to the third century.

> The theme of this prayer is absolute surrender, a personal, direct and uncomplicated cry (mantra) repeated over and over from the center (heart) of one's life. The focus is upon a profound recognition of need and an equally profound recognition that in any final sense the only resource able to meet that need is God. The cry is always simple: "O God, come to my aid"; "Lord, left to myself, I will be destroyed"; "Lord Jesus Christ, have mercy"; "Lord Jesus, mercy." This prayer is most often connected to our breathing so that as one breathes out, "mercy" is pronounced. To emphasize the heart is to find that place within us that lives out this intense and unending hunger for fulfillment.
>
> Consistently, this "Prayer of the Heart" brings us to a point of emptiness in our lives. At its most extreme this point of poverty is an experience of being lost with no recognizable hope of rescue save the simple cry we carry in our heart. It is here in our emptiness that God is gradually, in the words of Gandhi, reducing self to zero. It is here in our emptiness that God is increasingly able to work, because this moment of emptiness is the event through which God enters the world to transform the world. This is the meaning and power of Jesus, empty and crucified on a cross.[83]

The various types of mental prayer, ranging from awareness and contemplation, to meditation on the joyful and the sorrowful mysteries of one's life, to the healing of memories, are presented by Anthony de Mello in Sadhana: A Way to God. With an explanation of both the theological and psychological dimensions of each form of prayer, this handbook can well serve retreats or groups gathered to learn meditative and contemplative prayer. For younger learners A Peaceable Classroom: Activities to Calm and Free Student Energies can be used during catechetical sessions. Because the book presents prayerful activities as therapeutic strategies, it can be used even in public schools. All these types of prayer open one to the intuitive domain, also described as thinking with the right hemisphere of the brain.[84]

THE INTUITIVE DOMAIN. Carl Jung describes intuition as
the psychological operation by which a person can see beyond
the facts and so perceive the intangibles in a situation. Roberto
Assagioli states even more emphatically the connection between
intuition and spiritual reality:

> Intuition is a higher form of vision. Etymologically, it is
> related to vision and means to "see within" (in-tueri). At its
> highest it can be equated with a direct suprarational
> comprehension of the nature of reality, of its essence. It thus
> differs from what is commonly called "intuition" (hunches,
> psychic impressions, presentiments concerning people and
> events).

> The inner action of one who is endeavoring to
> perceive inner reality is called "contemplation" or the
> "contemplative state." The highest form of inner vision is
> illumination, which can be defined as revelation of the
> divinity in all things, in nature and in living beings.[85]

In A Spirituality Named Compassion, Matthew Fox makes
the following distinctions between the right and the left brain.
This book is a demonstration of how the world can be if we
develop both right- and left-brain spirituality.

Left lobe of brain	Right lobe of brain
Day, light	Night, dark
Clock time (control)	Suspended time (ecstasy and service in prophecy)
Linear time	Spiral time
Active (prophetic)	Receptive (mystical)
Intellectual, head cognition	Sensuous, guts, intuitive cognition
Straight	Curved
Yang, animus	Yin, anima
Sky, heaven	earth
mechanistic	organic
place	space
nouns	verbs
verbal	spatial
analytic	gestalt
literal	symbolic[86]

Fox quotes from Robert Ornstein's The Psychology of
Consciousness to emphasize the need for compassion, a

consciousness of interconnectedness, as the only route for a psychology of morality in our time. Ornstein argues that "the analytic mode, in which there is separation of objects, of the self from others (I-it relationship), has proved useful in individual biological survival; yet this mode apparently evolved to fit the conditions of life many thousands of years ago."[87] In contrast, the survival problems now are collective rather than individual: how to prevent nuclear war, overpopulation, pollution of the earth. Ornstein warns that in present-day problems a focus on individual consciousness, or individual survival, works against, not for, a solution.

Mortification of a self-centered, or individualistic, consciousness is the discipline pressingly needed. If we are to survive, whether affiliated with a religious tradition or not, we need to learn to let go our luxuries that imbalance the world. Six percent of the world's population, primarily in the United States of America, is consuming over forty percent of the world's goods. We need to relinquish our rugged individualism and competitiveness caught so keenly in the attitude of "every man for himself." In its place there needs to be introduced a new asceticism that shows itself in cooperation, in caring concern or compassion—that is, in a reverent *living* of the Lord's Prayer. This prayer is a verbalization of the belief that if God is our Father, then we all are interconnected as brothers and sisters. Therefore if our belief is not to be a lie, our life-style has to signify in everyday life a consciousness of the interdependence of each of us upon all others. When we have achieved this integration of prayer and action, of thinking and feeling, we have achieved peace of mind or integrity of life. We are living the virtue of wisdom.

WISDOM AND MATURITY OF FAITH. Wisdom is needed to translate love into effective action. Hermann Keyserling in *The Recovery of Truth* states that the Chinese, who know so much about wisdom, designate the wise by combining the ideographs for wind and lightning; for them, the wise person is not the serene old man bereft of all illusions but is "he who, like the wind, rushes headlong and irresistibly on his way and cannot be stopped nor laid hold of at any station of his career; who purifies the air in the manner of lightning, and strikes when there is need

for it."[88] We see the exemplification of wisdom in the lives of our
saints and heroes, such as Abraham Lincoln, Gandhi, and
Mother Teresa. Yet we do not have to be in the limelight of politics
or go to far-off missions to live joyous, full, saintly lives. Our
holiness is demonstrated in the healing touch extended to all
within a fifteen-foot radius that forms the perimeter of our lives.

Thus through prayerful meditation we are led to experience
the Incarnation as our intuition opens us to universality. To be
present to one another's reality nonjudgmentally is to be living
in love compassionately. This fundamental stance reflects
maturity of faith. It is the culmination of Kohlberg's and Fowler's
sixth stages, Teresa of Avila's seventh mansion, and Allport's
mature religious sentiment. It is the fullness of Eriksonian
psychosocial development as the cycle of one generation
concludes by commencing and maintaining the next, even as the
cycle of the individual's earthly life comes to conclusion.

Wisdom, or maturity of faith, has been described as a
second naivete, as is evident in Christ's exhortation that we
become as little children. Only then are we free to experience
expansive universality, a transcendence which saves us from
despondency and despair. Erikson recognizes wisdom as a
paradox. It is "the detached concern with life itself, in the face of
death itself."[89]

In a "wisened childhood" the individual has mellowed as he
or she has now understood the lessons of life's vicissitudes.
Forgiving of one's idiosyncratic follies, the wise are patient and
kind, outspoken too, yet neither rude nor selfish. Without
resentments or disgust, they are always ready to excuse, to trust,
and so to inspire hope as they endure and transform whatever
comes their way.

Maintaining a wholesome outlook while conveying the
integrity of their experiences, the wise can serve us well as
spiritual mentors. This they do simply by being true to
themselves. Living a faith that is full and mature, their joyous
allure will encourage others to risk the adventure. In this way,
wise mentors are responding to the need of the upcoming
generation for an integrated heritage. As younger ones look up
to us and recognize that we have made it gracefully, our model in
turn inspires them to be all that Life is calling them to. And so
the intergenerational cycle of Christianity perpetuates itself.

IMPLICATIONS FOR RELIGIOUS EDUCATION. Fowler warned that Stage Six faith can lose itself in universality and transcendental prayer and so become oblivious of the earth and people we are called to tend, to nurture and take care of. Neither does staying in the confines of discussion groups and logic's rationality do justice to Our Lord's prayer. To witness, to change and be changed, to have the Lord exchange our hearts of stone for ones that care calls for moral courage. Conversion calls for a transfusion in which Love's blood pulsates through our veins as we incarnate the Christ, each in our unique way. We will know we have been transformed if the world can say: "See how they love one another!"

Margaret Wold expounds rather poignantly:

> To be incarnationally in mission in a community means to enter into relationship with the people of that neighborhood, walking among them, talking with them, listening to them, being concerned with their concerns, and being willing to run the risk of being changed oneself. Programs are static; incarnation is dynamic. Programs impose; incarnation is relational. Instead of busying themselves with maintenance and survival matters, incarnational congregations become sharers of the pains and the celebrations of the people. Loving and caring replaces preserving and guarding. Sitting in an office or in committee meetings is exchanged for dialogue in the streets and identification with the issues that affect the life of the people around the church.[90]

LIVING WITNESS: AN APPROACH. This type of living witness calls for sponsors, or mentors, for people going two by two, and maybe leading younger groups, to encourage one another along the way. The social Gospel calls for more than asking confirmandi, or high school classes, to spend a number of hours in social justice to fulfill a requirement. Although good is intended, such an approach is myopic as people become objects serving to fulfill other people's requirements in order for these strangers to receive some magic form of sacrament. As a senior citizen once said, after the fifth seventh-grade kid came in to see her over the course of a few years, "Well, am I your Confirmation or your Lenten project? And how much time do you have to put in with me?" Christianity and a healing morality are not semester songs. They call for some commitments that may be lifelong.

A truer approach may be to begin parochially to build self-esteem. This will enable each to see his or her unique gifts or charisms and then, with others whose talents are consonant, to pray and venture forth to find where their skills fit in so that there is a mutuality and not an exploitation. For example, the president of a university spends a day a week in prayer, cutting hair, and ministering to Skid Row men. A therapist gives a worker needed rest and recreation once a week as she assumes her responsibilities for child care for those struggling to go beyond welfare. For both of these the needed change of pace from matters heady to more physical action provides many a blessing. The shifting of energies builds a heartiness instead of harmful stress and comes about in a relaxed fashion. Working with little children or indigent men helps each to see more readily the reality of Christ, since numberless encounters with grace come through meeting these people face to face.

To get this process going a parish group can start retreats entitled "Walk With Me" or "Come and See." Participants (led by a priest who legitimates the Gospel imperative, since most of us are at Stage Three) would go and spend a weekend in the inner city. With hearts open in prayer they welcome the Lord incarnate in the poor to awaken their social sensitivity. Exposure through a second tour, or a variety of speakers such as those listed in the resource book *Education for Peace and Justice: A Manual for Teachers*,[91] can round out the spiritual holiday.

From there, continually bolstered by those whose ministry is prayer, clusters can form, or individuals who care can begin in a committed way to share on a regular basis their time and talent and prayer. Pennington suggests "walking together," finding a fellow traveler or forming a small group with whom to share along the way. In this manner the travelers serve as spiritual guides to one another.[92]

CATECHESIS FOR WISDOM: TO CONCLUDE IS TO BEGIN. To conclude this book I must repeat the plea that education in faith and morals needs to be approached holistically. We need to engage the head and heart and hands and spirit of the individual and the community, both serving reciprocally as catechists and catechized. It is a lifelong process which needs the support of the faith community to be effective. A holistic catechesis calls for guidance from the Spirit, coming from personal and communal prayer. To open up and let the Spirit be our guide calls for a balanced life of simplicity, to allow natural joys to fill us. We also have to learn not to hide from our emotionality; hence the need perhaps for therapy or affective encounter groups to free what is repressed so that we can express a fullness of love. In this manner we will be enabled to hear the heart throbbing in fear or pain and no longer dread it or respond vainly. For it is only through our cooperation that the Lord will renew the face of the earth.

My attempt to approach catechesis holistically has led me to treat it philosophically, theologically, and psychologically, to touch on methods, on morality, and on spirituality. The task is so huge that obviously it is not possible in one volume to do justice to each area and subject treated. And so I pray for those who serve as catechists, whether they be parents, clergy, professors, or anyone else, as I do for myself—that we embark both individually and communally on a lifelong journey or conversation with some of the ideas and authors contained herein in order to bring home for the benefit of all the insights they have to offer.

NOTES

1. Erik H. Erikson, ed., *Adulthood* (New York: W. W. Norton & Co., 1978), p. 20.

2. José Comblin, *The Meaning of Mission*, translated by J. Drury (London: Gill and Macmillan, 1979), p. 36.

3. Ibid.

4. National Conference of Catholic Bishops, *Sharing the Light of Faith: National Catechetical Directory for Catholics of the United States* (Washington, D.C.: United States Catholic Conference, 1979), p. 84 (#148).

5. Ibid., p. 59 (#105).

6. Ibid., p. 58 (#102).

7. Ibid.

8. Erikson, *Adulthood*, p. 29.

9. Erik H. Erikson, *Insight and Responsibility* (New York: W. W. Norton & Co., 1964), p. 114.

10. Department of Education, United States Catholic Conference, *Position Papers and Recommendations from the Symposium on the Parish and the Educational Mission of the Church* (Washington, D.C.: United States Catholic Conference Publications Office, 1978), p. 2.

11. Ibid.

12. Erik H. Erikson, *Childhood and Society* (New York: W. W. Norton & Co., 1964), p. 263.

13. Ibid.

14. See Carl R. Rogers, *Freedom to Learn: A View of What Education Might Become* (Columbus, OH: Charles E. Merrill, 1969), chapter 11, "Being in Relationship."

15. Erik H. Erikson, *Identity, Youth and Crisis*, (New York: W. W. Norton & Co., 1968), pp. 135-136.

16. Erikson, *Insight and Responsibility*, p. 130.

17. Evelyn Eaton Whitehead and James D. Whitehead, *Christian Life Patterns* (Garden City, NY: Doubleday & Co., 1979), pp. 73-84.

18. Erikson, *Insight and Responsibility*, p. 231.

19. Whitehead and Whitehead, *Christian Life Patterns*, p. 79.

20. Erikson, *Insight and Responsibility*, p. 129.

21. Morton Kelsey, *Can Christians Be Educated?* (Mishawaka, IN: Religious Education Press, 1977), p. 46.

22. Ibid., p. 63.

23. Ibid., p. 64.

24. Among the many very easy to read yet practical and inspiring books on building self-esteem in one another are: Thomas A. Kane, *The Healing Touch of Affirmation* (Whitinsville, MA: Affirmation Books, 1976); Jean Illsley Clark, *Self-Esteem: A Family Affair* (Minneapolis: Winston Press, 1978); and Michele and Craig Borba, *Self-Esteem: A Classroom Affair, 101 + Ways to Help Children Like Themselves* (Minneapolis: Winston Press, 1978).

25. See Marcia Lasswell and Norman M. Lobsenz, *Styles of Loving: Why You Love the Way You Do* (New York: Doubleday & Co., 1980).

26. Whitehead and Whitehead, *Christian Life Patterns*, p. 100.

27. Ibid., p. 101. The authors note that the Reverend James Young, C.S.P., has been a catalyst in this ministry and in the establishment of the North American Conference of Separated and Divorced Catholics, now headquartered in Boston.

One of my students, a religious who is a parish coordinator and member of the diocesan marriage tribunal, reported that until a support group was formed for divorcing and single parents, their involvement in parish activities, especially in preparing their children for the sacraments, was nil. Their feelings of alienation and shame and fear of censure by those in authority kept them away. With the formation of the support group, and the sincere acceptance of them as they are, the majority of such people are becoming reconciled to the community to the point where they are the backbone of parish activities.

28. Whitehead and Whitehead, *Christian Life Patterns*, p. 106. Among the lilterature now appearing on homosexuality, the authors suggest that the following books be consulted: Donald Goergen, *The Sexual Celibate* (New York: Seabury, 1974) and John McNeill, *The Church and the Homosexual* (Kansas City: Sheed Andrews and McMeel, 1976).

29. Erik H. Erikson, "Identity and the Life Cycle," *Psychological Issues*, Vol. I (New York: International Universities Press, 1955), p. 97.

30. Milton Mayeroff, *On Caring* (New York: Harper & Row, 1971), p. 5.

31. Ibid.

32. See Erich Fromm, *The Art of Loving* (New York: Harper & Row, 1956), pp. 26 ff. The substance of *On Caring* is an explication of these virtues.

33. Mayeroff, *On Caring*, p. 30.

34. Kahlil Gibran, *The Prophet* (New York: Alfred A. Knopf, 1923), p. 18.

35. Henri J. M. Nouwen, *Reaching Out* (New York: Doubleday & Co., 1975), p. 56.

36. Ibid., p. 60.

37. Ibid., p. 62.

38. Daniel J. Levinson et al., *The Seasons of a Man's Life* (New York: Ballantine Books, 1978), pp. 331-335. Chart 8 is taken from Rita Preszler Weathersby and Jill Mattuck Tarule, *Adult Development: Implications for Higher Education* (Washington D.C.: ERIC Clearinghouse on Higher Education and American Association for Higher Education, 1980), pp. 6-9. Also in: Rita Weathersby, "Life Stages and Learning Interests," *The Adult Learner*, Current Issues in Higher Education 1978 (Washington, D.C.: American Association for Higher Education, 1978), pp. 23-25. She acknowledges that "sources for this chart are Levinson (1974), Gould (1972), Neugarten (1969), and Sheehy (1974). Category titles and time designations are Levinson's. Classifications for the later periods were developed from the data in Weathersby (1977)." See also Rita Weathersby, "A Developmental Perspective on Adults' Use of Formal Education" (doctoral dissertation, Harvard University Graduate School of Education, 1977).

39. Levinson, *Seasons*, pp. 317-318. See also Roger Gould, *Transformations, Growth and Change in Adult Life* (New York: Simon & Schuster, 1978); Alan B. Knox, *Adult Development and Learning* (San Francisco: Jossey-Bass, 1977); Gail Sheehy, *Passages: Predictable Crises of Adult Life* (New York: Bantam Books, 1976); George E. Vaillant, *Adaptation to Life* (Boston: Little, Brown, 1977).

40. See John A. Sanford, *Dreams and Healing* (New York: Paulist Press, 1978) and *Healing and Wholeness* (New York: Paulist Press, 1977); and Dennis T. Jaffe, *Healing from Within* (New York: Alfred A. Knopf, 1980).

41. C.G. Jung, *Modern Man in Search of a Soul*, translated by W. S. Dell and Cary F. Baynes (New York: Harcourt, Brace & World, 1933), p. 109.

42. Ibid.

43. Ibid.

44. Ibid., p. 229.

45. See Roberto Assagioli, M.D., *Psychosynthesis* (New York: Penguin Books, 1965). See also Morton Kelsey, *Healing and Christianity* (New York: Harper & Row, 1973); and, specifically for vision, Margaret Corbett, *How to Improve Your Eyes* (New York: Crown Publishers, 1938) and Charles R. Kelley, *New Techniques of Vision Improvement* (Santa Monica: Interscience Work Shop, 1971).

46. Diagram 5 is taken from Roberto Assagioli, M.D., *The Act of Will* (New York: Penguin Books, 1973), pp. 13-14.

47. See Ira Progoff, *At a Journal Workshop: The Basic Text and Guide for Using the Intensive Journal* (New York: Dialogue House, 1975).

48. Jung, *Modern Man*, p. 236.

49. Assagioli, *Act of Will*, p. 128. It is interesting to compare this with the hologram theory of Einstein's protégé, D. Boehm, the physicist renowned for *Quantum Mechanics*. He spent ten years in serious meditation on the basic building block of matter before realizing that all that appears is relationships of energy, whether they be waves or particles, and that the *unity of the entire physical universe is infolded in the brain system*. In turn, it is interesting to note parallels between Boehm's theory, Teilhard de Chardin's thought, especially in *The Phenomenon of Man*, and Assagioli, who has incorporated the best of Eastern and Western mysticism into his work and writing.

50. Abraham H. Maslow, *Toward a Psychology of Being* (New York: D. Van Nostrand Co., 1968), p. 26.

51. Maslow, as quoted in Assagioli, *Act of Will*, p. 120.

52. Jung, *Modern Man*, p. 225.

53. William Johnston, S.J., *The Inner Eye of Love* (New York: Harper & Row, 1978), p. 139.

54. Cardinal Léon-Joseph Suenens and Dom Helder Camara, *Charismatic Renewal and Social Action: A Dialogue* (Ann Arbor, MI: Servant Books, 1979), p. 9.

55. Ibid., p. 10.

56. Joseph Chilton Pearce, "Holistic Education: The Foundation of Holistic Health," address given to the Mandala Society and The National Center for the Exploration of Human Potential, at San Diego, on August 2, 1980. (Available on tape #103 from Mandala Outer Circle, P.O. Box 1233, Del Mar, CA 92014). See also Joseph Chilton Pearce, *The Crack in the Cosmic Egg: Challenging Constructs of Mind and Reality* (New York: Pocket Books, 1973).

57. Hans Selye, M.D., *The Stress of Life* (New York: McGraw-Hill, 1956), p. 296.

58. Ibid., p. 3.

59. Ibid., p. 299.

60. Ibid., p. 285.

61. Ibid., p. 284.

62. Ibid., p. 286.

63. Ibid.

64. Ibid.

65. Comblin, *Meaning of Mission*, pp. 74-75.

66. John R. Donahue, S.J., "Biblical Perspectives on Justice," *The Faith That Does Justice*, edited by John C. Haughey, Woodstock Studies 2 (New York: Paulist Press, 1977), p. 109.

67. Ibid., p. 68.

68. Ibid., p. 69.

69. Ibid.

70. Ibid., p. 95.

71. Ibid., pp. 95-96.

72. Nathan Mitchell, O.S.B., "Ethics and Earthiness: Elements in Liturgical Spirituality," NCR Cassettes (National Catholic Reporter Publishing Co., P.O. Box 281, Kansas City, MO 64141).

73. Morton Kelsey, *Dreams: A Way to Listen to God* (New York: Paulist Press, 1978), p. 74.

74. Ibid. See also John A. Sanford, *Dreams: God's Forgotten Language* (New York: J.B. Lippincott Co., 1968).

75. Meister Eckhart, quotation taken from Catholic Worker, Los Angeles House of Hospitality, 1976 Christmas card.

76. Henri J. M. Nouwen, "The Monk and the Cripple: Toward a Spirituality of Ministry," *America*, March 15, 1980, p. 207. See also Henri J. M. Nouwen, "Spiritual Life: Do Not Worry; All Things Will Be Given," *The Catholic Agitator*, September 1980, pp. 1-3.

77. Ibid., p. 208.

78. Ibid.

79. Johnston, *Inner Eye of Love*, chapter 16, especially p. 156.

80. Herbert Benson, M.D., "The Relaxation Response: The Key to Healing?" Address given to The Mandala Society and the National Center for the Exploration of Human Potential, at San Diego, on August 1, 1980. (Available on tape; see note #56). See also Herbert Benson, *The Relaxation Response* (New York: William Morrow & Co., 1975).

81. Ibid. See also Jaffe, *Healing from Within*.

82. M. Basil Pennington, O.C.S.O., *Daily We Touch Him: Practical Religious Experiences* (New York: Image Books, 1979), p. 71. For a pithy explanation of the varieties of personal prayer and their connection with charismatic prayer and social action, see George Maloney, S.J., "Exploring Prayer," an NCR interview, *National Catholic Reporter*, November 3, 1978, pp. 9-16. See also Abbot Thomas Keating, O.C.S.O., M. Basil Pennington, O.C.S.O., and Thomas E. Clarke, S.J., *Finding Grace at The Center* (Still River, MA: St. Bede Publications, 1978). Any or all of these three references can be used privately or with a group to become acquainted with the theology of prayer and to learn the practice of mental prayer.

83. Kent Hoffman, "The Dark Night Ongoing Surrender Survival Kit," *The Catholic Agitator*, September 1980, p. 6.

84. Anthony de Mello, S.J., *Sadhana: A Way to God* (St. Louis: The Institute of Jesuit Sources, 1978) presents forty-seven different Christian prayer exercises. See also Merrill Harmin and Saville Sax, *A Peaceable Classroom: Activities to Calm and Free Student Energies* (Minneapolis: Winston Press, 1977). The bibliography at the end of this book provides the reader with an easy introduction to the intuitive domain (thinking with the right brain).

85. Assagioli, *Act of Will*, pp. 225-226.

86. Matthew Fox, *A Spirituality Named Compassion* (Minneapolis: Winston Press, 1979), p. 87.

87. Ibid., p. 86.

88. Quoted in Assagioli, *Act of Will*, p. 103.

89. Erikson, *Insight and Responsibility*, p. 133.

90. Margaret Wold, "Incarnation in Mission," *Changes*, Vol. 1, #3 (Spring 1980), published by Institute for Changing Ministries, University of Southern California, School of Religion, p. 4.

91. Mary Beth Gallagher, James B. McGinnis, Kathleen R. McGinnis, Mary Ann McGivern, and Luanne Schinzel, *Education for Peace and Justice: A Manual for Teachers*, 5th ed., Spring 1976 (Institute for Education in Peace & Justice, 3700 W. Pine, St. Louis, MO 63108).

92. Pennington, *Daily We Touch Him*, p. 129.